D0408309

The Man
Who Moved
a Mountain

The Man Who Moved a Mountain

by
RICHARD C. DAVIDS

FORTRESS PRESS   PHILADELPHIA

Library of Congress Catalog Card Number 75–99609

2299H69   Printed in U.S.A.   1–237

To
the family and friends of
Robert W. Childress

Those Who Helped

The story of Bob Childress and Buffalo Mountain would be impossible to tell without the help of a great many people. I am deeply grateful to my mother, my brother Thomas, and my cousin Mae for their constant encouragement, and to Ralph D. Wennblom, Gertrude Dieken, and Mary Zeigler Glockner for valuable editorial aid and counsel. I offer a special thanks to Nineveh Willis for her vast knowledge of mountain lore. My friends in the mountains gave me more of their time and patience and understanding than I can adequately acknowledge: John Alderman, Carroll County historian; Doc Burnett and the Reverend Samuel Query; the Willises and Ed Gardner of Bluemont; the Ferry Hyltons of Willis; Charles and Euna Jessup of The Hollow; Howard and Maggie Webb and the Spanglers and Webbs at Mayberry; John Whorley and the others of Slate Mountain; Blaine and Cora and Hobert Quesenberry of Indian Valley; and especially the men and women of Buffalo Mountain —the Moles, the Harrises, the Weddles, the Kemps, the Sutphins, and the Goads. Most of all I thank the wonderful Childress family who have given me their constant and generous help, and something more—the gifts of friendship and inspiration.

Contents

Prologue

Shrouded in the mists of the Virginia Blue Ridge is a place called Buffalo Mountain. On a clear day you can see its rounded summit some five miles west of the Parkway. From that distance it is not an impressive peak. But to the people who have lived within its long shadows it casts a powerful spell. There are those who say a devil used to dwell there.

Walled in by surrounding hills, the people of the Buffalo lived in a land of Brigadoon, captive to the unchanging ways of generations past. Theirs was a heritage of proud independence —but also of poverty and ignorance, fear and superstition, violence and sudden death. Tales of dark deeds on the Buffalo spread through the mountains and beyond.

Then a man named Bob Childress came to live there. He had grown up a mountain man with mountain habits. He drank. He fought ambush-style, with rocks and pistols. He was scarred from many brawls and twice wounded by gunshot. But something happened to change Bob Childress, and the change in him shook and transformed Buffalo Mountain.

I first met Bob Childress by accident when I was in the Blue Ridge in 1950 on a magazine article assignment. He was an overwhelming, magnetic kind of man. Over the years I went back again and again to visit him and to talk with his family and neighbors. Almost all of this book comes direct from Bob, his wife Lelia and their seven children, his brother Hasten, and from the scores of mountaineers to whom Bob Childress was counselor, friend, and brother. In a very few cases names or minor details have been disguised to protect the innocent. Only in these isolated instances is the book anything less than factual.

It could not be otherwise. There are too many people who can tell you what life was like on Buffalo Mountain and the difference Bob Childress made. At first I found many of the stories hard to believe, the people odd and unreal. The strangeness only began to wear off after I lived there for a time, listening as at least a hundred mountaineers shared their memories with me, sitting on their doorsteps and turning to face the Buffalo as they searched for words to describe the anguish and tragedy, the humor and irony of their lives, but most of all to tell about the man who came to live on the mountain that prophetic year the chestnuts began to die. I have vowed to tell their story truthfully and as fairly as any outsider can. I pray that I will not disappoint them.

The Man
Who Moved
a Mountain

Peaks of Otter, near The Hollow.

Dark Shadows of the Blue Ridge

There are few places in America more beloved than the Blue Ridge, rising like an ancient Great Wall across a third of the breadth of the nation. It has the burnished beauty of a country long lived in, of doorsills worn thin, of deep cool footpaths beneath the poplars. It has memories of a big young surveyor named George Washington who rode a hundred miles from home to look it over and to survey the Natural Bridge, memories of a statesman and inventor named Thomas Jefferson who lived in the valley to the east.

A highway coils along the very summit of the Blue Ridge through a countryside of serene beauty, with patches of corn and cabbage interrupting forests of mountain oak and red spruce and pine, and here and there the ash-white steeple of a dead chestnut. Woodchucks feed on the roadside clover, skunks stroll along the paving, and in the corner of a field a deer comes to feed in the friendly shadows. Now and then from the ridge there's a glimpse of the fertile Piedmont to the east and the blue valley of the Shenandoah to the west.

In the coves are proud frame houses, here and there a log cabin. Flowers fill the yards. Grapevines follow the eaves of the houses, encircling them. Smoke rises from the fat stone chimneys. It is a place of mellow beauty.

One after another, rising like watchtowers above the wall of the Blue Ridge, are mountain peaks of slate and basalt and granite, with names worn smooth by the generations who have lived and died on them: Stony Man, Bent Mountain, Hawks Bill, Groundhog, Rocky Knob, the Pinnacles of Dan, the Peaks of Otter, and, tallest of all, Buffalo Mountain.

This is Bob Childress country.

The people of the Blue Ridge are descended from the Scotch-Irish—those rugged six-foot men and gaunt, prolific women whom James I induced to leave Scotland for Ireland in hopes that they would intermarry and convert the Irish to Protestantism, but who there did more quarreling than courting, more fighting than converting. King James went back on his promise of cheap land and low-interest loans, instead levying heavy taxes on the poteen the Irish taught them to make and forbidding them to bear arms. Believing that freedom to bear arms and to still whiskey were part of every man's birthright, they migrated to America in the 1700s, bringing their muskets and their thirst with them, to settle an area vaster than all of New England, a roadless wilderness of crags and coves.

The first to arrive were educated, God-fearing Scots who took up the rich bottomland along the streams and built churches and schools and even colleges. As their sons grew tall and took wives to themselves, the old men helped them build cabins farther up the creeks, for no good Scot would let his clan be scattered. Communities of kinfolk grew up to marry among themselves, cousins to cousins. As one generation succeeded another, little cabins climbed farther up the creeks, where the soil was shallow and the bare bone of the mountain showed through. Near the summit the hollows were barely a stone's throw from ridge to ridge, leaving only a few steep-sloping acres to a farm, walled in by a jungle of tulip and oak so tall that the sun at noon could barely wipe away the shadows.

Each generation found life a little harder than the last. Schools, even churches in some places, were forgotten. The few roads were scarcely more than animal trails, used only by the folk who lived there. So the mountaineers' life became more remote and lost, as changeless it seemed as the mountains themselves.

Much of their language remained unchanged. Some words were straight out of Shakespeare: *sallet* for *salad,* *sech* for *such,* and *afeard*—a word Lady Macbeth used. They rhymed *yet* with *wit,* and changed *it* to *hit* for emphasis—just as Chaucer did. They used double words for clarity's sake—biscuit-bread, ham-meat, ham-bacon, toad-frog, tooth-dentist, church-house, and granny-woman (midwife). An irritable man was techous, and a spotted horse was piedy. A lazy man piddlediddled his life away; an energetic one worked from kin-see to cain't-see. Some picturesque expressions evolved: morn-gloam, dusty-dark, a nothin'-doin' sort of day. A man given to boasting about his travels was journey-proud. And since Scots seldom made generalities, they would qualify: "Least I've heared it that way all my life," or "I never knowed it to happen out that way."

When sickness came they had to rely on their own remedies: pennyroyal tea to sweat you, boneset tea to clear you out, whey poured off buttermilk to cure a stomachache, parched beet leaves to draw a rising to a core, the liquor from red-stemmed ivy for the itch, stump water for warts, and a yarn pulled through mutton tallow and tied to the toe for dew cracks. If some cures seemed not to work, still you used them because there was nothing else, and because someone you loved was suffering. You dipped a red flannel rag in lamp oil and gave it to a child to bite down on when he had a toothache. You boiled a polecat and had a child drink the grease to ease the asthma.

Despite their isolation, the clan grew. Women married at fourteen to sixteen, nearly all by age eighteen, and bore great numbers of children. Folks say the biggest family had thirty-five, by two mothers. There was little promiscuity—only an occasional woods colt or brier-patch child, born on the wrong side of the blanket. Women barely took time out to have a baby. One was out picking berries when her time came. "There I was," she said later, laughing, "with a bucket of berries and a baby. I couldn't figure which to take home first. I had sweat over them both."

Now and then a woman complained of the work. "Menfolks want a woman that never sets down," she might say, "that'll work in the cornfield without getting tired, and be so rested when the day is done that she'll get the meals, tend the children, do the chores while he eats, have a whole passel of young'uns in her spare time, and milk the cows, 'cuz it's womanish for a man to milk."

Yet her husband had only to slip his arm about her and say, "Old lady, you're a right smart help to a man," and she was amply rewarded. No mountain woman wanted a hen-husband.

These were Bob Childress people.

They were proud of their land.

"Up here is the onliest place to live," they said. They looked with scorn on the bottomland. "Why, down thar the grass grows so thick you cain't never bust through it with a hoe. Takes a yoke of cattle. We'd a hull lot rather irk a livin' with a hoe."

A young man and his woman could start life with little more than a skillet and a hoe. They would go up the mountain where the trees were so big there was no underbrush and where folks said you couldn't hear a cowbell for the birds a-singin'. Together the young couple would settle in a fern-shadowed hollow where water was close by, deaden the trees by cutting off a ring of bark, then hoe down kernels of corn between. No need to plow the soil, it was that loose and mellow. After harvest they had the corn ground at the flutter mill, and in the embers of the fireplace they baked it into johnny ashcake.

Food was abundant in summer. Folks say there was a God's plenty of game—wild turkeys gobbling from the oak thickets, deer and coon grown fat from acorns and chestnuts that fell to the forest floor. You could buy a shoat for a dollar, ear-notch him and turn him loose to forage, and in the fall go out and shoot him. As you found the means, you got a pair of oxen. They were the mountaineer's friend. They could work on land too steep and rocky for horses, and didn't need grain and store-bought harnesses as horses did.

But life at best was a struggle. Folks say it was a land of make it do, make it yourself, or do without.

The one thing that made life easier for the people of the Blue Ridge was the chestnut tree. It fed them, fattened their stock, warmed their fireplaces, cooked their corn bread, bought their luxuries—yard goods, pearl-handled pistols, and snuff. The more children you had, the more chestnuts you could gather to roast on the hearth on winter nights and to haul by wagon to market.

A boy could quickly pick up enough to buy shoes and clothes and a doll or other play-pretty that father would bring home from selling chestnuts in a valley town. Hogs fattened on chestnuts were walked down the mountain in droves of hundreds.

There was no better fireplace wood. Chestnut logs kept an even heat all night and didn't smoke. Blacksmiths used it instead of coal in their forges. Chestnut lumber sealed up a house; chestnut furniture was light enough for a porch-baby to move about; a broth of chestnut leaves could break up a deep-down cough. One mother who never bothered with a husband used to say, "A grove of chestnuts is a better provider than any man—easier to have around, too."

If you needed a footbridge to cross a branch, you simply cut a chestnut long enough and dropped it across. The slim stout pole was straight as an arrow, never sagged, and, if floods didn't wash it away, would last a lifetime. Nail a board atop it and stretch a wire for a handhold, and you had a footbridge fit for a preacher and his lady. The acid that suffused the wood halted all decay; drainage ditches made of chestnut didn't rot.

Most of all, rail fences made of chestnut fenced in your kingdom from your neighbor. Splitting rails and laying up rail fences was hard work, but it was reverent work, for it was something you were doing for your children, and their children, too. There was something venerable about rail fences, even new ones. They seemed like old hands folded protectively around a place.

The chestnut tree was a gift of God to the southern mountaineer, some said, a bounty so generous that people were stirred to awe—almost reverence.

Liquor was like that too. It seemed that nature had intended the people of the Blue Ridge to make liquor, for apples and corn grew on the slopes, and every fold of the hills had a tumbling stream of water to cool the coils. Most folks had family-size stills for their daily "usin' liquor," selling only as they might overproduce. They continued to operate them after it was legally forbidden. It took more than a ruling by distant lawmakers to stop them. Lord knows there was nothing wrong with it. The Lord made the corn and the apples. The Lord made the wood that fired the still, and made the creeks that cooled it. How in God's name could anyone call that wrong?

So folks hid their stills in a tangle of laurel and ivy. And if they didn't have but two bushels of corn, they made it into whiskey. They could carry it across the mountain a lot easier in a jug than in a sack. And if they didn't have but two bushels of apples, they made them into brandy. Apples wouldn't keep, folks said, and wouldn't sell—leastwise unless you hauled them miles down the mountain. But you could sell brandy right at home. And the home market was steady.

The Scotch-Irish revered all that they had brought with them —their land hunger, their language, the right to make whiskey —but most of all the right to settle their own disputes without interference of law. And the way to settle was with a gun.

Fathers taught their boys to use a gun when they were eight —and often, six. It was good for all the men to know how to hunt and gather food for the family—and you could never learn too early to protect yourself. So a gun became almost as much a part of a boy as shirt or pants, even while he was still in knee breeches. Young men were that proud of their guns that when they had their pictures taken by photographers who sometimes rode horseback across the mountains, they almost always posed with their rifles or pistols.

There were reasons for the killing habit. Historians have said that mountaineers first learned from the Indians how to fight from ambush. In the early days courts were far away, near the Atlantic Coast, and there was no sheriff or constable. To survive, a man took matters into his own hands. Good men—patient, cautious, and reserved—were also courageous, prompt, and thorough. They fought their own fights, and they fought to a finish. A half-beaten enemy was sure to seek revenge.

Even when courts did come closer it was hard to get a conviction in a population so intermarried that everybody was a cousin of everybody else. In the rest of America, men hired lawyers to defend them. The moneyless mountaineer used the only counsel he knew—his gun.

*Mountain men dressed up to pose with their pistols
for traveling photographers.*

Killing served as more than a final act of justice or safety,
however. Killings provided the excitement—almost the enter-
tainment—that lent savor to the dreary struggle of existence.
Tales of gunfights were told and retold wherever men met. There
was the story of the man in The Hollow, for instance, who sold
his head. Folks say he had gotten into an argument with a friend
who shot him down for dead and then urinated in his face, which
sort of woke up the dead man, who started in to cuss. That made
the friend mad all over again, and he fired another bullet right
into the forehead. They took him down to Mount Airy, where
two young doctors, Ed and Joe Hollingsworth, probed for the
bullet so deep they daren't go deeper. The man wasn't much
'count after that, but then he hadn't been before, either. Still, he
lived, and that surprised the doctors. They offered him five dollars for his head, and that was fine, for it was enough for a week's

drunk. But the doctors didn't get their money's worth. He out-lived them both. When he died, he took his head right with him.

The meanest tales of all were about a place called Buffalo Mountain. While the rest of America fought a war of indepen-dence, a war between the states, and a war in Europe, the people of Buffalo Mountain lived at war with one another. They stilled whiskey and drank and fought and stabbed—and shot each other with Owlshead pistols. Shot only people they knew well—their enemies, their friends, and their kinfolks. It was said that one man would sometimes shoot another at a frolic and then dance in his victim's blood. Curiously, a man might kill another and then feel remorse and take a gun to anyone who spoke ill of the de-ceased at his funeral. If they lacked knives or guns they fought with jagged, skull-crushing rocks. Killing was a habit of genera-tions. To argue was womanish. A Buffalo boy didn't become a man until he came to discard words for action.

Along with alcohol and guns, a third giant ruled the southern highlands. This was the Primitive Baptist church. Born of proud old Calvinist doctrine, but freed of the restraints of education and seminaries, it sprouted like mushrooms from the dark corners of every hollow and cove. It had roots in the Scriptures but thrived on superstition and fear and was kept alive only by man's ageless hunger for worship.

Its members called themselves "Primitive," meaning first or original, to distinguish themselves from the offshoot group known as Missionary Baptists. Because of their ironclad convic-tion that their faith was the only true one, their preachers—called elders—referred to themselves proudly as "Ironsides" or "Hardshells." On a Sunday three or four would gather to preach "from the lids of the Bible"—which few of them could read, yet which they believed implicitly. One said, "I'd believe it even if it ain't so." They spoke from visions or "experiences" instead of from a text.

Generally a preacher would start out: "I ain't got no text today. I'm just here ready to speak if God puts anythin' in my mouth. If he don't, I can't." This was "tuning up." As he mumbled on it was clear that a mortal man was talking, fumbling. He'd stop to drink a dipper of water from a bucket beside him, then page through his Bible searching for a text he couldn't have read had he found it.

Then, like a breeze beginning to stir, his words would come swifter. The phrases would start to sing. The words would begin to tumble out. The Lord was beginning to speak, and glory was pouring into the log church. The words were so lost in emotion that few understood more than a phrase now and then. The preacher turned his eyes heavenward, his words a chant soaring from velvety bass to tenor, from plaintive minor to melodious major. As the spirit increased in him, it seemed as if he would faint from the passion. For an hour, often two, he would go on. The words didn't matter. It was the voice and the drama that counted. Then suddenly the Lord would be through with him, and without warning he would sit down, and the next preacher would take over.

Sometimes the Lord supplied the words so fast that the preacher couldn't get his breath, and he'd gasp between each phrase, with an "ah" that turned his words into a kind of chant. A man might tune up:

"On these hills I've hunted the squirrels-a
"And in these valleys I've courted the girls-a."

After an impassioned two hours of preaching, he might conclude:

"Now I'll have to quit-a
"Because I cain't swallow my spit-a."

All during the service, which lasted the whole day, people walked in and out or went up to the pulpit for a swig of water. There might be half a dozen waiting in line. The confusion didn't bother the preacher, since God was supplying the words.

The shouting preachers gave excitement to the whole week. The preaching was something for mountaineers to talk about, and that was important, for since they were unable to read there was little to discuss beyond the bare bones of existence. Each preacher was in effect his own church, setting its rules. Few of them cared if men came drunk to church, for they themselves believed in drink. But all were forbidden to take any pay or salary, except for the gift of a jug of good wine or brandy—a boon to the timid speaker who might become a powerful mouthpiece for the Lord after a morning session with a jug. All were uneducated; that was a requirement. An uneducated man was sure to be a mouthpiece for the Lord, for he was without wit or words of his own. The Lord spoke through him. Anything that came out was God speaking, whereas a man with book learning might be tempted by the devil to speak words of his own. The more ignorant the man, the more faith folks had in him, for he couldn't fool them as a cunning city preacher might.

This was the life Bob Childress was born to, and was part of, and loved, and fought.

The Heller of The Hollow

His friends often urged Bob Childress to put down in writing the story of his life. Usually he would just laugh. Life was in the living, not the telling, he'd say. Besides, he was a man who found it hard to sit still for long, especially to think about himself. But one time he did make a start, beginning with his earliest memories of childhood. The words that follow are from that account, interspersed with recollections of his older brother, Hasten.

When I was not quite three, I got drunk. That's the first thing I remember in my whole life. I was wearing a long shirt that folks called a dress, and it was Christmas, the time when aunts and uncles gathered to celebrate with all the liquor they could hold. There was plenty, that Christmas, enough even for Uncle Tom and his nine who were visiting us: coffee lace, ginger stew, eggnog, and plain hard liquor. I had never felt so good in my whole life—until my stomach suddenly spun. The grown-ups told me to hurry outside, but I was too drunk to find the door. I tripped over my dress, fell and hit my head, and dropped off to sleep. Sometime during the night I lost my shirt, and I woke naked as a jaybird and with a hangover. But that didn't matter, the grown-ups told me. It was fine, just fine, to be drunk.

Brandy was god in our cabin. It was brandy that made life bearable. Food eased the stomach, but brandy filled the whole spirit. Twice a week a horse-drawn liquor wagon made its rounds past our cabin from a state-licensed distillery across the mountain. The most it could leave at one time was a runlet—that's just a shade under five gallons—and Pa often took the full amount.

We lived in Virginia on the eastern slope of the Blue Ridge, just above the North Carolina border, in a place called The Hollow. It's a crescent-shaped area about thirty miles long and twenty wide, walled in by the mountains.

My father Babe was a big, red-faced, boisterous man, generous and kind, a jokey fellow that everybody liked. His ancestors were Scotch-Irish who had lived in the hills for three generations. Pa's parents never got around to giving him a name other than Babe, and Ma said it was just as well, for big as he was he never really grew up.

Pa was a liquor-head. He worked hard when he was sober, as a timber cutter or as a farmhand in the tobacco fields or apple orchards lower down in the valley, but that wasn't enough that he could feed all nine of us children. At one place he got fifty cents a day, if he'd take half in pork at twenty-five cents a pound. No job lasted long. As a result we never did own any land or even a cabin, and we were always on the move, forced out of cabin after cabin for not paying rent. Sometimes there wasn't a bite of food in the house. But there was always brandy. One year Pa tried running his own distillery but couldn't make a go of it; there was seldom any surplus to sell.

My mother was named Lum. She was tall and slim, with fair skin and black hair, pure Irish, and sad most of the time. She worked hard, even when she felt poorly, washing clothes for people for twenty-five cents a day, and keeping the dirt floor of our cabin swept clean. Ma too was a heavy drinker, like many women in The Hollow. First thing every day she and Pa would have a "morning's dram," a few gulps right from the bottle, as regularly as they pulled their clothes on.

Later, at breakfast, Ma would pass the bottle around the table to the rest of us. Her mother had told her it was good for children and kept away diseases, and Ma could repeat her mother's teachings word for word, like many mountain people who had never learned to read.

I was born on the night of January 19, 1890. A real old-timey mountain blizzard was howling across the mountains. My oldest brother Hasten was fourteen, and he ran down the mountain to

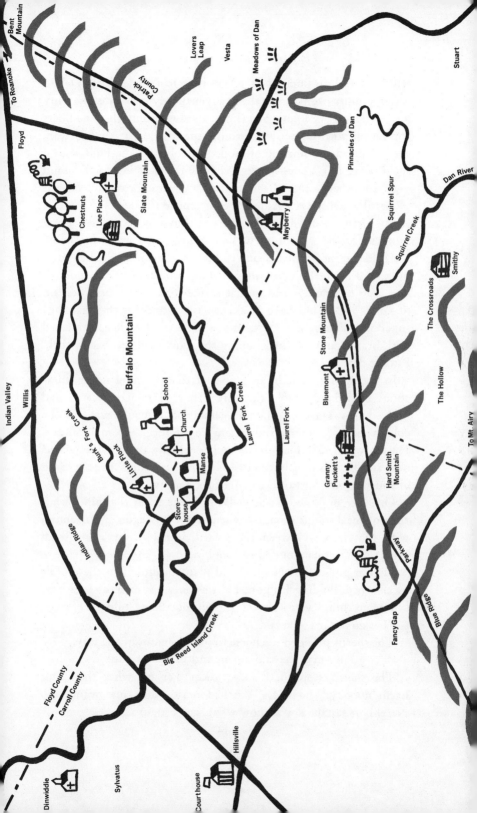

tell Aunt Orlean Puckett that Ma's time had come. Aunt Orlean was a granny-woman, a tall, rawboned lady who was the only sort of doctor we knew. She threw a shawl around her shoulders and set off with Hasten up through the drifts. To Aunt Orlean, every baby was a miracle of God, and folks in The Hollow said she'd never lost a one—though she'd birthed at least a thousand —or a mother, either. I don't know for sure. Anyway Ma was peaceful when she saw Aunt Orlean come in the door.

My birth was hard on Ma. She was thin and weak from going hungry for the sake of all us young'uns, and I was a big baby. Ma told me she was hard put to keep me alive, she had so little milk, and I had the colic bad. She'd dip a piece of rag in molasses and then in brandy, and give it to me to suck, to ease the pain of colic. She would have weakened the brandy with sugar, but sugar was a luxury we seldom saw. She tried to keep me eased with brandy until spring, hoping she too would feel better then. But she didn't.

In the spring something happened to Ma that I never knew about until Hasten told me only a few years ago. Hasten had noticed how sad-eyed Ma was getting. She would walk in the cold woods for hours, and often would forget to make meals. Hasten worried to himself about her. He always was the serious one, and Pa was mostly too drunk to notice things. Hasten, even at fourteen, was sort of the man of the family.

One day in June he was walking home from the mill with a turn of meal on his shoulder when he saw a wagon approaching, with Ma sitting between the sheriff and a deputy, out from Stuart. She was handcuffed and sobbing.

Hasten put down the meal and planted himself in the middle of the road, holding his gun. He was only a lean spear of a boy, but some things you knew to do without being told.

"Let go my ma," he said.

The sheriff prodded the horse to push him out of the way.

"Let go my ma," he said again, and lifted his gun.

The sheriff stopped. "We're takin' her off whar she cain't harm nobody," he said. "We had notice she's just wanderin'. Neighbors say she don't know what she's a-doin'."

Hasten looked up at the two men. "My ma is a sick woman. She had a young'un this winter." He leveled his gun at the sheriff, drew back the hammer, and deepened his voice. "Move any further, and I'll kill you both!"

The sheriff must have known mountaineers well enough to know when a threat was real. He hesitated, then loosed the handcuffs and helped Ma off the wagon. The men whipped the horses and hurried down the hill. Hasten put his arm around Ma to still her crying, and they walked on home.

That's how bad things were for Ma that first year.

As summer deepened and food was more plentiful, Ma's spirits and strength returned. They say I picked up and got brown as a berry from the sun.

Our home, at best, couldn't be called a happy one. Ma seemed to pick a quarrel with Pa whenever he came into the house, drunk or sober. And happy-go-lucky Pa was high-tempered and fought back. Sometimes it seemed they hated each other.

People in The Hollow took babies as much for granted as the coming of spring. If one died folks would say, " 'Twas meant to be, and when a thing is meant to be, it ain't no use to fret." But if the young one who died was getting some stretch to his legs, a man might think, even if he didn't say, "A shame—getting big enough to work."

Not so with my folks. They loved every one of us and were as good parents as they knew how to be. They hadn't been to school a day in their lives, but they were clean and they kept us clean, and that wasn't common in The Hollow, where folks didn't have the washrag habit. Pa carved what he called playpretties for us boys and corncob dolls for the girls. We respected our sad-faced mother, but it was our big, boisterous father we really loved.

After me came two more babies, so there were five boys and four girls growing up in our one-room cabin. We boys slept in the loft on straw ticks, the girls on ticks on the earth floor. Pa and Ma had the only bed. A stone fireplace cooked our food and warmed the room too. We generally had one opening for a window, but it had no glass, only shutters to keep out the cold.

There'd be a washstand in one corner and a homemade table with two or three oak-splint chairs in the center. It was crowded all right, but we never thought about it, because one cabin nearby had sixteen children—fourteen singles and a set of twins with not so much as a freckle's difference between them—and two other cabins had sixteen apiece too. The only time we felt

Lum Childress. "They loved every one of us," Bob said, "and were as good parents as they knew how to be."

crowded was when Uncle Tom came with his nine to spend the night. That made twenty-two of us. But we just thought it was fun. We'd pull as many straw ticks off Ma's bed as we needed and scatter them on the floor. Six or seven of us boys would sleep crossways on a single tick and think nothing of it.

It was food we were short of. Every day was different. Most were hungry, some full. There were plenty of apples while they lasted, but without jars to preserve them in, that wasn't long. In winter we lived mostly on hominy and corn bread, on strips of hog or deer or rabbit meat that hung in the smoke of the chimney, and on rings of dried pumpkin strung from the ceiling. But this would give out before spring, and there were lean cold months before summer came and we could get to grazing on wild berries and vegetables.

We were the poorest in a place where everyone was poor. If we came to a neighbor's house at mealtime the family would jump up from the table and the mother spread a dish towel over the food, explaining they were just through with victuals.

We didn't blame them. We knew that the family came ahead of friends and neighbors, ahead of everything else. A man's family was his kingdom. Loyalty to family was the first commandment of the mountains. At the gristmill, when Hasten scraped a little meal from the rim of an empty bin, the miller chased him off. Generosity was a luxury, something for rich people.

It seems I was most always hungry. Many times I stole outside to look at the mountains. Someday I'd climb up there to the top, where the stars lived. There'd be food there, and everything else I longed for.

There was one time of year when we had food. That was in late fall after the gusty winds of a chestnut storm left the ground strewed with nuts. Pa and Ma would take us out by lantern light to beat the hogs to them, for the hogs knew every tree as well as the humans did. The nuts stained our hands and feet a dark brown that nothing but time could remove, but no one minded. Hasten said that the chestnuts were like the manna that God sent to feed the Israelites.

It was on a day in June when I was six that a stranger came walking up the side of Hard Smith Mountain where we lived. She was a young lady with big dark eyes and a quick smile, and I thought in my whole life I had never before seen anyone so beautiful. When she asked for my folks, I explained they were away working but that I'd quick fetch my big brother. I raced up the ridge to where Hasten was grubbing out thorns on the face of the mountain. We hurried back.

The lady said her name was Miss Sally Marshburn, and that the Quakers at Guilford College in North Carolina had sent her to start a school in The Hollow, and Sunday school too, for all who would come. Hasten promised to come and to bring the older children.

I remember I spoke up in my biggest voice and said, "I'm six," and Miss Sally laughed and said, "We'll try to find room for you."

Ma was angry when she heard about it. Five miles morning and night was too far for young ones to walk. Besides, what good would school be? And who was this woman? But Hasten was a hard one to talk out of anything.

"Ma," he said, "you love those young'uns like a sow loves her pigs. But me, I want to make something out of them." The next week he herded six of us down the road to school, two hours away, carrying me on his shoulders when I got tired, and now and then playing the breath-harp to amuse us.

The school was the first glimmer of education to penetrate The Hollow—and Miss Sally quickly became the most important person in my life.

I loved school, and Sunday school too. The Old Testament heroes were my favorites, especially Daniel. I already knew about lions. Sometimes at night they screamed on the ridge above the cabin, and one morning on the way to school I saw one slip behind a boulder near the path. Most of my brothers and sisters got tired of Sunday school, but I never missed, and when spring came Miss Sally gave me a pair of red suspenders as an attendance prize. I had never seen any before. I had no idea what they were for.

"Galluses he's got, and nothin' to hitch 'em to!" my classmates taunted. And it was true. I didn't yet have breeches. Only my shirttail dress.

When Ma heard the joke that night she hurried to her sewing basket where she kept scraps of cloth, and in the firelight of the hearth sewed them together. The result was wondrous, like the golden calf that Aaron made of the jewelry his people brought him. There was no music or dancing to celebrate the day I put on my first pair of knee breeches. It was all in my heart.

The rest of my brothers and sisters would have gone to school oftener except for the humiliation of our raggedy clothes and the meager lunch pail that my big sister Annette carried. Sometimes we had only poor-do—milk with corn bread crumbled into it. Other days there'd be nothing but one biscuit apiece. At noon, when all the school was gathered under the oaks to eat, Netta would slide the cover back a little, reach in for the biscuits, and dole them out one at a time. When they were gone and the lunch pail was empty, she'd ask each one of us, "Wouldn't you like somethin' more?" And each of us would reply, "Nope. Had a-plenty." A mountain child, even though his stomach was hurting from hunger, had his pride to think of. When my father heard how we said we were full on one biscuit, he laughed his loud laugh. It seemed he often laughed loudest when he was most hurt.

Most of us were lighthearted like Pa. But there was no humor in Hasten. He worried over our parents, over the sack of cornmeal that was always running out, over the way we had to move almost every year as the rent fell due.

Hasten Childress, a week before he died,
reminiscing about his younger brother.

Hasten recalls that Bob was jokey like his daddy, and he too seemed to clown most when he had least reason to. He was forever trying to get his pa and ma to laugh together, making up little riddles and jokes. But as soon as the laughter died down, there were contrary winds in the cabin. Sometimes Bob would slip outside and cry.

Hasten found him one time back of a bush by the cabin wall and pulled him out gently.

"Bob, —that's just the way people are."

"But they hurt each other," Bob said with a catch in his breath. "They hurt each other."

"I guess all people do. They just got to fight. And nobody ever wins."

A couple of miles from where we lived when I was seven or eight was Squirrel Creek, a steep-walled cove full of colored folks. I loved to go visit them. The grown-ups were always so happy and laughing and gentle, never any quarreling or mean talk. I had lots of playmates my age there. Pa and Ma never minded that I went. Mountain folks never did feel kindly towards those rich tobacco planters who'd had slaves. The main reason the Negroes had stayed clustered in that one cove is that the walls were so steep it was hard to get in or out. They'd been brought there in the first place by an outsider, a tobacco planter from the Piedmont, a man who never married, whose prettiest slave girls had lived with him and had borne him great numbers of tall, handsome children.

In January just after my ninth birthday I walked to school in a sleet storm. I was the only one who made it from Hard Smith Mountain. I got to school chilled to the bone. Miss Sally stopped her class, took me alongside the stove, and put her arms around me to warm me. I remember yet how puzzled I was that anybody who wasn't kinfolk should care that much that I was cold. That night I took pneumonia, and for nine days I was out of my head. Ma held me in her arms most of the time, for she knew how hard and lonely a straw tick is to a sick child. Aunt Orlean came to spell her off. I still remember puzzling even in my delirium why she too should care so much about someone who wasn't even kin. I knew we never paid her, and a lot of others didn't either. She'd come when she was needed, no matter what time of night, even if a storm was crashing through the mountains, toppling trees across the path—sometimes for five, even ten miles by lantern light, or up some hogpath that would have made the stoutest man puff.

Just as I was recovering I found out that my favorite playmate, a little girl, had been burned to death when her dress caught fire from the hearth as she was fixing food for her three younger brothers. The parents were off on a weeklong drunk. No one blamed them. It was an act of God, folks said. But I was so grieved and confused that I had a long setback, and it wasn't until March that I could be up and return to school.

There wasn't much for a boy to do in The Hollow. Grown-ups did the planting and hoeing and harvesting, and tended the stills. We had to manufacture our own fun. We'd play cat-ball, a game where one team forms a circle around the other, trying to hit those in the ring with a rubber ball. We seldom had a ball, so we used rocks, and once in awhile we'd come home bloody. At molasses-making time we'd have taffy pulls that were fun. Most of the time, though, we'd just sit and swap stories. One of my friends was always seeing ghosts. "A whole passel of 'em—all in white—came a-floatin' down this very road, a-walkin' it seemed, and yit their feet never moved!" I'll admit I was scared even to listen.

The big event in the mountains—and one we all went to—was a Primitive Baptist funeral. Mountaineers—normally reserved—gave themselves up to wailing and weeping; even grown men sobbed and moaned. Funerals were actually festivals that brought a thousand—sometimes two thousand—people on foot, on horseback, or by oxen. If an old man died, there might be a wait of years until his widow went too, and then a double funeral. On such an occasion the bereaved family would serve dinner to all friends, neighbors, and relatives—and remember, in the mountains, we reckon kinship even to thirty-second cousins! The more preachers the better. Usually there were four or five who went on all day. Their message seldom varied: God had willed the death, long before the world began.

I'll never forget the first funeral I ever went to. A young man had come home drunk and tried to kill his stepmother, but shot himself instead. I remember yet what one preacher chanted out:

"Little Georgie-a, is a-walkin' the streets of glory-a
He done exactly what the Lord wanted him to do-a
When the Lord pulled the foundations of the world-a
He planned for little Georgie to be born-a
And to get drunk-a, and to try to shoot his stepmother-a
And to have the pistol go off and shoot himself-a
And he fulfilled God's purpose-a
And he's gone the way that God wanted him to go-a
A man cain't die before his time comes-a, nohow
Nor in any way nor at any time except as God planned-a
If he could-a, what would he do when his time comes-a
Would he die again?"

I suppose I was ten, but I puzzled over that question. Just what would have happened to little Georgie? I asked Hasten about it that night as I lay alongside him in the loft, but he only rolled over and fell asleep.

Every August the Primitive Baptists held their annual meetings at the church grounds with baptisms in the river and footwashings and a giant festival under the trees. Neither Pa or Ma were members. Pa couldn't take himself that seriously. Besides, before you could be accepted you had to stand up before the congregation and describe some vision or other divine "experience" to qualify you, and neither of my folks would do that. But we went anyway, for the free food and drink as well as the excitement.

Sometimes we went inside and listened to the preaching. I never will forget hearing one preacher sing out, "Praises be to God that I am igno*rant*. I'd only praise him more if I were igno*rant*er." I wondered to myself, did God hate learning? I knew without asking what Miss Sally would say. Then I remember that the preacher ended with a prayer that in heaven there'd be plenty of possums, sweet 'taters, and brandy, for heaven wouldn't seem right without them. Pa was already outside, having a foretaste of that heaven.

After services one preacher, sharing a bottle with Pa, said, "I never do prepare me a sermon. I just wait to see what the Lord tells me." And Pa said, "I'd hate to throw that one of yours back on God Almighty!" Then he laughed his loud laugh.

It was hard for me to know what to believe in. Haunts and visitations seemed more real than church religion. Folks saw strange sights. Others possessed strange powers. If along past midnight a glass fell from the table, rolled across the room and broke, a man would say to his wife, "I've a coffin to make tomorrow." And it seemed he always did. Another neighbor woman when she threw out her dishwater at night would sometimes hear a sound like someone throwing down the shoulder load of planks that cover a coffin, and she would say, "Tom, they'll be a buryin' tomorrow." And sure enough, it seemed there was. Sometimes in the fogs that hushed The Hollow the spirit world seemed more real than life itself. I kept picturing God dressed in white like the ghosts folks kept seeing. And though I kept going to Miss Sally's Sunday school, I was just as devout with mountain superstitions. I kept a piece of lead on a string round my neck to keep from the nosebleed, and I buried a hair of my dog's ear and one from his tail to keep him from running away.

Hasten didn't believe such stuff. He ridiculed Ma for switching the cream to chase out witches. He even ate berries out of a graveyard to prove to all of us he wouldn't die of the bloody flux. But I never outgrew some of those old superstitions. Even today, strange sounds at night bring me bolt upright. Foggy nights make me uneasy.

When I was eleven I saw something that made me wonder what life was all about. My brothers and I were on our way out hunting when we saw a crowd at Hunter's Chapel, a little church in the woods near us. They were gathered around a gumwood tree. Hanging from a limb was a man with a note pinned to the body: "We kilt him. Hunt us." Many in the crowd were smiling and laughing. I couldn't take my eyes off the swaying body. Didn't the others know that the Lord said, "Thou shalt not kill"? I knew that buried near that very tree there were already thirteen men who had died by guns and knives. Was death any more than a careless mistake, or did God really plan it that way? How could he be a kind God if he burned little girls at the fireplace and made grown men kill and then laugh about it? The others hurried away to hunt, and I had to run to catch up. I never did forget that hanging man, swaying and turning.

Hasten began taking over as head of the family, and we had more to eat. He rented a patch of ground for beans and had us all stringing beans through the middle of the pod to dry into "leather breeches" that we hung from the ceiling for the winter. We picked pails and pails of wild berries and dried them on bark that we rived from trees. He bought chickens and saw to it that the extra eggs were traded at the store. He got a job as a timber cutter and promised Pa that someday he'd buy a farm for him. But even with Hasten in charge we still all drank, and got into trouble for it. Hasten himself would come home with bruises, though we never heard that anyone ever bested him. I looked up to Hasten. I wanted to be like him, and begged to go out with him, but he never let me.

When I was thirteen I got the second pair of pants I ever owned—knee breeches made of wool my mother had spun. Along with them I got my first pair of new shoes, bought with chestnut money. I told Ma my feet were so tough from going barefoot that I'd wear out the shoes from inside long before the rocks did.

I was in seventh grade now and loved school as much as ever. Some mornings I'd come an hour early so I could talk with Miss Sally alone. She'd tell me about her home and her parents and life in North Carolina. I did everything I could to please her, memorized dozens of poems because I knew she liked them, and read every book she brought me. My favorite was Emerson's *Essays*. I loved the one on friendship. Miss Sally tried her best to make something out of us, and when one boy spoke of himself as nothing but a poor mountain boy, she scolded him. Why, didn't he know that the blood of knights and even kings ran in his veins? And in this very county a young man had practiced law, a young man with pure fire in his speech, named Patrick Henry. Jeb Stuart had been born here. Daniel Boone had farmed in a valley to the south. And a young woman named Nancy Hanks had been born here, though she moved away and married a man named Lincoln. All these were mountain people, she said—and fire seemed to spark from her.

The year I was fourteen, Hasten married and left home. I missed him terribly. And then a few months later, Miss Sally married a Quaker preacher from Guilford and left The Hollow for good. I mourned her almost as if she had died, and didn't go back to school except for a day or two now and then.

It was then that I started my hell-raising. I already knew how to claw and bite and kick where it did the most damage. Now I practiced throwing a rock so it counted. Being able to "rock" an adversary was a mighty useful skill. There was never a lack of ammunition—jagged rocks the size of a fist. In my first big fight a rock caught me behind the ear, knocking me out and nearly killing me. I learned to fight mean—mountain-style— from ambush. I longed to be grown up. Here I was, still in knee breeches, the fuzz on my face getting dark and thick, and I had no gun. Someday I'd have long pants and my own pistol, and I'd be feared.

There wasn't much for a boy to do in The Hollow. Sometimes I'd go over and help Hasten on his new farm. More often I'd join friends at a still to drink and play poker. For a while a couple of us looked for a lost silver mine that had been discovered years before in the slickenslides near the Pinnacles of Dan by a Civil War deserter. The fugitive had hid out there and made silver bullets to sell to the mountaineers for warding off witches. Then he began making silver dollars, and the law heard about it, and the man disappeared as suddenly as he had showed up. Mountaineers said that his dollars were purer than the government's, so he couldn't rightly be called a counterfeiter. We never found a trace of a mine.

The year I was fifteen, Hasten bought a farm for my father and a cabin—the first he had ever owned. Pa was so moved he decided to give up drinking, and did too, for some months, then suddenly took pneumonia and died. All the laughter and fun were gone from our house now. Ma grieved the way I couldn't believe she would over someone she hadn't seemed to like.

I was drinking more and more now, and going along with my big brother Sam, joining up with other boys whose sap was rising. Sam had to stay sober enough to look after me, for I was always getting into trouble. Sam was a peaceful boy, but could lick any boy in The Hollow who threatened me. I was right proud of the way Sam could fight, and sometimes I'd start a ruckus just to see what would happen. One Sunday there were seventeen boys, and when I started trouble, Sam jumped in and propped for me. Soon everyone was after us. Sam knocked one boy out with a rock and we ran for it, rocks bombarding us for a mile before we escaped. It was then that Sam announced that he was through with fighting and I would have to look out for myself.

Soon after, with the first five dollar bill I ever held in my hands, earned from cutting timber, I walked seven miles to Mount Airy and bought my first pair of long pants. They cost two dollars. Then I went to a gun shop. I knew exactly what I wanted: an Iver Johnson .32 caliber nickel-plated pocket revolver with a four-inch barrel and an owl's head on the grip. It cost exactly two dollars. A hundred cartridges cost thirty cents. At last I was a man! On the way home I splattered a few shots against the rocks beside the road.

I started teaming up with my big cousin Jess, twelve years older, who was counted one of the meanest men in The Hollow. I liked the way people looked at us when we walked to the woods to cut logs. We were tough, not to be trifled with. On Sundays we would join others at some still where we gambled and drank, guns at our sides. Once I was watching a poker game when two good friends started arguing over a five-cent stake. In a flash, one shot the other dead. At the funeral the preacher said, "This is a fearsome thing, but since it be the Lord's will, it had to be. Man ain't got nothin' to do with it. He dies when his time

*Young Bob with a girlfriend
from The Hollow.*

comes, and he cain't die before." I didn't know what to believe. I wondered if the Lord planned for me to kill a man—or to be killed.

A month later I was playing cards by candlelight in a tobacco barn. All of a sudden a short man jumped up and stabbed one twice his size in the neck—a man who carried neither gun nor knife, for he could whip two men. The big man died in the arms of the one who stabbed him. There didn't seem to be any reason why it happened. It was like that many times—a small argument, a secret resentment, or an imagined slight, and a man would be dead. We had no family feuds, no hatreds passed down from father to son. I couldn't figure it all out. Sometimes I would look up to the top of the mountains and think that up there I would find the answers, so I'd climb up. But it never helped much, and I'd come right down. I guess I never was one to worry or fret very long.

Hasten says that at seventeen Bob stood six foot one, and was lean and hard as a chestnut tree. His face was strong-featured, a mite too rugged to be handsome, with hazel eyes that smiled at you from under thick brows and black hair that he always kept trimmed. Folks said he didn't have a care in the world. Everyone liked to cluster around him. He was a live one. At a gathering, when the boys would stay outside, wrestling, footracing, and otherwise showing off even after the girls had gone inside, Bob herded everybody in and started up fiddles and guitars and banjos and got everyone going at cotillion or Virginia reel. He sang his father's songs, in a voice that was big and mellow.

More and more he was taking to alcohol. Anyone who could joke and laugh and carry on as he did could get all he wanted, mostly free, from the liquor wagon as it made its rounds from the Williams still at Trot Valley. All eighteen of John Williams's sons who took turns driving the wagon looked forward to the stories Bob Childress could tell. Hasten wondered if he shouldn't warn his brother that his friends probably liked him mainly for his jokes and his whiskey bottle.

I was getting to be known as a heller. Much of the time I was either getting drunk or sobering up. One day I was playing cards in a blacksmith shop with half a dozen friends when one of them hit me over the head with a whiskey bottle. When I came to, hours later, it was dark, and my friends—even my cousin Jess— had all left me. My head throbbed, and my hair was sticky with blood, but it was my heart that was in pain. Wasn't there a one of my friends who cared whether I lived or died? I wondered if friendship wasn't just a pretty word. It was like the lines on a tombstone that I used to repeat for a joke:

> Beneath this stone John Anderson lies
> Nobody laughed and nobody cries
> And where he's going or how he fares
> Nobody knows and nobody cares.

I knew what the man was saying. I felt just that alone. I wondered if the man had committed suicide.

Hasten was a heavy drinker too, and a fighter, and though he could put away whole bottles, he never got wild-drunk or came home hurt. One day he said to me, "Bob, I believe drink is bad. It makes a little man biggety and a big man a fool. I believe I'll give it up." I couldn't have been more surprised if he'd said he was quitting the mountains. Then he told me he was going to be a county police officer.

I kept right on drinking, and fighting. I got my jaw broken in a fight, and though it mended all right, there's a deep scar on my cheek to this day. Often my friends and I would fire back and forth at each other in fun, and though I somehow never killed or seriously wounded anyone I was shot once in the leg and once in the shoulder. They were surface wounds that healed quickly. Time and again I saw men kill each other, men without hate in their systems, but drunk and with guns and knives always handy.

The year I was twenty I was hardly ever sober, not even in the morning. I was miserable and sick to my soul. For days I didn't eat a decent meal. My cousin and I got to whipping out our pistols and daring men to shoot us—hoping sometimes they would. Once a man did yank out his gun and hold it in both hands, aim, and fire at me from less than ten feet away. I wondered why I felt no pain, why I didn't fall. When I realized he was so drunk he had missed, I cried. It is hard to tell the agony of those days except to say that twice I went out into the woods and put my pistol to my temple. But each time I put it down. I can't tell you why.

Then one day, after playing cards and drinking for hours, I found myself six miles from home outside a little church. I never did know how I got there. But I could hear singing. I went in and sat down. It was a Methodist church, and there was a revival. I don't remember how it happened, but when the altar call was given, something inside urged me to go forward to the rail. As I knelt I felt no sudden revelation, only a sense of peace. For the first time in my life, it seemed, I rested. I slipped out of church quietly, not wanting to shout as some did, but only to rest. That night I slept like a child, without having a pull of brandy. Next morning I left my pistol off. I didn't seem to want it.

I returned the next night to the church with my cousin, and

walking home afterward along a dark mountain path I said, "Jess, somethin's happenin' to me. I don't know what it is, and I don't know how, but I want to kneel here, and you with me, and I'll try to pray." Big Jess nodded silently.

We knelt, and I prayed, and afterward Jess said he felt something happen inside him too. When we started up again he began telling me what he said he had never before told anyone—that in spite of his reputation as a dangerous man he was a coward, scared whenever he dared a man to shoot him. And he was too sick of himself to stay sober.

The revival lasted a week, and I didn't miss a night. Once I came early and saw another boy I knew sitting on a log outside the church, a brier-patch child born without a father. I just had to speak to him. The boy listened, head turned away, as I explained my strange experience. When I stopped he turned a cold look on me and said, "If you're a-tryin' to convert me, save your breath. Work on those as have already j'ined."

But I kept right on talking. I just had to try to share the wonderful peace that had come to me. This time the words came easier. And during the services that night—to my amazement—the boy made confession.

That week of revival didn't change me into a new man, but it gave me the first real peace in my whole life. For the first time I had felt a power stronger than the power of liquor and rocks and guns.

Blacksmith Lawman

Bob was twenty-one when Hasten faced him with a choice. "Bob, what you doin' with your life? You log a little, blacksmith a little, and a little this and that, but mostly drink and raise hell. Now I'll tell you. You're a learner. You got to go back to school. You're one Childress who can make somethin' of himself."

Hasten had prospered. At the time he was married he had borrowed money for the license, and a year later his home was burned out down to the last skillet, but he was hardworking and thrifty, and his fields of tobacco were always well tended.

Bob hesitated. "Well, I've wished sometimes I hadn't quit. But Hasten, I'm twenty-one. And there's Ma and the others who need someone to—"

"To what? Go off roisterin' and come home drunk? Let me tell you I can keer for them—and for you too. I'll see you get enough for clothes and food as long as you're in school."

Bob had no answer. The next week he entered eighth grade at Friends Mission where he had left off six years before—a strapping hulk of a man among skinny youngsters. But he had hardly a chance to get back into studying. For Pearl Ayers, a timid, brown-eyed slip of a girl he had known all his life, was there, too. He fell in love in his headlong, headstrong way, and decided he was going to marry her, and right now. But Pearl's mother, the postmistress, wouldn't hear of her being tied to a big rowdy drunk. Pearl herself acted like she didn't quite know what had happened, only that the world was all different since Bob Childress had come into her life.

So one day Bob just drove up to the Ayers cabin and began piling things into a buckboard. Pearl's sisters were screaming and carrying on, and one went to get her brothers from the woods. But Pearl climbed up beside him, and off they rattled, scattering loose garments in their wake. They ended up at a Methodist parsonage down in the valley, and the ceremony was just over when Pearl's two brothers rode up on muleback. There were lots of angry words but no fighting, and that night the brothers even showed up among the crowd who came to Bob's sister's cabin to serenade the newlyweds.

Pearl Ayres a year before she married.

It was the end of schooling for Bob, and for Pearl too. Now he had a woman to take care of. Hasten was so sad about the wedding he couldn't talk to Bob for weeks. But Bob felt happier than he could remember. And he began drinking and carousing less often, and started thinking about doing steady work.

First, he went to work for his sister Georgia's husband, Hayes Jessup, and lived in a cabin on Hayes's farm. It was hard work, and Hayes wondered if Bob would return to heavy drinking, but Bob didn't seem to mind. He joked about everything, or so it seemed.

"Hayes," he'd say, "this land of your'n is so steep that goin' up you can mighty nigh stand up straight and take a bite out of it, and goin' down you need hobnails in your breeches." Then he'd laugh, so loud that everyone around laughed too.

Hayes's ten-year-old girl Euna loved her big raucous uncle who helped give her doll a fine funeral and a week later helped search for the grave. He taught her the lore of the mountains and how, if she counted ten stars for ten nights, she would dream of the boy she would marry. But all she ever dreamed about was Uncle Bob.

Bob was starting to be more content than he had ever thought he could be. Within the walls of his log cabin was a miracle: a woman who never complained, who sang at her work, who comforted him even when he came home drunk. Out in the fields of corn and tobacco he would send up a prayer for his good fortune. A year passed.

Then a storm of violence hit the Blue Ridge. The law that year had decided to put a stop to the Allens, a well-off family who lived at Fancy Gap, a few miles from The Hollow, but whose reputation for toughness and generosity and daring went far beyond. When two young members of the clan were arrested for breaking up church services with rocks, Uncle Floyd Allen beat up the deputy sheriff. It seemed sure he'd be sentenced to a year in prison for the assault, and no Allen had ever gone to jail. What happened made front-page headlines for the next year all over America.

The report that follows is from the *New York Times*:

> ROANOKE, VA., MARCH 14. Down to the quaint old red-brick
> courthouse at Hillsville, Va., where sentence was being pro-
> nounced on one of their number, a troop of twenty mud-
> splashed mountaineers galloped in with rifles from the sur-
> rounding hills, raced up the steps and, in less time than it takes
> to tell it, killed off the court, the judge upon the bench, the
> prosecutor before the bar and the sheriff at the door. Several
> jurors were shot, one mortally, and the prisoner and two by-
> standers also wounded. Before the smoke of their rifles had
> cleared away, the mountain outlaws leaped into their saddles
> and, putting spurs to their horses, galloped through the stunned
> village. Troops have been ordered held in readiness at Roanoke
> and Lynchburg and the Second Virginia Regiment has been
> ordered to Hillsville. A witness, a girl of 19, started home, not
> knowing she was shot through, and collapsed and died a quarter
> mile from town. The prisoner's familiar boast was that he had
> thirteen bullet holes in his body, and that five of them had been
> put there by his brothers.

Bob decided to join the posse, mainly for the excitement.
Before long there were a thousand men in pursuit. Bob was
amazed at the hullabaloo. Newspaper reporters—in hordes from
all over the country—inspected the courtroom and found two
hundred bullet holes. They reported every rumor.

> The Allens may be hiding out in Devil's Den, a cave guarded by
> huge, insurmountable rocks where a small party of men could
> defy a regiment for days. The Allens are well supplied with arms
> and ammunition and no one believes any of them will be taken
> alive. The outlaws have recruited a big band. There is a saying
> among revenuers here that every pine tree shelters a moonshine
> still.

The hunt shifted to Squirrel Spur, the high shoulder of the Blue
Ridge above Bob's cabin. Reporters called it impregnable.

Bob couldn't get over the commotion.

"But sure you must have shootin' scrapes up North?" he asked
a magazine editor at the hotel lobby in Hillsville. The editor only
shook his head and showed Bob an editorial.

> The majority of mountain people are unprincipled ruffians. They
> make moonshine, 500 horsepower, and swill it down; they carry
> on generous and gentle feuds in which little children are not
> spared, and deliberately plan a wholesale assassination, and when
> captured either assert they shot in self-defense, or with true

coward streak deny the crime. There are two remedies only—
education or extermination. Mountaineers, like the red Indian,
must learn this lesson.

It was Bob's turn now to shake his head. That night he talked
about the editorial with Pearl long after the fireplace embers
turned to ashes. Now he knew that some of his doubts about killing were not so strange after all, that other people, outside the
mountains, didn't believe and act that way. But he still could not
understand the frenzy and the harsh accusations. "That's what
they think of us—and they mean *all* of us," he said. "But it ain't
so. We're not evil like they say—even the worst, they're good
underneath."

Bob read other papers that came to reporters.

"A flash of Sicilian vengeance," commented one. "These wild
Christian clans take the same view of law as Bedouins on a
cattle raid."

A magazine equipped: "The Allens prove that the family that
preys together, stays together."

Bloodhounds took up the Allens' trail, pressing so close to their
hideout in a cave near Buzzards Roost that they fled, leaving
blankets and food. The tracks began separating in many directions as the fugitives scattered to different hills and coves.

The Allen clan made national headlines
after the Hillsville courtroom massacre.
Left, *Sidna Allen's home near Fancy Gap;* right, *the courthouse.*

After weeks of hiding, they were caught one by one. Reporters, expecting to see ogres, were amazed.

> A boy of 22, a splendid type, who stands more than six feet high, with dark hair and blue eyes, was brought in without handcuffs, as carefree as a schoolboy. Another, Claude Allen, 16, stumbled out of a thicket, sleepless and starving, and gave himself up. He is an outgoing, handsome boy.

On his last day with the posse, Bob stopped at the hotel. He liked to talk with the men there. He liked to listen, too. The men seemed so different. They all had things to do and were eager to do them. He read all the newspapers he could find. There was one with an editorial that concluded:

> The Scotch-Irish mountaineers are more ignorant than vicious, victims of heredity and alcohol, and now that their isolated region has been invaded, must change or perish.

All the way home Bob pondered. Was he one of those victims of heredity and alcohol, an ignoramus who must change or perish? The newspaper wasn't describing just the Allens, but the whole Blue Ridge, his friends and neighbors and kinfolk. He stopped in the road, his temper flaring. His people were good people; they just didn't behave. Then he cooled. The paper had said they were more foolish than mean, he remembered. That evening after supper he talked again with Pearl about the strange world outside the Blue Ridge where it seemed that most men never thought about drinking and fighting. Perhaps this was where they should live, especially now, with a child on the way.

Suddenly he turned to his wife. "Pearl, I think I'll give up drinking."

She stared a moment, then started to cry softly. Seeing Bob's worried frown, she said, "It's only I'm so glad."

Tears came to his eyes too. "I didn't know," he said. "You never said anything." A wife who asked so little—what wouldn't a man do for her?

Quitting drink was a struggle. Sometimes the urge within him was a torment. His friends would offer him a pull at the bottle for old time's sake. "We takened to teasing him about being womanish," one recalls, "but he just laughed."

Sundays, when he wasn't working and when the Blue Ridge took to serious drinking, were the hardest. One way he tried to keep occupied all day was by renting a horse and buggy and driving with Pearl from one church service to the next. There was Hunter's Chapel, the Methodist church five miles southwest, and another, Carter's Chapel, just above The Crossroads, besides the Quaker Meeting at Friends Mission, which Hasten had joined. Other than that, The Hollow was all Primitive Baptists, with little churches at intervals of every two or three miles where they sometimes stopped in for the old-fashioned preaching. The speaker at one was known to have helped forge a legal paper claiming he owned a corner tree that marked a boundary line. After a service Bob heard a man confront the elder with his misdeed, asking him, "Posey, don't you call yourself a preacher of the gospel?"

"Yessir," he replied, "but religion don't have nothin' to do with corner trees."

Bob suddenly thought of Miss Sally. She had said that religion was the way you talked, the way you worked, the way you helped your friends and neighbors—and even your enemies. It wasn't something you only thought about on Sundays. It was Aunt Orlean and the way she came to help, no matter what. It was doing right.

In the fall of that year a boy was born. They named him Conduff. Holding a son in his arms made Bob think about the future—something he realized with a start that he had seldom done. He decided he should aim toward saving some money and trying to work at getting land and his own home. He worked all winter in the woods, and in the spring helped several farmers with their plowing and sowing. In spare moments he helped out in a blacksmith shop, and during the summer he even taught in the Kimball elementary school, three miles south. This was something he liked. He found that the children appealed to him, and they seemed to like him. In fact, they took to following him around. They believed everything he said—which was pleasing and yet frightening.

Bob thought even more seriously about the future when a daughter, Evelyn, was born. What chance did a child have in the Blue Ridge, he thought one day when Lum brought brandy for the baby and he had to turn her down. "We're trainin' our young'uns to be dry at both ends," he joked, trying to ease her feelings. But Lum seemed hurt.

When World War I broke out, Bob got a letter from his sister Netta urging him to move to West Virginia, where she and her husband had gone to work in the coalfields. Bob loaded his family and all they owned, including the cow, onto a flatcar bound for Coalwood, West Virginia. There he set up a blacksmith shop.

Only three months later he got word that a flu epidemic was sweeping through The Hollow and that his sister Hattie had died. So had Hasten's wife, and Hasten himself was lying helpless, no one daring to care for him. Bob hurried with his family back to the Blue Ridge. He found Hasten near death, and spent night and day for two weeks in his frame house, nursing him back to health.

Only three weeks later, his beloved Pearl took sick herself. She had always been frail, and the flu, strange to the mountains, found her defenseless. She died quietly in a few days.

Bob felt paralyzed. He was worn out, body and spirit. Pearl had given the joy, the sense of worth, that kept him from aimlessness and drunkenness. Now, here he was, with two motherless babies. He went into the woods. He thought of drink and its gentle forgetfulness. He thought of suicide. Up to this moment in his life he had generally got what he wanted by persuading or working or fighting. Now he was helpless.

The first night he lay in bed between his baby girl, a year-and-a-half, and boy, three-and-a-half.

The boy whispered, "Papa, are you there?"

"Yes, son."

"Let me feel you."

Bob reached out his big arm and laid it over Conduff's covers. Then Evelyn woke up and began to cry for her mother, and the boy joined in. Bob patted them both. Then he too began crying, and right away the children dropped off to sleep.

More weary than reverent, Bob found himself repeating the Lord's Prayer. "Our Father," he began dispiritedly, then stopped at the line, "Thy will be done." Not his own will, which till now had somehow always been served, but *thy* will, God's will. Perhaps in this awful moment, God had another plan, one so distant there was no hint of it. Perhaps when his own will could do nothing, he should let God do the planning. A surge of peace came over him as it had on that strange night of revival, and he slept.

Next morning Bob heard of a mountain couple so sick with the flu that they couldn't tend their little girl, who was thought to be out of her head. Folks were that afraid of the flu, that no one went near the house. Bob was upset.

"There's no one—not even kinfolk—goes near them?"

As far as anybody could tell there wasn't.

Bob couldn't stop thinking about them, even in his grieving over Pearl. He went over to his mother, who was living alone now that her children were all married and gone. It took no urging for her to come live with him. She was feeling poorly and didn't like to be alone. As soon as he had moved her in, he set out up the mountain through drifts of snow so deep he often had to dismount. He found the house icy cold, without a stick of wood for a fire. Both parents were huddled in bed, alternately freezing and burning with fever. Bob hacked off enough splinters of wood for a fire to warm his own numbed hands, then went out and cut up bigger logs and got a large blaze going. The only food was a sack of potatoes under two loose boards in front of the fireplace. He boiled them and fed them to the parents. The child was too ill to eat. He made poultices out of the mashed potatoes and kept warming and applying them to the child all night. In the morning he found milk left by a neighbor at the edge of the clearing. He mixed this with the mashed potatoes and fed the parents. Then he went to a neighbor and begged leather-breeches and dried beef and made them into a broth that he coaxed into the little girl's mouth. The second night the child grew deathly pale. Bob was afraid he had done something wrong. He asked the parents to pray with him for her. Sometime during the night, as Bob watched by candlelight, the little girl sighed, her color returned, and she started to breathe evenly. Bob muttered a quick prayer of thanks and—as a kind of partial payment —sprang outdoors and in the light of the stars chopped up a mess of firewood. By morning the parents were on their feet, and by evening the little girl was sitting up in bed. It was almost a miracle, Bob thought, then quickly dismissed it. No man could think so bold.

As Bob rode down the mountain in the icy darkness he felt strangely exhilarated. He realized with a pang that for long stretches he had forgotten about Pearl and about his motherless children, and though he felt this was wrong, he wasn't quite sure. He wished there were someone he might ask about it. He knew that after two days and nights without sleep he ought to be tired, but he wasn't. He felt buoyed up, yet peaceful. He thought of Aunt Orlean. Was this how she felt as she pulled herself through the winter drifts? Was this what Miss Sally had meant when she spoke about doing for others? It was something Bob Childress had never felt before.

Lum stayed with Bob and the children only a few weeks. Bob saw she was sick and ought to be near a doctor, so he put her on a train for Pilot Mountain, North Carolina, where she could stay with his brother Everett. She died after only a few months.

In The Hollow, tradition ruled that when a young mother died the children must be given away to the nearest relatives. Bob would have none of this. He rented a house at The Crossroads from the Quakers and with money borrowed from his sister put up a blacksmith shop just behind. One room of the house he decided to turn into a grocery store that he could tend at night. That way he could work all day and into the night and yet keep watch over his children from the time he dressed them and fed them breakfast until he undressed them and heard their prayers. When relatives continued to demand the children he would say, "My young'uns are fatter than your'n." Then he'd laugh. "Got better manners, too."

On Sundays he would polish his children, folks say, till a fly

could ski off their noses, slick down the little boy's sandy hair
and tie a ribbon around the little girl's yellow pigtails, boost
them onto the horse, and then swing himself up, the girl ahead,
the boy behind. Then they would set out for one of a number
of churches they went to alternately. But increasingly Bob was
drawn to a young preacher named Roy Smith who had come to
The Hollow fresh out of seminary. He was the only educated
man in The Hollow, and Bob liked to be around him. He wasn't
so much interested in getting converts as he was in starting Sunday schools, and he got Bob to teach whenever he came. He kept
his denomination a secret even from Bob.

No matter which church Bob attended, the minister would
usually ask him to lead the congregation in prayer. His voice was
powerful, his manner dramatic, and he had a natural way with
words that made them seem somehow noble and majestic. A
delegation of Primitive Baptists came to the blacksmith shop urging him to join them. With a voice like his he was predestined by
God to be a Primitive preacher. They were willing to overlook
the fact that he could read and write. But Bob had no urge to
preach. It was Sunday schools that interested him—and to the
Hardshells these were a curse in God's eyes.

The blacksmith shop prospered. Folks say that Bob's horseshoes
were a marvel for form and fit, and that hard as he hammered
away at the glowing metal, he kept everyone in hearing amused
with his stories. Hasten was proud of his brother. "I just tell him
what kind of tool I need for my tobacco patch, and he makes it—
even tools that never were before!"

Bob loved his fiery forge and the showers of sparks and the
clean strong objects that took shape beneath his hammer. He had
stopped both drinking and brawling now. Yet all the while he
kept thinking of his friends, still drunk and fighting, and of the
torture he knew they felt in their sober hours. He had hoped it
would be different, especially when prohibition was voted in. He
thought this was what the mountains really needed. Now there
was a law to help cure the curse of the hills. But nothing happened. Liquor was as plentiful as ever, though the stills were con-
cealed and deliveries were secret.

Lawmen smashing a still during prohibition.

The day a drunk man dazedly grasped a glowing horseshoe in his shop Bob raked back the coals, doused them with water, and closed the door. There was other work that needed doing. He sent for his niece Euna to look after the children, then donned his black homespun suit and rode off for Stuart, the Patrick County seat. The next day—June 4, 1919—he was sworn in as a deputy sheriff, pledged to uphold and enforce the laws against drink and shooting. The court that week had a busy calendar: seven mountaineers for miscellaneous shooting scrapes, ten for felonious shooting and murder, not to mention twenty-six misdemeanors, mostly for "U.M.A.S."—unlawful manufacture of ardent spirits. It was a heavy docket for a county of seventeen thousand people.

The sheriff was glad to have such a mountain of a man as Bob Childress, so quick to move, so sure of tongue. He immediately sent Bob after a boy in liquor trouble who said he'd shoot it out before he'd be dragged to jail. Anther deputy had refused to go. Bob talked to the boy from outside his cabin, finally persuading him to come quietly to town. A few weeks after that, Bob trailed and caught a fugitive in North Carolina, disarmed him and started home, riding awhile himself, then letting his prisoner ride. Twice the man tried to charge the horse over him. When they got to the justice of the peace at three in the morning, Bob thought of sleeping, but just as he'd doze off the prisoner would try again to escape.

"It 'pears to me," the justice told Hasten, "that every time they got a roughneck to go after, they put it off on Bob."

Bob took Hasten along one time to a cove towards the Dan River to see about a man who had been shot while asleep behind a log. They found him with his head smashed, Hasten says, like a busted watermelon, and his brains spread out on the ground. There was a boy, too, shot right through but wide awake.

"Well, Hasten, we've got a job getting this boy out to the road and a hospital," Bob said.

Hasten looked at his brother in disbelief.

"Look, Bob, that boy's done gone. You can see it by his eyes." The boy looked up and said no, he wasn't going to die.

Hasten whispered, "On top of that, Bob, he's a stranger. And if we touch him, we'll be obliged to pay the hospital and burial bills."

But Bob paid no heed. He took the boy in. Luckily for Bob, said Hasten, the county paid the burial costs, but Hasten never forgot the incident. Bob always seemed to think with his feelings instead of his head.

It wasn't long before Bob began to feel prohibition was futile, especially the way it was carried out. He discovered that most times the sheriff and his deputies would find a still, smash it, arrest the man, and then and there—along with the prisoner—get drunk on the evidence. In most cases, the sheriff had no intention of making arrests. Bob felt foolish for not having guessed it earlier. On one of his last raids the posse surprised a moonshiner and five of his sons at the still—a fine man except for the liquor, Bob knew. There was considerable shooting, though no one was hit. Taking out after the moonshiners in the dark of the forest, Bob scrambled over rocks, slid down fallen logs, and stopped beside a big chestnut log to catch his breath. Then he decided to give up and go back to the still. There he found his fellow deputies all drunk. He wondered what he was doing on their side.

Later, after federal agents had imprisoned the moonshiner and his boys, Bob visited them in prison, bringing gifts. He always hated to see anybody cooped up.

"Bob," they said, "do you recollect our battle, when you got separated and was a-restin' by the side of that chestnut log?"

"I sure do," Bob said, "for all I could think of was how disgusted I were at myself."

"Bob, you were in a bad fix then, wuss than you know."

"How's that?"

"All six of us were a-lyin' t'other side of that log with our guns a-pointin' at you. If you'd a-looked over it, we were all a-goin' to shoot."

"I wouldn't a-blamed you much, neither."

Two years as a deputy was long enough to convince Bob that the law would never conquer the proud people of the Blue Ridge. The killing and drinking would go on and on, no matter how tough they made the law. He turned in his badge, went back to his home, and opened the smithy again.

Free Lance in the Brush Arbors

Lelia Montgomery was twenty-three, a slender girl with chestnut hair and eyes as blue as flax blossoms, and it was spring and the purple haze of redbuds was blowing across the mountains as she walked home from church one Sunday.

She had stopped to talk with Bob's sister Georgia outside the Jessups' cabin near The Crossroads, when Bob drove up in a buggy with his two children. He pulled up sharp and stared. He had seen her before, even talked with her, but only now did he realize what folks meant when they called Lelia the fairest girl in The Hollow. She smiled with her eyes, they said, and her laugh was pure as the jest of God. When Bob told her how pretty her Sunday dress was, Lelia blushed and turned to go. Bob stopped her by asking if she knew of a good washwoman to help him.

"I'd rather shoe a yoke of cattle than scrub shirts," he said, with a grimace.

Georgia turned to Lelia. "They's a woman up the cove from you, ain't they?"

Lelia recalls that she started to redden, for she knew he'd ask her to ride there, and she should say no, for she wasn't that well acquainted.

He did ask, and she did say no, she'd rather walk.

Bob tipped his hat and started off the other direction, but she was no more than home when he showed up at the door, asking the way. He had a lot of washing to do in the next few weeks. Then he asked if she would be at home the next Sunday when he came by with the clothes. She said no, she was going to see a sister in Mount Airy.

"Let me carry you there," said Bob. That surprised her so, she couldn't think what to say. It was a full twenty miles from The Crossroads to Mount Airy. She nodded.

Lelia Montgomery (left),
"prettiest girl in The Hollow,"
with her sister Maggie

Bob arrived right after church the next week. It was a fine day in May, and the dogwoods were stealing like haunts through the hollows, lighting up the thickest forests. The horses were high-steppers. The rented surrey was smooth and quiet. To Lelia it was a pleasant ride. To Bob it was heaven. How could a girl be so easy to talk to without being bold, so sweet and feminine without being coy, so unaware of her beauty? He felt a numbness almost like that of alcohol creep across his face. Even when they weren't talking he felt easy, comfortable. Once during the trip an image of Pearl flashed to his mind's eye, as it did so often, but Pearl seemed to smile her approval. By the time they returned to The Hollow Bob knew for a certainty that he was in love again. He had never thought he could be.

On Wednesday evening he came to take Lelia to prayer meeting. This time he had a single horse and a buggy with a narrower seat that would leave less room between them. Lelia hesitated, but then considered it might be a sin to refuse to go to prayers.

On the way, the horse balked at the bottom of a hill. It just wouldn't move. When he slapped it, it looked back and kicked.

Lelia cried, "Let me out of this thing. I'm skeered."

"Just sit tight," he said, "I'll get her movin'."

Lelia got out anyway, and when Bob left the buggy to cut a switch the horse ran away up the hill. Bob chased after, roaring at the beast. Lelia could see he was a high-tempered man. He caught up at the top of the hill, a long way off, then hollered for her to stay until he could return, but she hollered back, "No sir, I'm a-walkin' up!"

When she reached the top she said, "Mr. Childress, if you're a-countin' on going with me again, don't bring this balky horse. I'm skeered of him!"

Bob started to laugh, and Lelia reddened. She had all but asked him to come again! He laughed until she had to tell him to stop.

During services that evening, someone slashed Bob's new harness to pieces, hoping to provoke him to fight; all The Hollow knew of his fighting skill, and some liked to irk him. Usually he was patient and joking, but now he was furious, and while Lelia stood trembling beside him he dared the men who'd done it to show themselves. "I tried to hush him up, for I saw how mad he was," says Lelia. "I was afraid someone would answer." No one did.

That spring and summer there were other threats. The very next Sunday night some men barricaded the road Bob normally took from church, waiting to waylay him. But Bob happened to have taken a longer route home.

"The Lord just plain looks after you!" said Lelia, when she learned of it.

Two weeks later, as they drove home in the dusty-dark from

Mount Airy, an admirer of Lelia's was waiting with his father by the road. Both had guns, Bob could see. Lelia whispered their names to him and he called them out right friendly, asking if they wanted a ride. The men walked away silently, apparently surprised he knew them.

That night Bob asked Lelia to marry him. Without a minute's pause, she said no.

"Is it the children, Lelia? Would it matter if I got them placed out among their mother's people?"

"No," she said. "If I loved a man enough to marry him, I'd love his children enough to make them my own. It's just that I don't reckon I'll get married at all."

Bob was in despair. Lelia hadn't meant to hurt him. She vowed not to go out with him again, but he persisted and she finally did.

Their next time out she told him why she knew she should never marry. When she was seven she had contracted tuberculosis of the bone, or what folks called the white swelling, in one ankle. A doctor had come a few times by buggy from Mount Airy, but all he could do was give medicine to ease the pain. It was her mother who doctored her with poultices made out of the reddest clay she could find, mixed with vinegar and applied as warm as she could stand it. Small slivers of bone worked their way out through the skin. Her grandfather kept the ankle wrapped in the pitch from white pine, while her grandmother would light fire to a saucer of whiskey, let it burn a few seconds, then weaken it with water and sugar for her to drink. Gradually, as the bone rebuilt itself some, she was given wild cherry bark, sassafras, pignut, and sarsaparilla root ground fine and mixed into water and whiskey. She was ten before she could return to school at The Crossroads—three and a half miles from where she lived—and since it was too far for her to walk on crutches, her father arranged for her to live there.

Her voice was soft with affection as she described the love and care her family had given her. Bob longed to take her in his arms.

"So you see I'm a cripple," she concluded. "I can walk all right, but slow, and I can't run and jump and dance as other young folks can. I should have told you before this. I never planned to marry."

Bob wept. For once he was wordless.

Lelia said it was unfair to go out with him again. This time Bob just got up and left. But he was back again the next evening, saying he wanted just to sit and talk. So it went all summer. She felt she couldn't just turn him away. And soon she didn't want to.

It was on a Sunday evening in August driving home from church that Bob stopped to pick an apple for each of them from a branch above the buggy. He saved the seeds from his, and started to count them, while he said the old rhyme:

> "One I love, two I love,
> Three I love, I say,
> Four I love with all my heart,
> And five I cast away;
> Six she loves—"

He paused and grinned at her.

"Bob," she said, "you've more seeds between your fingers!"

He went on counting.

> "Seven he loves,
> Eight they both love;
> Nine he comes,
> Ten he tarries;
> Eleven he courts,
> And twelve he marries."

He looked at her and tried to seem surprised.

"Lelia, that old apple settles it. You're bound to marry me."

"It appears that way," she said quietly, her blue eyes sparkling. He didn't speak for a long moment. Then he let out a bellow of joy that startled the horse into a gallop, and they charged off down the woodland road.

Next day, when Lelia told Aunt Orlean she was going to get married, the old granny-woman tried to discourage her. "He's a good man, child," she said finally, "but you've got plenty of time to get married."

Lelia knew she was thinking of her own marriage, of how her man got drunk and beat her, and of her own babies. As magnificently as she cared for others, she couldn't keep her own children alive. Of the twenty-four she bore, only one had lived seven months, and she had had such hopes for him. But then one day he lost interest in things and just faded away. She buried him alongside the others in the old Dunkler Puckett burying ground below the mountain. What they died from nobody knows for sure, not even Aunt Orlean. She dug slabs of gray rock into the ground to mark each grave, twenty below the mountain in a single file and four on the mountaintop near her cabin.

Aunt Orlean patted Lelia gently and said, "Honey, hit's for you to decide. Hit's not for me."

Lelia could not bring herself to tell her mother of her decision, for the family had assumed she would never marry. It was Bob who broke the news while Lelia sat looking at the floor.

Lelia's mother listened to him quietly.

Aunt Orlean Puckett's cabin is preserved in memory of the tireless midwife who lost no babies but her own.

VIRGINIA CHAMBER OF COMMERCE—PHOTO BY IRBY HOLLANS, JR.

Then she spoke. "Mr. Childress, Lelia would do all she could for you, because she's a good girl. But you must remember that she is a cripple. There are other girls who would be better to work than she is."

"Mother," said Bob, "if I were lookin' for someone to work, I'd hire someone. I'm not marryin' a slave."

Then he went on to tell about his work at the smithy and the store, of how he'd been able to manage so far. But suddenly he found himself talking of other things they would do together, of holding Sunday schools and prayer meetings. He hadn't really thought about it much until he spoke, and he began fumbling for words as he considered the effect this girl, so gentle, so deeply and honestly devout, was having on him. He was telling of dreams and hopes he had never been fully conscious of—and meaning everything he said.

They were married in August and went to live in a cabin that Lelia's grandfather had built at the foot of the mountain. Bob began a new period of discovery about himself, and about his wife. Lelia had the gift of serenity. And though she was soft-spoken and mild, she didn't hesitate to disagree now and then. Bob respected her judgment. She had a logic and wisdom that was akin to Hasten's—something he knew he was often lacking. The children loved her. Bob thought to himself: the Lord had taken away, but had provided someone too good for any man to deserve. "Thy will be done," he thought.

In the spring they moved back to The Crossroads, where he resumed blacksmithing in his little shop. The world looked good to Bob Childress. His singing rose above the clanging hammer as he pounded out horseshoes and wagon rims. He sang so loud that some folks wondered if he had gone back to drink.

On Sundays he would hire a horse and buggy and, with Lelia and the children beside him, maneuver along some mountain trail to a spot in the forest where folks had built a "brush arbor" —a thatch-roofed canopy that served to shelter a Sunday school. A Methodist preacher had two or three such arbors, the Quakers had a few, and Roy Smith had another. No matter how primitive the arbors—they were often no more than cleared-off spaces where people sat on the ground—they were sacred ground to Bob Childress. From the very start he had a feeling he must protect them against profanity and drinking. "He was like a dog a-standin' guard on his yard," says one mountaineer.

To mountaineers, brush arbors were no sanctuary. Men fought in them, and even killed. Some of the Primitive Baptists, determined to keep out alien beliefs, especially Sunday schools, encouraged the conflict.

Bob's presence usually preserved order, but once half a dozen drunken youths began caterwauling while he led a class. He warned them to be quiet.

"They ain't no law agin' it," they said.

He grabbed two of them by the shirtcollar. "If I can't teach the love of God into you I'll beat the devil out of you!" he thundered, and gave them a mighty shaking. There was quiet.

In June Lelia gave birth to a hazel-eyed daughter. They named her Marie. Bob brought home an armful of red lilies from up the mountain for the bedside. How much a woman could do to show her love, he thought, and how little a man could do! He kept the woodbox and waterpail filled—chores only a hen-husband did in The Hollow. And he urged Lelia to let him take the clothes to be cleaned elsewhere, but she insisted she enjoyed being outside with the black kettle and the fire.

With Lelia caring for the baby, Bob went alone to the brush arbors on Sunday. There was such a need of him there, to keep order as well as teach. Bob liked especially to go up with Roy Smith, who was becoming his closest friend. Roy finally confessed that he was a Presbyterian but had been warned not to reveal the fact, since anyone who sprinkled and called it baptism was an infidel to the Primitive Baptists. He had started a Presbyterian congregation, and was slowly building a small group of followers who appreciated his Sunday schools and his calling on folks. Bob would often go there to teach, to listen to Roy preach, and then to talk with him about almost anything, but especially about what Roy believed in and what he hoped could be done in the mountains. Sometimes they would talk late into the night at Roy's cabin, about one of the books Bob had borrowed from Roy's shelves or about his belief in educating the young for a new and different life than their folks had known.

Bob began thinking more about what he was teaching in the arbors, especially about Jesus and what he'd said and done. His confusion about what God was like began to clear up as he read the Gospel stories over and over again. He came to see Jesus as someone who always looked inside every person for the good that was there and tried to bring it out, no matter how mean or ornery he might have been. God didn't want a man to get crazy drunk and to kill or be killed by a gun. He wanted men to *live*. He loved them, loved all men. That's what Jesus said, and showed people too. If they could only see it, they could change and act the way God wanted them to. Even robbers, even prostitutes, even tax collectors. Even gun-toting, whiskey-stilling mountaineers. It was all right there in the Scriptures, plain to see, but for Bob it was a new discovery.

It had always been easy for Bob to talk and laugh and be friendly with most folks, but now he began to look at each one a little harder and to see a little deeper. One Sunday after an early snow Bob went with Roy up the mountain to a brush arbor in the farthest woods. Sitting on a log in Bob's class that day was a wrinkled little woman who listened intently. Afterward he spoke to her.

"Mother, it's good to see you," he said, slipping an arm around her small shoulders. And then by way of conversation he remarked about the snow and asked, "You ready for winter with plenty of wood up?"

"No, and I'm bound to act lively," she said, "but the joints are a mite stiff."

Bob was shocked. She was almost sure to be eighty years old. "Why mother, you can't handle an ax, or a saw either! Isn't there someone—"

"I've got along so far," she said proudly.

Bob walked home with her that day, and as they went she told him of her life on the mountain, from the time she was fourteen and a bride. Impulsively, he said, "Wouldn't you like to come spend the winter at my house?"

She shook her head sadly. Then she brightened. "Hit's been a good year, and I thank the Lord. I've got enough to last me the winter."

PHOTO BY DAVID GREEAR

Mountain worshipers gather at a brush arbor in the woods.

When Bob asked for her ax and saw, she hesitated. Wasn't it wrong to work on the Lord's day? Bob said the Lord would understand. He cut and sawed and split enough wood to last a few weeks and, as he kissed her good-bye, promised to be back.

It was only a short while later that she died and her life's riches were sold at auction. Bob chanced to see the sales report, recorded in the courthouse at Hillsville.

1	cow	$51.00
1	haystack	12.00
1	pitchfork	.65
1	oggar	.35
1	hoe	.25
1	shovel	.75
1	cradle	.45
½	bushel grass seed	2.65
2	bushels buckwheat	1.75
1	saw	3.50
1	ax	.75
1	lard pail	.10
1	calf muzzle	.25
1	churn	.50
1	sword	.25
3	straw ticks	1.00
1	pickle dish	.15
1	butter mold	.25
	snuff	.20
	clothes pins	.10

It was probably as much as she and her man had ever had. Bob admired the tough independence of her character, but he knew that just a little effort by someone else would have lightened her load. He began visiting some of the isolated cabins just to get to know those who never left their little hillside plots, and whenever he saw a need he tried to help.

Word traveled fast across the Blue Ridge of the blacksmith who came to help people. What kind of a man was he? He taught Sunday school, but he obviously wasn't a preacher, because preachers of any denomination seldom stirred outside of church.

He was sometimes received with curiosity, often with indifference. But usually his easy ways and ready laugh won over the suspicious. When Bob heard that old Aunt Jude Idey Bowman lay sick six miles across the mountains, he decided to go visit her. He clutched his Bible under his arm and set out feeling —he had to admit—a bit proud. In his new black suit he knew he must look every inch a preacher. He found Aunt Jude's house full of grown boys—grandchildren and great-grandchildren. They expected her to die, and to keep her from feeling lonesome were having an old-timey frolic, drinking and singing, playing the breath-harp and dancing. The wizened old lady lay on her back under the patchwork quilt, not moving a finger. She was reputed to be a hundred and five.

A grandson said, "Ma, we done fetched the preacher."

She opened her eyes and whispered, "Did he bring whiskey?"

Bob explained that he never brought whiskey, that he had used to drink but had left off.

The room grew quiet. Here was a chance, Bob thought, to preach to the whole family. So he lectured them on the evils of whiskey. It was a right pretty speech, he thought proudly.

When he was done, the old woman closed her eyes and sighed.

"Preacher, you're dead right about whiskey," she said. "It never did come up to brandy."

When Bob told her, Lelia laughed until the tears came.

It was in May that Stase Duncan died. She was a tall, dignified woman with the look of an Indian about her who lived atop Squirrel Spur, the high crag which newspapermen on the Allen case had called an impregnable fortress. Stase rarely left her mountaintop except when she walked nine miles to market with plump red cherries and dusky-blue huckleberries and the brooms she made out of stiff grass—brooms with three feet of sweep to them that would last for years. A Negro named Joe Tuggle came to live with her, and folks said they were evil. But when Stase died, Tuggle sent word that he couldn't bury her without a few words said over her. No preacher responded.

So Bob went. He left home before sunup on a strong mule, picking his way along Squirrel Creek. When the creek gave out he followed deer trots, leading the mule. When the way was too rough for the mule he tied it to a chestnut tree that towered above the forest, hoping it would prove a landmark on his return. Then he fought his way up the rocks to the mountaintop through a jungle of fallen trees and grapevines.

He found the man waiting, and crying. Someone back on the

ridge had made a coffin for Stase, and Tuggle had dug a grave down the mountain at a place she was right fond of, where the flowers bloomed so pretty. But when the two men tried carrying the coffin and Stase down the mountain on their shoulders, they found the footing too unsure and the turns too sharp. The only thing was to dig a grave on the mountaintop alongside the cabin. The two men dug, but it wasn't long till they hit bedrock. So there they buried her and piled stones over the thin layer of earth that covered the coffin. It was deep night when Bob got home.

Lelia was waiting up, a lamp in the window. When he told her about the day his voice was full of sadness. "They're not bad people," he said. "They're lonely, they need love, someone who cares. Every one of them, even the folks others call bad."

In June, Lelia had a second child, a boy they named Bryan. Bob brought an armload of daisies into the house, and Lelia said the whole place smelled like honey. Lelia seemed so happy, and she said she felt stronger than she had in her whole life. There were no bounds to Bob's joy.

He had all that earth could offer a man, he thought, as he paused on the doorstep on the way in with water. A redbird was singing from a honeysuckle bush, and from inside the cabin came the music of children's laughter. From up the mountain came the clean fragrance of blooming basswoods. It was good to be alive.

One morning soon after Bryan's birth Bob looked out from his shop and saw a swarthy, bearded stranger coming up his path, leading a horse nearly as bony as the man himself. Bob knew from the four-cornered hat and blue overalls rolled to the knees that he was from Buffalo Mountain, eight miles north. Sometimes Buffalo men would pass through The Hollow on their way to or from the market in Mount Airy.

The horse had a loose shoe, and Bob said he'd tend to it right away.

"The Buffalo," said Bob. "That's a right wild place, ain't it?"

"Yes, 'tis," said the man proudly, and immediately began a story as he eased himself into a seat while Bob began work. "Why

only last fall I was a-fiddlin' the roll-down at a frolic when
bullets started flyin' so fast the blast put out all four coal oil
lamps." He paused, savoring every word. "I just lay down agin
the wall to keep from getting shot. The shooters takened off, but
after that the party seemed to break up." The man chuckled, as
Bob took the horse's foot between his knees.

The man went on. At an apple butter boiling a little later,
one of the shooters came in drunk and asked polite-like if he
could stay. Directly he took a whiskey bottle half full, held it
in front of his pistol, and fired. It splattered glass into a girl's
face. The host took the man by the arm and said, "You and me
has somethin' to talk over," and led him out beyond the firelight
—so as not to offend the guests. "Presently we heard two shots
—bang bang—fast as that," the man went on. "Everyone else
takened off fast, but my brother and I lifted the kettle off the
fire to keep the apples from burnin', then went over beside a
sprangledly tree where the man lay a-dyin'. He lasted quite a
spell."

The stranger obviously enjoyed telling his stories, and Bob
knew from past reports that most of them must be true. He
was halfway mad at himself for liking to hear them. Like any
man of the mountains, he was a teller of the tales that made
the lore and heritage of the people. But now his feelings were
mixed, and as he thought about it later he wished he had spoken
out against the man's relish of bloodshed. He thought of the
lonely women and frightened children, of the twisted ways that
would lead people not just to kill, but to enjoy telling of it.
He could see it in himself and in the people of The Hollow, not
just in the Buffalo man.

That night he went and talked with Roy Smith.

"I've been thinkin' hard, Roy, and I can't let it alone. We
need help here. We're poor and ignorant and lost, and most folks
don't even realize it. But ever since they caught the Allen boys
I knew other people don't live this way. And ever since I've
been helpin' you out I knew there was lots of things to be done
for folks." He paused. "So, Roy, I've made up my mind. I want
to be a minister."

Roy looked startled, but Bob went on.

"And not just another old stomper and thumper either, just as foolish as the ones he preaches to. I want to be trained, like you."

Roy was silent. Bob knew what he was thinking—a man of thirty with four children, a man who hadn't finished eighth grade.

"I ain't afraid of the work, Roy. I know it means more schoolin'."

"But do you know how *much* more? You've got all of high school, four years of college, and only then could you start seminary. And there'd be Greek and theology and. . . . Look, Bob, a man doesn't need to be a minister to serve the Lord and help people."

They talked some more, but Bob went home deep in thought and discouraged. There had to be a way, but right now he couldn't see one.

That winter when the blacksmith trade slacked off Bob got a job teaching the lower grades again at the Kimball school. He loved the work and the children, and it gave him a chance to do some extra studying on his own. He also started up a Sunday service at the school. Later, he began preaching at a little community south of The Crossroads and even helped form a congregation there that had no denominational tie. They called it Free Union Church. And Bob began going some Sundays to Squirrel Creek to lead services in the Negro community's little chapel. The urge to become a minister was growing in him, a force he felt he could not resist. Yet he hadn't even settled on a denomination yet. In fact, he'd never been baptized. What he really wanted was to be trained, like Roy, to be someone who could teach and lead folks. But the way seemed closed. So when the Methodists sent a delegation offering to baptize and ordain him, and the Missionary Baptists offered him any church he wanted, Bob was tempted and confused. "I'm too dry for you Baptists," he would say, "don't have enough religion for Methodists, and am too ignorant for the Presbyterians." He wasn't opposed to immersion, but he couldn't go along with the importance that many of the local preachers placed upon it. And he found it hard to believe in closed communion.

But one day Bob settled on the Missionary Baptists and was scheduled to be baptized. Before the time came, though, he filled in for Roy Smith in the pulpit. This made the Baptists furious. "Don't have nothin' to do with them infidels," he was warned.

That settled it. "Look friends," he said, "I can never join you."

On the following Sunday he and Lelia and the children were baptized in the Presbyterian church.

The urge to preach grew stronger in him. Wasn't there some way, he kept asking Roy Smith, that the church might ordain him? He would keep on studying the Bible and all the books he could lay hands on. He begged his friend to speak for him at headquarters, but Roy's efforts were no use.

A delegation of Quakers went to Hasten, urging him to intercede with his brother to accept leadership of their meeting.

"But I can't," said Hasten. "I know what a sorry life he's led. A man doesn't change that much. Besides, he doesn't have good judgment.

"I've heard him in the pulpit. He blows out a lot, but I have too many doubts about him. I know what a heller he was. I tell him, 'Bob, a minister who isn't sincere is an awful mean man. As for me, I'm going to preach right behind my mules in my tobacco patch. Many a preacher would do better for his fellowmen there than in the pulpit!' "

But Bob had been spending long hours thinking as he hammered the red iron on his anvil. He came to Lelia with his thoughts.

"Look, Lelia, all I know is blacksmithing. I just don't know enough to preach in any congregation. How can an ignorant man preach anything but ignorance?"

He went on. "You know, Mother, one time Hasten said he'd see me through school as long as I wanted to go. And I like school, I really do. It would take time, but it would go fast, don't you think?"

Lelia hesitated, hiding her fears. She had always been shy of new places and of new faces. "I reckon it wouldn't be too hard, maybe. But eleven years? That's a long time, Bob."

Bob went again to Roy Smith. He was set on starting the long, long trip to the ministry. He couldn't be satisfied with less than seminary. Roy could help tutor him at night through eighth grade so he'd be ready for high school in the fall. Roy looked grim. Bob went on: Hasten had once promised to see him through school. Maybe if they asked him again . . . .

A delegation from the Presbyterian church went with Roy and Bob to where Hasten was grubbing weeds in the red clay of his tobacco patch. But Hasten shook his head.

"Look, Bob, you've got a wife and four young'uns. The best preachin' you can do is carry wood and water for them. We need preachin', but we need honest workin' men too." He paused, then added with finality, "I'm sorry, Bob. I can't prop for you."

When Bob came home, sick with disappointment, Lelia only smiled. "Bob, if it's a Presbyterian preacher you must be, we have no time to lose."

Hasten, the guiding force in his early years, could not serve him now. But with Lelia's help and his own determination, he suddenly felt sure he would one day be a minister—and a trained one.

So with Roy he studied nights with the same fervor as if he were pounding out plowshares in his smithy. He bought a big black mule, and on the day school opened at the Friends Mission, six miles away, he mounted the mule and set off to begin high school. Behind him, clutching his pants pockets, was Conduff, who was starting first grade. Lelia stood in the doorway and waved. To Bob it seemed a silent benediction.

To Beat the Devil

All that winter the mule carried Bob and Conduff together the six miles to school. Often the snowdrifts or rushing streams made the trip slow and tricky, but they almost never missed a day. Bob found it hard to study at first, but threw himself into the work with impatient determination and within a month was put in tenth grade. At night, he read far ahead of lesson assignments in all the textbooks, borrowed other books from Roy Smith, and sometimes even went over to Mount Airy to the library. One teacher tutored him in Latin.

In the spring, the school told Bob he had learned all they could teach him. But college? They weren't too sure about that. Finally they agreed to certify and recommend him. He sat down that night and wrote to Davidson College, two hundred miles away in North Carolina. It was Roy Smith's alma mater, and that must have helped, for a letter of acceptance came in June.

Lelia's people couldn't believe what was happening. What was wrong with a man to give up blacksmithing? It was just about the best-paying trade in The Hollow, and legal too. What need was there for schooling? Why, anyone could preach if the Lord chose to call him. Besides, Lelia would have her third child in November. Come home with the young'uns, they told her. He'll get through wandering someday.

But Lelia was set on going too, to be with Bob and keep the family together. In September the Childress family migrated to Davidson, North Carolina.

In November a boy, Paul, was born. Bob could see that the little money from his savings would soon be gone. He bargained with a Mount Airy merchant to send on credit several hundred bushels of apples, which he stored in unused rooms of the big drafty farmhouse they had rented for next to nothing. Every morning he was up at two, polishing apples, burnishing each one to a mirror shine, and by sunup he had a load ready to take from house to house and store to store in a rented truck. As he drove, he'd have a textbook beside him, ready to read any moment he could find.

The bruised apples fed the family. Lelia would cook them into applesauce, roast them, fry them with brown sugar and a little butter to brown them. The Childresses ate apples for breakfast, dinner, and supper. Lelia tracked down like a bloodhound every apple recipe she got wind of.

As it came time for Christmas, though, after paying the doctor and buying clothes and textbooks, they were down to their last ten dollars. Bob couldn't bring himself to tell the children, who were wide-eyed with talk of Santa Claus.

By the time Christmas Eve came, the children had stopped asking for anything. Bob didn't know why. He hadn't talked to them about being penniless, nor had Lelia, but they must have guessed it. As the family sang carols around a tree Bob had cut in the woods, Lelia's eyes were bright but Bob's were downcast. He was aware as never before that his children were growing up as poor as he had been. Was he really meant to preach, or was he only vain? How could he be sure? There had been no blinding flash, no sign from above, just the feeling that he had to try to do it.

Suddenly there was the crunch of wheels in the snow outside. When Bob opened the door, a tall Negro was lifting two big boxes off the back of a truck. Bob told him he was at the wrong house, but the man insisted that what he had was for the Childresses. How he did chuckle as he brought in package after package! And when the five-year-old said, "Mama, is that Santa Claus?" how the man laughed! There were clothes and toys for every child from the breast baby on up, and food to last for days. The children clapped and shouted. Bob and Lelia could only look at each other in speechless surprise. To this day no one knows where the gifts came from.

Bob managed to sell enough apples to keep his family in food, and made a little extra as a substitute elementary school teacher, but in the spring his professors called him in for a talk. Time was fleeting, they said. He was already thirty-two. They knew he was all but penniless. Why didn't he quit college and leave for seminary? Bob was flabbergasted. The studies had come hard for him, and he knew he was doing only average work. Was he ready in a single year? They were reluctant to answer. As he searched each face he began to guess their real reason, and he reddened as the realization came to him. He knew that he must look and talk like anything but a minister. His manner was rough and loud, often raucous. His speech was still pure mountaineer. In class there were often snickers when he spoke. His teachers wanted him to learn for himself that he wasn't suited for the work. That was it. Why not try a summer as a student pastor, they said, to make sure that was what he wanted? There was a place not far above his home in The Hollow, a community known as Mayberry near Meadows of Dan, that needed someone right now.

All right, he would do just that, he said. He thanked them and left.

So it was that Bob bought a T-Model Ford coupe and set off for the mountains, leaving his family behind, hoping to return in the fall for college. He headed for Mayberry, Virginia, a picturesque rolling plateau at the crest of the Blue Ridge halfway between The Hollow and Buffalo Mountain. He had been there once before, walking up from The Crossroads with Roy Smith, who had held services now and then in a small schoolhouse.

He began preaching in the school and also in Union School at Vesta, a few miles away. Occasionally he held a prayer meeting in a brush arbor, using a portable pulpit someone had made out of a tree stump.

Sometimes he would preach against drinking and shooting, and some didn't take it kindly. Several young men met him outside after one sermon and told him to be more careful what he said. Ernest Boyd was among them, and Ernest carried brass knucks and knives and a gun, and, perhaps because he was so short, was quick to use them. Folks were right worried, because it was clear that the new preacher was high-tempered, too. But Bob just talked easy that day, and soon had them chuckling at one story after another.

He was not always so mild. When a man came drunk and noisy to services one night at Vesta and refused to leave, the preacher whipped off his coat so fast the breeze blew out the lamp behind him. By the time it was relit the drunk man was gone.

The next Sunday night three men were drunk and swearing, and that made the preacher boil.

"I've been just as bad as any of you," he roared, "but I've never misbehaved in church, and I aim that you don't neither. I'm stout enough to take care of you all!" The men quieted.

Sometimes he got so riled he completely lost his temper, and regretted it later. Once he sent a chair flying over the congregation at two drunken men carrying on in the back. Close after it he went, so fast the pulpit teetered and almost tipped. He grabbed them by the collar and led them out, and when they struggled at the door and the congregation got up to help, he shouted, "Go on a-singin'. You know the hymn." He returned and finished the service.

"We'd be so nervous," one woman said. "We were sure the new preacher would get into a fight."

He might have, too. With his portable pulpit that he carried over his shoulder like a club, he looked as if he was armed to take on sin single-handed. His muscles were hard and strong. The more he preached, the surer he got that he had to tackle evil head-on with powerful weapons. And his voice could be shattering. At a revival at The Bent, ten miles away, when no one responded to an altar call he shouted, "Devil, get out of this church. You're not a-goin' to stay here. I'm a-goin' to run you right out!" He picked up a chair and hurled it down the center aisle. People thought he had aimed at someone. There were seventeen who made profession of faith that night. He won more converts with the same rough-and-ready methods at a revival at Danville, a hundred miles away.

Word was traveling that this was a powerful strong preacher. At Mayberry, people were making profession. Roy Smith came up from The Hollow many times to baptize them. Once there were twenty-five. Curious crowds came to watch the odd sprinkling ceremony, and to hear Bob.

As the summer wore on, Bob got louder and stormier. Most people liked it. "I declare that man's going to be another Billy Sunday," one said. "He ain't much of a preacher," said another, "but he can sing and shout to beat the devil." When the preacher heard that, folks say, he laughed till he shook. "That's what I aim to do—beat the devil!"

Bob was living at Abe and Lila Webb's house, and sometimes Lila tried to quiet him down a bit. "Mr. Childress, I do believe you must preach the loudest of anybody in the Blue Ridge!" Bob laughed, then gave her a quick look. There was no smile on her face.

As stormy as he was in the pulpit, folks said it was a caution how gentle he was outside it. He was always doing something for people. There was Aunt Empress Spangler, who did his laundry. She was only a young woman, but she weighed more than three hundred pounds and was painfully shy. She had come to him hesitantly, asking first, "If you don't be afeared to risk it, let me press your black broadcloth. I never seen such a fine one."

And when she had finished, the preacher said, "Why, Empress, that's the nicest it has ever looked." Words like that meant a lot to Aunt Empress, folks said. When he urged her to ride to church with him, she hesitated at first. Feared she might break the springs, she said. When they got to the very door of the school, the engine died.

"Aunt Empress," Bob said, "you mash the little car's nose in the dust so it can't get its breath!" How she smiled!

He took her for many other drives. There weren't many people who paid attention to Aunt Empress, he could see, and she was just one of many lonely, overlooked people. During the week Bob sought them out.

Aunt Empress Spangler was fearful
Bob's T-Model couldn't carry her.

In one family, nearly all the men had been born without feet and had to crawl about on their knees. Even the proud Spangler clan, who traced their ancestry to English royalty, had an affliction. Half the children in that family grew blind from glaucoma in their teens or early twenties.

Tall, handsome Aunt Josie, who had married her cousin Babe Spangler, thought she would escape the disease. When it hit her, she couldn't be comforted.

"I'm a-goin' to die," she told Bob. She had been bedfast a year, with a small child, and was so thin she was barely alive.

"Oh, no, you're not," he said. "You're a-going' to your

daddy's, where your sister can take care of you and the baby."

"I'll die there," she said.

And all he said was, "If you do, you'll be as close to heaven there as here."

Bob carried a portable organ from one service to the next.

He drove her to the doctor at Mount Airy, a forty-mile trip she had been making by covered wagon. He kept talking and joking all the way. And when he found out she had a reed organ and knew how to play it, he pulled the car to a stop. "Josie, I declare the Lord has work for you. You've just got to play for us." Josie only moaned and shook her head. But the next Sunday she was in church with her organ, and she didn't miss a service from then on.

Then there was old Mattie Spangler who had fallen and broken her hip and lay bedfast. Bob went and asked her, "Grandma Spangler, if you had a wheelchair, do you suppose you could sit up in it some?"

"Sit up in it, son?" she said. "Why I reckon I could drive myself to church in it!"

On a trip to North Carolina to visit his family Bob found a secondhand wheelchair and brought it back. All the while he helped her learn to use it, she was puzzled. Mountaineers care for their own, not for strangers. And preachers don't do anything but hold services and revivals.

"Son, why do you go to all this bother just for an old woman?" she asked.

"Why, 'cause you're my Grandma, and I love you," he said, and kissed her.

It was soon after Bob brought Roy Smith up for a baptismal service in the schoolhouse that folks started talk of needing a church. The schoolhouse was little bigger than a cowshed, the floor was breaking through, and the foundation was rotting out where it rested on the rocks.

"Fine," said Bob, "but before that we need a new school. So let's do both." He promptly drove down the mountain thirty miles to the county seat of Stuart and talked to the superintendent of schools. If Mayberry folks could build a two-room school with their own lumber, what cash outlay could they get for windows and doors and desks and equipment? About two thousand dollars. And how about boosting the school term from four-and-a-half months to a full nine? Not a chance. He made three more trips to Stuart, but without success.

He wrote presbytery headquarters asking that they send teachers so school could open in September, but got no answer. Discouraged, he walked down the mountain to The Crossroads for a talk with Roy Smith.

"Bob," said Roy, "those men at presbytery don't know you. Besides, they likely get a flock of requests like that from lay workers."

"But when I'm a minister in their church they'll have to listen, won't they?"

Then he suddenly turned to his friend. "Roy, I can't take time for more college. I've got to start seminary right now!"

Roy smiled.

"Roy, I'm just beginnin' to see how much there is to do," he said, and as he looked up the slopes, he could feel his heart beat faster, could feel it clear up in his temples.

"Why, with you here in the valley and me up there, we could be a team for the Lord. There's lots more we could do than just preach. We could start up schools, and get enough teachers to keep them open all term. Mountain young'uns need them a whole lot more than city children. We could even send some of 'em to college, too—and do it before they've got a cabin full of kids. We could pry them loose from their ignorance. We ought to give folks somethin' to do, too, besides stillin' and fightin'. Most of the time these folks just sit around, even though there's a fortune in timber up there just waitin' for the axe and the saw."

He turned to his friend. "You've got to go help me get started at seminary. Maybe I won't be the fanciest preacher in the mountains, but that isn't what they need. They need to know that someone cares whether they blast each other's brains out. And I can help, I know I can."

Roy saw that this time there was no use in trying to hold him back. The next week, as the dogweed leaves began to redden, the two set off for Union Theological Seminary at Richmond, a Southern Presbyterian school.

The registrar was amazed—a man asking admittance who had had only one year of high school and one year of college? Impossible! And with a wife and five children—and no money? Incredible!

The president of the seminary, Walter W. Moore, had the same response.

"We'd like to help, Mr. Childress," he said, "but our responsibility is turning out qualified ministers. We can't relax our standards. Maybe you'd better give up the idea of the ministry. There are other ways of serving."

Bob swallowed hard, but he really wasn't too surprised. He had another question ready. "Is there any rule," he asked, "that would keep me from renting my own house and just going to classes?"

The president considered. "I don't know that there is. We've never had another case like it."

So Bob rushed back and packed his family onto a train bound for Richmond, armed this time with a hundred-dollar loan he had talked out of Hasten. Bob opened the windows, took a seat ahead of Lelia, and closed his eyes. He needed to think. The house he had rented was six miles from the seminary. That meant streetcar fares every day, and the rent was forty dollars. He was thankful for the loan from Hasten, thankful, too, the kids were well clothed for the first time.

"Bob. Bob." Lelia poked him. "Bryan threw his shoe out the window."

"Well, I guess I can't have 'em stop the train," he said, annoyed. Then he turned around and managed a grin. "Have him throw the other one out."

As school began, Bob realized he was amusing to his classmates. He was ten years older than the others, his suit didn't begin to cover his big wrists and ankles, and when the others stopped at the ice cream parlor after school, he had to hurry home to help with his babies. More than once when he spoke up in class during the first week there were snickers. Each time, he would puzzle over just which word had betrayed his mountain ignorance. He worked harder than he ever had on his books, and time after time risked exposing his background by asking questions about something he didn't understand.

Twice a month during his first year at seminary Bob drove to Mayberry, leaving Richmond at noon on Saturday. The roads were punishing. Mostly they were hardly more than trails that followed old animal trots. A few had been laid out by men working in teams. One man on a spur above the others had a cowbell that he kept ringing until the others hacked out the best path up to him, and so they went on up the mountain. Few roads had been designed for cars, and winter made them even worse. Often when the roads were fender-deep in snow he would need to try one trail after another before he could make it up to the crest. Then it would be two or three in the morning when he reached the Webbs'. Abe would be waiting up with bricks and flatirons warmed for his bed—which Bob sometimes didn't use, talking instead with Abe until morning.

"We need roads, Abe, maybe more than shoes or houses," he would say with real feeling. "Roads are our hope of gettin' this place civilized. I'm beginnin' to think we can even do without schools before we can do without roads and bridges."

After his final service on Sunday night he would set out for Richmond about nine, arriving there barely in time for class Monday morning. Once on the way back he grew impatient with the way the road zigzagged slowly down the mountain. He remembered how folks with a load of tobacco or apples would sometimes urge their oxen straight down the side of the mountain, with a tree tied to the wagon as a drag. Bob nosed the T-Model over the brink, jammed on the low pedal, and rattled to the bottom without mishap. From then on he often used the shortcut.

In October Lelia had another child, a son that they named Bill Joe. Money was running low. After school hours Bob sold razor strops house to house, but as Christmas approached he spent the last of Hasten's loan. He didn't tell Lelia. Fact was, he thought to himself, he wasn't going to tell anybody but the Lord. He lay awake nights, and when he he went to a doctor about it he was told nervous strain was the reason. That didn't help him to know what to do about it.

But he felt lots better when a letter came from Danville the week of Christmas. "Dear Mr. Childress," it read. "You have been on my mind ever since I heard you speak last summer. I have inquired about you and find you are in seminary. I don't know whether or not you need it, but I am sending you three hundred dollars." The letter was signed by a Mrs. D. A. Overby.

He had hardly known Mrs. Overby, but now he knelt to thank her and the Lord. Without telling Lelia he went out and bought groceries.

"There must be a mistake," Lelia said to the delivery boy. "We didn't order anything—"

Then there behind him was Bob, beaming, his arms full of

bags and bundles. Again, it was going to be a real Christmas.

Things got even better before the year was out. This is the way the *Presbyterian Survey* later described the event.

> When he entered Union Seminary no one thought he could do the work. He was refused a scholarship or a house rentfree as would normally have been his due as a married student. Nevertheless, in the first semester he made a high record in every class. After having made so splendid a start, Mr. Childress attracted attention, and that great judge of men, Dr. Walter W. Moore, who at first had advised him against the ministry, came to him and personally apologized. Instead of giving him one scholarship, Dr. Moore gave him two, and his choice of all the houses on the campus. The first Presbyterian Church [of Richmond], to their eternal credit, gave several hundred dollars a year to keep him in the seminary.

His teachers had seen that Bob Childress was no simple-minded mountaineer with an urge to preach. He studied hard and did well in classes, despite his lack of preparation. In tests that he took along with the others he stood well above average. And his stories, told in twangy mountain lingo, usually made a worthwhile point.

When a big Richmond congregation asked for someone to fill in on a Sunday, the seminary suggested Bob Childress. "At least he'll keep you amused," they told a delegation from the church. Bob was leaving assembly hall when the representatives approached him, asking him to come. "We'll give you fifty dollars," a woman spokesman said. Bob's eyes widened.

Then, soberly, "Ma'am, I am not for sale." He pretended to reflect for a minute, then laughed. "But make it sixty and I'll come!"

The following Sunday, as he watched the congregation file in, he frowned. Such clothes-proud people! He had never before seen such finery. Then he had to chuckle as he recalled how his own mountain people would come barefoot to church and brush arbors, shoes across their shoulders until they reached the grounds, where they sat and pulled them on before entering. The spirit of wearing your best was the same here as in a brush arbor.

When his first year of seminary ended, Bob moved his family to Mayberry for the summer. They lived in a rented house at nearby Vesta. Within a week Bob had folks building the school he had set his mind on. The first morning a dozen people came to help lay the foundation, and it wasn't many days before there was a crowd, with tables of ham and chickens and biscuits and corn bread spread out under the trees to feed the working men. Children were in such a hurry to get to the grounds that

Bob Childress was ten years older than his seminary classmates in Richmond.

they would dip the well dry getting water for the house and cattle. Folks with chores to do had to leave before dark. The rest stayed for the preaching service Bob held every night.

When money for paint ran out, Bob asked the womenfolk to raise more. "I always say that if men can't do it, leave it to women." That was strange talk for the mountains, where women had never counted for much. Bob knew that few people had money, so he had women and girls go out with horse and buggy on what he called a chicken drive. "Tell 'em you're after a chicken to sell for the school," he said. "If that doesn't work, tell 'em you're hungry. And if they still won't give you a chicken, tell 'em you'll be back to see 'em after dark."

Law, how the chickens came in!

"Don't worry about gettin' too many," he said. "What we don't sell, well, we'll just build us a flue and have a chicken stew."

After buying the paint they had money left over, and with it they bought a portable organ.

Men built the scaffolds, and women painted, and everyone found it was fun to be around the place, especially with Bob Childress there. A woman spilled some paint from a can just as Bob was walking beneath.

"Oh, Mist' Child'ss, did it hit you?" she called down.

"It would have, right in the face," he said, "except I had my mouth open." Then he laughed, and others laughed, and sometimes it seemed there was always laughter all around the grounds.

In the fall a fine two-room school was ready for use, built for twelve hundred dollars cash. The superintendent at Stuart finally agreed to extend the term to nine months and to get teachers for the job.

During his second year at seminary, Bob began to learn the fine points of organizing a sermon, of phrasing, delivery, and voice modulation. But his friends on the mountain were of even more help.

Bob was explaining a lesson from his class in theology to Abe Webb.

"Moses gave us the laws, Abe. Jesus gave us love. Without love there can be no forgiveness. Where law strikes, love heals. Law and love walk side by side."

Lila Webb was listening. "Why don't you say that tomorrow in church?" she asked. "Just the way you said it now. We'll understand." He tried it and wondered as he spoke as if a sermon couldn't be a kind of conversation with his friends. But somehow it didn't feel like real preaching. The week after, he was shouting once more.

Lila Webb talked to him at dinner. "Mr. Childress, I do think you'd better take things a little easier in the pulpit. If you're going to hold out you'll have to slow down. It may be just me, but I get a mite nervous—"

Bob broke in. "Lila," he said thoughtfully, "you're the second person who's called me down for preaching too loud. The other day it was Thursday Banks, and now you. I'll have to do something about it."

His sermons grew more subdued. Slowly he was realizing that he couldn't holler or bully or threaten mountaineers into real religion. More and more he began putting humor into his sermons, often the raucous humor of The Hollow, and often personal.

He would stand up to the portable tree-stump pulpit, and begin.

"I love you all, better than anything else in the world," he would say, "even with all your faults." He sounded sober and serious. Then his mood would change and he'd say, "Sally over there, I love her, even though she does dip snuff and I hate the stuff."

Sally was a Spangler, and someone he could joke with. He found he could be stern now and then if he mingled his admonitions with humor. Humor, more than oratory, was healing balm. He saw that his jokes were often more effective than his most spirited pleas. The mountains—more than the seminary—were molding his preaching style and ministry.

It was during his last summer there that Mayberry built its church. Some folks donated lumber, others their work.

Grandma Spangler, now no more than a little bitty body curled up in bed, no longer able to use her wheelchair, called for Bob. She pulled three one-dollar bills from under her pillow.

"I'm not a-goin' to need them," she said. And when he declined and told her how much he needed her on that front pew, she reached for his big hand, put the bills in it, and closed it. A week later, she died. Folks remember things like that, for there wasn't a hundred dollars cash within five miles.

All that summer Bob kept preaching regularly at the school at Buffalo Knob and at the Stuart School near Slate Mountain, taking Aunt Josie with him to play the portable organ. The sight in her second eye kept declining, but she could bear it now, for she had something to live for, she said.

Bob would say, "Your family needs you, Josie, all the poor little churches need you, and God needs you." They would drive in the T-Model from early Sunday morning until night, from one place to the next. As they got out of the car Bob would shoulder the portable organ—which folks said looked for all the world like a casket—and lead Aunt Josie to the cabin or school or brush arbor for services.

Many times during the summer Aunt Josie said to him, "Mr. Childress, you saved my life. But you changed it too, and sometimes I think that's more important."

Those words began to echo in the hills and coves near Mayberry. How Bob Childress did change folks! It wasn't that he got Aunt Josie's boy the first suit he ever owned, or started her daughter Margie to singing. It was that he showed them and lots of others they were important, and could be useful. He taught them how to laugh, even when things seemed to call for tears.

The Mayberry church was one of the first Presbyterian buildings in all the Blue Ridge. The congregation began to grow. The new school would soon reopen. People had learned to work together. Bob Childress had changed a small piece of the Blue Ridge.

When fall came and it was time to leave Mayberry for his final year of seminary, folks loaded the car with hams and potatoes and chestnuts. Someone gave him a bag of meal, for he was so fond of corn bread, and another family gave him quilts. There were tears in the big preacher's eyes when he said good-bye and headed his T-Model down the mountain.

It was during Bob's last year at seminary that Hattie was born, a child with a head too big for her frail body. The doctor urged an operation, saying otherwise the child would grow up an idiot, but he warned that the chances of survival were small. Lelia shook her head. She didn't believe it. As they took the baby home, she said softly, "A person needs to have more faith in the Lord than that."

Bob's final year at seminary was his busiest and best. He was feeling more confident now, in his studies, his preaching, and—most satisfying of all—his calling. He was sure now the Lord had work for him to do and that he had been right to give up everything for the ministry. The rough edges were coming off his speech and sermon style, but the humor and warmth and powerful voice remained. Bob Childress was ready for the ministry. His words and manner could be polished when he wanted them to be. He had outgrown the shouting hellfire of his brush arbor days. His voice was deeper, and controlled. He knew the fine points of organizing a sermon, of delivery, of emphasis. He had one good suit that covered his wrists and ankles. He had put on more weight, too, and with it seemed more impressive.

He got high grades in all his subjects, and in systematic theology, the most difficult, he stood far ahead of anyone else. His professors rated him "an excellent mind," "an individualist, with facility in speaking and a rare sense of humor." He towered above his classmates in physical stature, vigor, and maturity, and it was perhaps natural that they looked to him for his advice and views and, often, his personal help. "He could be as discouraged as the rest of us," a classmate, Sam Query, says. "The difference was he could laugh instead of cry. There was no shallowness about this man; he just knew when laughter was good for the soul."

Richmond churches kept asking to hear the rawboned mountaineer who had such a gift for humor and narrative and pathos. There was even an invitation to speak in Washington at Central Presbyterian—Woodrow Wilson's church—and it was Bob's biggest thrill yet. Afterwards, Bob talked to the people about the mountains, and they told him how much they wished Mr. Wilson were still alive. Bob had admired Wilson ever since he had started reading, and he listened raptly as the President's friends talked about him. He had been born at Staunton in the Shenandoah Valley, little more than a hundred miles along the Blue Ridge from The Hollow, and had gone to Davidson College, too. His father, a minister, had lamented to the end of his days: "My boy, my boy, if only you had gone into the ministry!" Central Presbyterian invited Bob back several times. It was a heady experience—a mountain man preaching in a President's church.

The day came for Bob to deliver his final sermon before the whole student body. Sam Query, a classmate, says, "I'll never forget that sermon, and I doubt there's a man in the class who couldn't quote from it even now, after thirty years. When Bob's turn came, he awakened the subject.

" 'I have chosen a deep subject,' he said.

" 'Woman.

" 'Behold, how low she can sink.

" 'Behold, how high she can rise.'

"Then he began to describe Mary Magdalene, and I felt like I knew her myself. She was vivid, triumphant, alive, as real as someone here and now," says Mr. Query. "The sermon was on love and service, nothing so new, but he made it new for all of us, every man and woman whose ears could hear and heart could feel."

On the day of graduation, a North Carolina church where Bob had once delivered a sermon sent an elder to him to offer him its pastorate, a fine manse, a new car, and a salary beyond anything he had dreamed possible. He still had some debts to pay, and this would be the answer to them. It was hard not to accept. He was a man with a wife and seven children, who all his life had been poor. And, too, he had an afflicted child to consider. His close friends urged him to accept. Lelia's grandfather had once visited there, and all her life she had heard how fine and pretty a place it was. She would feel safe there, with the baby close to a doctor.

And yet from the time he had gotten the urge to minister and preach Bob had felt he must return to the mountains. These were his people, and they were in need of help. But nobody there had asked for him. He promised the elder an answer in the morning.

That night, late, a stranger stopped at his table in the seminary library and introduced himself as Peter Cunningham Clark of Montgomery Presbytery. He had been sent, he said, by seminary professors who had told him about Bob Childress.

"I'm sorry I'm so late," he said, "but your professors told me I must reach you before tomorrow morning."

Bob offered him a chair beside the library table.

"We've got a field in the mountains," said Dr. Clark, "where they're shooting each other, they're ignorant, they don't have a chance, they have no schools or Sunday schools. There's enough work there to kill you, but we'll furnish you a living while you're at it."

Bob leaned back and smiled. The mountains were calling.

"I don't want to make it seem like a nice rustic life. The killing is real. Right now in the county courts there's two up for murder, three for attempted murder, three for maiming, twenty-two for moonshining, a half dozen for breaking jail or the road gang, and a slew of others for everything from knifing to buggery. Almost every one is from the Buffalo, and most of the cases never reach court."

"Buffalo Mountain?"

"That's right. It's up in Floyd County, right near—"

"I know. I grew up just hollerin' distance below it."

"Oh. Well then you realize a little of what you'd be getting into."

"I'm a mountain man, Dr. Clark." Then he said, "I believe that's where the Lord wants me to go."

"Well, I'm glad, Mr. Childress, very glad. But if you should change your mind for any reason, you can still let me know in the morning."

Bob all but ran home, he was so filled with excitement. He

found Lelia in the bedroom with the ailing baby. He was surprised to see her shrink as he told her the news. She didn't look at him, but kept her eyes on the crib.

"Bob, do you really mean it? The Buffalo? It's so far from anywhere. There's the children, and especially little Hattie. I just don't want to go there. Not at all." She began weeping, something Bob had hardly ever seen her do. He put his arm around her shoulders and pressed her close.

"I'm sorry, Mother, but you know it's the mountains I want to go to. Together we can do it, I know it. I feel it deep. I think the Lord means us to be there, and I think he'll watch out for us, all of us. And we're needed, Lelia. We can help."

"I can't help what I feel, Bob, and I'm plain frightened. No amount of talkin' is goin' to make me *want* to go. But talk isn't goin' to change you either. You're set on it. So we'll go, and I'll try, and we'll hope you're right."

Three days later, June 3, 1926, they had packed up and were on the road to Buffalo Mountain.

The Heritage of the Buffalo

Y ou'd better wear a gun up here. Most folks do." It was a tall, serious man talking. The morning after they arrived at Buffalo Mountain he came to the Childress house—looking for a lost cow, he said.

"Why, friend," said Bob, "I haven't worn a gun since I was a young fella. I don't believe I'll start now."

"Things are bad here," the man said, shaking his head gravely. "Worst of any time I've ever seen. Lots of folks sleep with guns under their pillows."

There was a hush. The children had been listening.

Bob laughed loudly. " 'Pears to me that'd be bumpier than sleepin' on the floor." The tall man didn't smile.

The first visitor had hardly left when another came up, a short, redhaired man who introduced himself as Johnny Sutphin. He was a kindly man, you could tell from his voice.

"Oh, yes. You're the one who's been looking after things for the Presbyterians, aren't you?" said Bob. "Why don't we go look at the school?"

As the two men walked the mile to the school, Sutphin told Bob about the efforts the Presbyterian church had made during the last half dozen years to establish Sunday schools on Buffalo Mountain. Every summer they sent lay workers. Few of them stayed. One woman from Mississippi took sick within a month of her arrival, and with the roads so bad, she had to be carried a mile to a buggy and then to town, where she died. The next —a rawboned, plucky woman—stayed on a few weeks until the tallest man on the mountain, who stood six foot six and whose brother was a Primitive Baptist preacher, served warning he'd blow her brains out with his shotgun, and named the day he'd do it. Well, no woman, no matter how plucky, could stand up to that. The last one was a man, a lay worker out of Roanoke. He had lived at Nattie Burwell's house, on the old Lee property. That was too bad, for the Burwells associated only with the first families of Floyd, fifteen miles off, where people served tea and spoke fine English and kept away from the Buffalo. He was cautioned never to sit down to meals in any mountain cabin, and most certainly not to stay overnight. Dapper and city bred, the little man was courageous. He went right on preaching when mountaineers threatened to shoot him. During one service a deputy sheriff grabbed hold of two men, and the congregation, expecting a fight, started to leave. The little preacher stamped his foot and bellowed, "Sit down, and let the officer make his arrest!" The following Sunday, when a shot was fired outside at the close of the service, folks again got to their feet, and he shouted: "The first man going outside is me, and I'll swear out a warrant on everyone who goes ahead of me!" He was blunt in his preaching. He told Buffalo people they were going to hell, and quoted Scripture to prove it. He said he never had believed in preaching about the sins of Gomorrah when he meant the Buffalo. But as often as not, he just made folks mad, and after three summers he left for Texas.

The Presbyterians were bent on getting a foothold on Buffalo Mountain. To them it seemed a colony of the devil. And so they had built the school, completed two years before Bob arrived. It was a mammoth three-story structure that straddled the line between Floyd and Carroll counties. The basement and first floor had classrooms to hold a hundred and fifty students, and upstairs floors had living quarters for teachers and six to eight resident pupils.

As Bob walked from room to room with Johnny Sutphin he felt his spirits soar. "This is where we'll start," he said. "We'll pack it full of young'uns all week and give them something to think about besides guns and old red-eye. And on Sundays we'll preach the word of God to everyone we can crowd in here."

Johnny Sutphin said nothing, Bob noticed. They said good-bye on the steps outside the school.

Across the road Bob saw a small one-room grocery store (what mountaineers called a store-house). He walked over to introduce himself to the proprietor. The man seemed uneasy as they spoke, and not very friendly.

Bob hurried home. He must help Lelia fix up the old house they would live in until a manse was built.

It hadn't been an easy trip. They had arrived at dusk the night before, after three days of travel. Ahead of them down the road had gone their furniture and clothing, piled high on an old solid-tire Federal truck that Bob had gotten from a junk-yard. Posey Sutphin, Johnny's brother, had come from the Buffalo to drive it. First thing, Posey had run into a streetcar in Richmond, for the truck had no brakes to speak of. Twice he went into the ditch and was hauled out, and once a wheel came off. Periodically, they'd stop to soak the wood-spoked wheels to keep the rims tight. Finally the truck just hissed and stopped, and the Childresses went on ahead, leaving Posey to cope as best he could.

They were crowded in the T-Model touring car. There were six children besides Bob and Lelia and the two-month-old baby. When they forded the first stream, the children squealed with delight at the splashing. And when the older ones had to get out and walk so the car could labor up a steep hill, they laughed. But the novelty vanished by the third day. As the roads grew narrower, following the animal trots, and thickets of rhododendron purple with bloom scraped the car on both sides, the children grew quiet. The first whippoorwills were starting to call as darkness fell.

Suddenly, across an open valley, they saw Buffalo Mountain, a great broad mound, bright in the last sunlight. They got out and looked. Almost at once a man in a black hat and blue overalls broke out of the bushes, stopped, and stood there staring at the car.

Bob went to him and reached out his big hand. "My name is Bob Childress. I'm a Presbyterian preacher, and I aim to live here."

The other nodded, glanced again at the car, then at Bob, and disappeared into the laurel. The older children looked at their dad.

"It's time to see your new home," he said quickly, and hoisted the little ones back into the car. As they went on they passed through a swale that smelled of sour mash. Half a mile farther on, they came to the old house that was to be home. It looked dark and forbidding, but it was lots better than a log cabin. Lelia hadn't known what to expect, so she was relieved to see as they entered that someone had swept and even made up beds. In a few minutes Bob had a fire going. Lelia had packed a basket of food, and when they sat around the table Bob asked a blessing.

Then he looked up, and his smile swept around the circle.

"Well, children, this is home."

That night as the others slept Bob couldn't help think how his family might right now have been snug in a much finer home with electricity and running water. And here he was, thirty-six, his life already half spent, taking on Buffalo Mountain.

Only a handful of people turned out at the schoolhouse for his first service.

"Look, dear friends, I am a Presbyterian," he began. "I don't believe there are many Presbyterians around. On the way up here I stopped at a cabin, and by way of striking up a conversation with the woman at the door, I asked, 'Any Presbyterians in these parts?'

" 'I don't rightly know,' she replied. 'Jeb does a lot of trappin', and tacks up all his hides on the smokehouse door. Whyn't you just go down and have a look?' "

No one laughed, except Lelia and the children.

"My friends," Bob went on, undaunted, "I aim to live here a long time as your neighbor, providing you don't tack up my hide on the smokehouse door. I aim to get this school a-goin', and fill it full of your nice, smart young'uns. I aim to hold services and preach and help any way I can, and someday, God willing, we'll build a church together."

Then he preached from the third chapter of Galatians: "Who hath bewitched you?" A bewitched state is a sad state, a dangerous state, he said. Some witches: selfishness, pride, strong drink, bad companions, and anything else that blinds our hearts to the truth.

When he was through he had an announcement. Twice a week he would drive into Willis for his mail, and anyone who needed to see the doctor or run an errand was welcome to go along.

After service, a young woman waited on the steps to talk.

"Mist' Child'ss," she said, "I want to join your church."

Bob brightened.

"You see, it's like this. I'm mad at our preacher. Well, not exactly mad, but I've lost confidence in him."

"How's that?"

"Well, let me tell you what he done. He charged my husband two gallons of liquor to marry us, and everybody else he's charged just one. Now tell me, can anyone have confidence in a man like that?"

Bob smiled, thinking she was joking, but she was in dead earnest. At home, when Lelia heard the story, she was hard put to believe it wasn't one of her husband's jokes, but Conduff too had heard the woman.

During the week the furniture and clothing came, though the old Federal truck never again budged on its own from the field where Posey had it pulled. Soon the little house began to seem like home.

From the start, Lelia was so occupied with Hattie that Bob took over much of the care of the rest of the children. He would start the fire under the black kettle in the backyard to boil the day's supply of diapers. He took other laundry to a mountain woman to be cleaned and ironed, kept the pantry stocked, and ministered to the children, rubbing sore limbs and stomachs, taking temperatures, consoling hurt feelings, and trying to keep the home serene.

Right off, he started making calls, driving his car as far as possible and then walking, urging people to send their children to Sunday school and to come themselves for the preaching. In two cabins to the north and one a mile south of the school he began to hold preaching and teaching services, too.

As he traveled about Bob realized that athough the area known as Buffalo Mountain wasn't too different from other parts of the Blue Ridge, it was more inaccessible. Most other places you could reach from east or west, but north of the Buffalo the Blue Ridge splayed out, so that the Buffalo and the region around were stockaded by other mountains and ridges.

The summit itself, 3,970 feet high, lay along the Blue Ridge no more than fifteen miles above the North Carolina line and no more than ten miles north of The Hollow—with Mayberry in between, only five miles away. The nearest towns were Willis, at the northern edge of the Buffalo; Hillsville, ten miles to the west; and Floyd, fifteen miles to the northeast. To the east and south was the unending wall of the Blue Ridge. In between—in a sprawling, crumpled land of rocks and hardwoods and rushing streams—was the eight-mile-square region called Buffalo Mountain.

The summit of the mountain looked like a charging buffalo, head lowered, hump bulging a thousand feet above the surrounding hills. Great slabs of black rock, nearly vertical, formed its neck. Its hump was furred with a growth of hardwood. In the early mornings soft mists caught in the trees on its slopes, and all was quiet. But Bob sometimes saw clouds of blinding white gather above it in midafternoon, climbing higher and higher until they grew black and exploded into lightning that stabbed at hilltops, fences, and houses, killing cattle and sheep. Winds could whip up with barely a moment's warning. Rain washed off the mountain like water from a roof, spouting across the roads, sometimes with such force that fence rails from fields above came shooting down the slopes.

Around the edges of the mountain itself, for several miles in some directions, lived the people—most of them in Floyd and

The profile of the mountain is like a buffalo's hump.

Carroll counties, but a few in Patrick. The area was settled in the coves and meadows and along the streams, but there were no towns or villages, only store-houses litte bigger than a shed at intervals of every two or three miles along the rutted roads.

Buffalo life was like most mountain existence Bob had known. The people grew corn and apples for their kitchens and stills, besides beans and potatoes and buckwheat and greens and a few other vegetables. They kept a cow or two, and a small flock of chickens, and ear-notched a litter of pigs and let them range the forest for food. But Buffalo farms were smaller and rockier than any he had seen. Some fields were little bigger than a city lot, and so steep that apple drops would roll downhill. The land wasn't fit for the money crop, tobacco.

88

There was little for a man to do but saunter down the road to the store where other mountain men gathered. Sometimes they went hunting quail—which mountaineers called partridges—and now and again they went fox hunting. A favorite sport was to chain a raccoon to a floating log in a millpond and send a dog in to fight it. There weren't many get-togethers, and families living less than a half mile apart with a ridge in between might not see each other for months, especially in winter. Occasionally there'd be a frolic with dancing, and in the fall there'd be apple butter boilings. But the real sport, at any time, was a fist fight.

Fighting with fists might start out as a friendly match, but just as often it took goading to get men going, and that's when rules might be broken, and the knifing and shooting begin. If someone was killed it was too bad, but accepted as part of the game. No long-standing feuds resulted. Families were so closely related that it would have been hard to draw lines. Most shooting "scrapes" never got to court, and if they did the accused men were usually set free. The reasoning went that since everyone was armed, any shooting was sure to be in self-defense. And if a man had been drunk, he was often not held responsible and was punished lightly—even excused—for crimes up to and including murder. So men prepared for conflict by drinking.

One day on the way in to Floyd a mountaineer pointed out to Bob an old cemetery on the mountainside. "You'd never know it," Bob said, peering. "There's nothing but trees. No headstones."

"That's right. Not a one there was buried with a church service—folks just didn't have preachers, not even Hardshells, in those days. Most of 'em died in a fracas."

At the courthouse in Floyd, Bob made a point of introducing himself to the commonwealth attorney. The man squinted and asked, "Buffalo Mountain? You're not going to live there?"

Bob nodded. "I am."

The man was unbelieving. "They give us the most trouble of anyplace. That's the most lawless region in all the southern mountains. Why, people there think it's worse to kill a man's cow than to kill the man himself! You don't have a family?"

"A whole houseful," said Bob, getting up to go. "And we are going to live there, all of us."

In Willis, Bob went to meet Doc Charles Burnett, the only man from outside who ventured onto Buffalo Mountain with any frequency.

Doc was a gentle man with a voice soft as a whisper. As he talked, he punctuated every sentence or two with a bullet of chewing tobacco that clanged against the copper spittoon in his examining room. He'd started chewing tobacco about the time he stopped wetting his pants, he said, and had chewed it sixteen hours a day ever since, stopping only long enough to eat. Bob wanted to hear everything he could tell about the Buffalo.

"Mr. Childress," he said, "I wonder if you aren't the first stranger to move onto Buffalo Mountain since the day of the Lees—and that would be a hundred years or more ago." He went on slowly. "Oh, a few drummers come to the store-houses with wares, but they always leave before dark." He chuckled. "I'll tell you, not even politicians go there."

He explained about the Lees. During the Revolutionary War there was a lead mine on the Buffalo from which men fashioned their own bullets. The exact site had been lost, he said, but now and again when timber cutters would skid logs to a mill they'd find bits of lead ground into the bark of the logs. It was word of the mine that brought General Henry "Lighthorse Harry" Lee to Buffalo Mountain, just after he bid good-bye to his friend and commander George Washington. He bought a major part of the Buffalo—some six thousand acres—only three years before he was called to deliver the eulogy before Congress upon the death of the President, when he used those long-remembered words: "First in war, first in peace, first in the hearts of his countrymen." His two sons became joint owners of Buffalo Mountain. One was the beloved General Robert E. Lee. The other was his little-known brother Charles Carter Lee, who had lived at the Buffalo for several years.

"Folks say forty-two slaves are buried on the Lee property," Doc said, "one with a sugar poke of money in fifty-cent pieces and hog dollars, and everyone up there just knows it's haunted. And sure enough sometimes your footsteps echo back at you as if someone is following. A man was riding across the place one night and saw a flashing light come down a tree. His horse was knocked to its knees. He got it up. It went down again. He got it up. The third time it knelt he said he knew he had met his Savior, and ordered that on his death he be buried there and that afterward if a light shone above the tree, it would mean he was in heaven. And they tell that a light did shine there after he was laid away, and his faithful wife went every night to see and marvel. You might get someone to lead you to the grave and the tree if you want to see them. No one lately has seen the light shining, but they still keep the grave poled off so cattle won't walk across it."

Doc didn't really like his visits to Buffalo Mountain, especially after dark. But sometimes he'd hear about somebody lying sick or shot up, and he'd just have to go. "A man remembers the stories he's heard—of balls of fire that flash across the cove and disappear in the ivy ahead of you, of hands that reach up and grab your horse by the bridle," he said. "So often I'm out on a black-cat night so dark even my horse gets lost. I'll circle to the right, then to the left, before I hit some little hog path of a road. It's a right spooky place."

Then, remembering he was talking to a man who was fixing to live on the mountain, he laughed softly. "Well, tell you the truth, Mr. Childress, the trouble is I'm a wee bit afraid of 'ha'nts'!"

Bob leaned forward and whispered, "Me too."

"In fact," said Doc, "the house you're living in is haunted, folks say, by Johnny Sutphin's daddy-in-law, who lived there just before you. He fell out of a tree picking cherries and broke his neck. Two years ago, it was."

"So I hear tell," said Bob, unsmiling.

There were people waiting in the outer office to see the doctor, but he went right on talking—"No emergencies out there." He used to have two Kentucky saddle horses, he said, and often rode twenty miles a day. One night he went to the Buffalo to visit an old man, tied his horse to the fence, took off his saddlebags, and dropped them as he went in the door of the cabin. The old man was on his back in bed, drunk and naked. "I guess he didn't know I was coming," said Doc, "because when I got out my stethoscope and started to lean over him he sang out, 'Ma, whar's that pistol?' He had one hand under the covers, and I watched it like a bird. If he had made a move, I had one fist doubled up to make his two eyes one. What I heard in the 'scope didn't sound good at all. I told him his heart was weak, and he'd better ease up on drinking. He didn't say a word, his eyes following every move I made. I folded up my 'scope, edged back towards the door, sort of sideways, picked up my bags, opened the door, and backed out fast as I could, watching the window 'cause I was still in shotgun range. I backed up so fast I fell rear foremost over the fence, then

Doc Burnett came out from Willis
to patch up gun and knife wounds after a fracas.

scrambled onto that horse and lit out. Those Buffalo patients don't make you feel like following up, and I never did find out how he fared."

One day while Doc was a young doctor and still courting, he got word at his girl friend's house of a shooting scrape at the Buffalo. He hopped on his horse that stood saddled at the gate, raced to his office for probes, forceps, dressing, sutures, and needles, and galloped off for the Buffalo eight miles away, arriving just as the justice of the peace galloped up. Together they held an inquest. Two men were dead, and another was near gone. These were the first of about twenty killings that Doc had attended, two or three by rocks and knives, the rest by guns.

Doc went on for an hour, until finally Bob excused himself and left. He was getting a little upset and tired of all the tales of violence. He had been hearing them all his life. He didn't want to know which persons had—and which hadn't—wounded or killed someone else. It might make a difference in how he treated them. But wherever he went—the store-house down the road, a remote cabin, or Willis or Hillsville or Floyd, he would hear the stories. Most often he heard of what had happened on that Easter Sunday of some seven years before, a scrape that still seemed to hang over the Buffalo's slopes like a thundercloud.

Bob heard it first from the storekeeper. Every Sunday during spring, young folks would spruce up and climb to the very top of Buffalo Mountain, where emerald mosses and bird's-foot violets carpeted the windswept rocks. The view did a person good. You could see spring touching the treetops. You could see an indigo strip to the west that was the Alleghenies. You could see all the way to Pilot Mountain in North Carolina. You could see the whole world, it seemed, and that was important when you had been walled in by snow and ice in your own small hollow all winter.

Men brought their guns and hunted for wakening rattlesnakes. In "the Kettles" on the west, where the rocks dropped off sheer, there were dens full of rattlers that men shot with pistols or else tied to the end of a stick and led along like a dog on a leash.

Some Sundays were pure fun, but on others there was fighting, and many times bullets would sing out that weren't just for the snakes. If you showed any fear you'd be run off the mountain. If you wanted to stay, you had to threaten to whip the lot.

Mothers would plead with their sons to stay away. But where else was there to go? So every Sunday they would look toward the top of the Buffalo, and whenever the boys saw the bright dresses of the girls, up they went. Wives urged their husbands not to go. But the mountain had a powerful attraction, especially on Easter, when crowds of people—young and old—climbed the mountain to celebrate spring. It was a time of coming alive on the mountaintop.

Easter came late in 1919: the twentieth of April. It was a perfect day on the mountain, folks say. Apple trees were beginning to explode white in the warm coves, and the air held warm layers of spring-smell between layers of chill. Men, and women too, had walked, ridden horseback, and driven in buggies—some relatives had come from as far as North Carolina—and climbed to the moss-covered top of Buffalo Mountain.

Most men were from the Buffalo itself, though the white shirts and blue pants of some marked them as being from Shooting Creek. All told, three hundred people were atop the Buffalo that Sunday, the men and boys drinking and shooting at trees and rocks and other targets, the women sunning and gossiping.

Among them were two brothers, Amos and Emmett Sutphin; Claude and Giles Harris, also brothers; two of Claude's brothers-in-law, Mack Moles and Deck Talbert; and Wib Jackson, who had stopped in at Giles's place, where they'd hunted up some liquor. Giles's wife Nancy had begged him not to go, for the sake of their five children, but the two men had headed up the Buffalo on horseback.

Around noon, Amos and Emmett and Wib decided to scare everyone else off. They hoorahed and hollered and fired their pistols, splashing bullets against rocks. Women screamed and ran, dragging their children, and most of the men began easing down after them.

Claude and Giles and Mack and Deck decided they weren't

going to let their friends bluff them off. They pinned them down behind some rocks and forced them to retreat down the side. They stayed on the top till three in the afternoon, then started down the mountain. Halfway down, at a place called the Stomping Ground, where cattle were salted, the other three were waiting, blocking the path. Amos, a middle-aged man with raven-black hair and mustache, spoke.

"All right," he said, "we're a-goin' to fix all your troubles."

There was a blur of action. Bullets sang out. Onlookers fell over logs getting out of the way. One man, hit through the chest, ran like a wounded wild animal down the mountain. Then it was suddenly still. Three men lay quiet: one with two bullets through his chest, another with four bullets through his belly and others through arm and thigh, and a third shot twice through the neck. As they lay dying one called out to another. "You got me, Deck. Who got you?" But Deck could no longer answer. Someone had run earlier to tell Doc Burnett there was going to be more shooting, and when he came galloping out from Willis he found two dead and a third gasping his last in his wife's arms. Someone brought a haywagon to carry the bodies down the mountain.

In a farmhouse at the foot, Doc found the man who had run down the mountain, unconscious from drink and shock. The bullet had entered the chest below the collarbone and plowed through, lodging just under the skin of the back. "Those old Owlshead pistols," Doc said, "never did pack much of a wallop." Doc cut out the bullet right then, without even numbing the spot. But the bullet had rammed ahead of it a patch of the man's black sateen shirt the size of a dime. Doc hesitated to probe further. Then he saw a fine black basting thread protruding from the wound. He pulled at it slowly, carefully. It brought out the patch of black sateen as pretty as you please. All the while Doc worked, the man slept. It wasn't but a few days until he was up and about.

After that things got worse in the hills. There was a difference this time—so many shot, and then the law getting in on it. Mack Moles and Giles and Claude Harris were taken in to Floyd for

*Giles Harris (top) and friends at the mountaintop,
not long before the fateful Easter Sunday there.*

trial. It didn't really matter that they were let go finally. Something fearsome was now in the air.

The Buffalo had known terror for generations, but never like now, Bob was told. Before, there had been temper killings, spur-of-the-moment shootings or knifings, where whiskey was doing the fighting. Now it seemed to be like the feuding western mountaineers they had used to make fun of, who kept alive the hates of generations and were proud of it. Buffalo people hadn't been like that.

It had never really let up since that Easter, and even now Bob saw signs that it might break out at any time. Old Noah Dodd, as kind a man as ever lived, had testified about a shooting in court, and the next night had been taken out and beaten until he nearly died. Kinfolks of dead men sometimes galloped up and down the roads, hoorahing and shooting "Wild hog!" They would make as if they were going to burst into a man's yard—anyone's yard—then stop at the gate and shoot in the air. There were more fistfights among young folks, more knifings. One boy stabbed his brother "plumb to the hollow" of the knife handle so you could see right inside him.

When men were late to come home, their women would wait, hidden, beside the road. At every rifle shot of squirrel or rabbit hunters, they trembled.

As Bob started home from the store-house in the gathering dusk the feeling of hidden violence seemed to be all around him. He stopped to look up at the bulging hump of the mountain. It looked like a brooding monster of evil.

"There is no more violent, troubled land in all the southern mountains of America," Peter Cunningham Clark had said that night at seminary which seemed so long ago. "They're an island untouched by change." Now Bob understood.

People were marooned there as effectively as if they were living on an island in midocean, and they liked it. Over the long years a million people had drowned in China's flood, Charles Duryea had invented a gasoline buggy and Thomas Edison a kinetoscope, McKinley had been killed and Teddy Roosevelt made President in Washington, just 220 air miles away, but it made no difference to Buffalo Mountain. They were free of authority, free to still whiskey, to fight, and to raise their families as they saw fit. A few, very few, had been down into the slumbrous valleys below the mountains, where turkey buzzards softly circled over pastures of fat cattle, and where life seemed easygoing and slow. But they were glad to get home, to get back to their lean cattle that braced themselves against the rocky slopes, back to the cool air and the breezes that swept up the Buffalo, lifting the eagles that nested there into the wild white clouds above the peak.

The plans Bob had made seemed so futile. After a few weeks only handfuls of people gathered for services at the school and at the two cabins, and a few small children at the teaching classes on Sundays. The school itself—well, that was pretty certain to begin. And quite a few parents had promised to send their children. But he wondered if it would make much difference. And when he talked about roads and sawmills—why, people only stared, hardly hearing him, wrapped up in their hates and fears, unable to imagine anything different.

As he walked home, he prayed. He wasn't much of a one for kneeling prayer. He could do it just as well on the move, he said. But now he knelt and asked God to show him the way and give him the strength somehow to shake the Buffalo to its granite core. When he rose he knew one thing he had to do was go straight to the heart of the Buffalo.

The Fear and the Fearless

B ob was sitting on the front porch of Claude Harris's frame house down the hill, a few hundred yards below the school. As he spoke, Claude listened without moving a muscle of his thin, delicately formed face.

"I sure do agree that someone needed to do something," Bob said. "I just would have done it differently."

Claude had brought up the subject of the Easter Sunday killings himself, almost as soon as the preacher had arrived. "I reckon you heard about Giles and Mack and me and what we done," he said, glancing up quickly at the dark summit of the Buffalo above them.

"Yes," said Bob, "and I don't know what I'd have done, except I'd have tried talking them out of it. But then I guess I'm long on talk," he said, laughing. There was no change on the man's lean face as he studied the broad, big-boned preacher.

Bob turned serious and pulled his chair closer. "You know, Mr. Harris, the Good Book says that those that live by the sword will perish by the sword, and I really do believe that, don't you?"

The man appeared to nod.

"Mr. Childress," he said, "without a gun I'd be kilt in a week."

Bob thought he was probably right. He knew how the three men had hid in the woods for a long while, secretly fed by their children. Wherever they slept there was a pistol beside them. Later, when they met the dead men's kin on the road their wagons would ease past one another, eyes riveted on eyes, heads swiveling like owls'. Men were probably waiting even now to find them unawares and unarmed.

Claude and the others had been acquitted of the murder

charges on grounds of self-defense, but Claude had been con-
victed of "maiming" the man who had lived and run down the
mountain. He was fined five dollars. For a moment, Bob thought
of making a joke of it, but reconsidered. Instead, as he was getting up to leave he said, "I declare we'll have to run you for
president. You look that much like Woodrow Wilson."

*Claude Harris with his wife
(Mack Moles's sister) and grandson.*

The man's face lit up with a smile. It was a face, Bob thought,
as finely chiseled as one on a coin. Somehow, for no real reason,
he felt that here was a man he could trust.

"Well, I hope you'll come to church and bring your
young'uns," said Bob. "And I hope you'll let 'em come to school
this fall, too."

Claude didn't promise, but he said he'd see.

Giles Harris was a lot easier to know. He lived along the road
to Willis, five miles from the school, just before you turned to
go down the hill into a picture-book valley through which ran
a sparkling stream known as Burk's Fork. He was a handsome,

outgoing rogue with a ready wit, as quick to speak and act as his brother was reticent. But Giles had a reputation as a dangerous man. Four years earlier, outside a store-house where services were being conducted, Giles' gun had gone off and killed a young man. There were almost as many stories about how it happened as there were people who watched. There had been no argument, no fighting, no drinking. Most people said the gun had fallen on a rock, discharged, and killed the boy on the spot.

Now, though, Giles was a deputy sheriff, and Bob was glad of that, he said laughing, for Giles could keep the peace at church services. They had hardly started talking before they were joking, and Giles said he'd be in church the very next week with his whole brood. He was so open and easy, Bob wondered how he could have been so feared.

Mack Moles was a lean, sun-weathered man who lived just down the hill in a cove no more than a quarter of a mile from the school. Normally a great hand to talk, he sat silent now as Bob told about his two years as a deputy sheriff, and how he had learned one thing he would never forget—that good people often get in trouble with the law. He also spoke of his belief that the troubles would be fewer if there weren't so much drinking and gun-toting. Mack said nothing, but when Bob asked he did say he'd bring his family to Sunday school and church.

Then, as Bob was getting up to leave, Mack stopped him. It wasn't easy for a man to leave off wearing his gun, he said. It had been only last fall that he was driving home a load of shucks when two bullets sang past him. Ahead were two men on horseback barring the road. It was clear they had been drinking, and that looked bad, as if they meant business. Mack did some fast thinking. If he ran off, they were bound to shoot him or follow till they did. "If I kept on a-goin', they knew I'd get one of them, so I switched my cattle team, held the lines in my left and my pistol in my right. The men didn't move. I clucked at my cattle till they bunted the horses out of the way. As I passed, I turned plumb round to keep watch and let my cattle pick their way, but after fifty yards they lost the road. The second I turned to guide them the bullets came a-flyin'. The men passed the

bottle back and forth to get up their nerve, then started followin'
me. Well sir, the road ahead went down a long hill. I'd have all
I could do to keep the load from runnin' over my team. I
couldn't tend wagon and shoot both, so I tied up the lines, pulled
on the brakes, and jumped off into a field of corn shucks. Two
bullets hit the shuck I was hidin' behind. They kept firin' at me
for quite a spell, then one takened out to circle me so I lit out
fast as I could, they after me." Mack lost them in the woods and
went on home. He and his father found the oxteam next day.

"I don't like shooting neither. 'Least, not anymore. But there
ain't much I can see to be done about it."

Bob shook hands as he prepared to leave. "Mr. Moles, I think
you and I are interested in the same things. We can work together to make this place a better one to live in."

It was becoming obvious to Bob that the three killers—no, he
must never call them that, even in his thoughts—the three men
were responsible people who wanted to do the right thing. They
were people who mattered to the mountain—were, in fact, its
leaders. They were feared, but they weren't as fearsome as he had
thought they'd be, and they were respected. They were men he
already felt he could depend on.

For their part, they didn't quite know what to make of the
preacher. Lots of people began to be puzzled about him. There
was the way he would dicker for a horse or a cow or a pig—and
then give things away. He was a sharp trader and hated to be
cheated. But on a day that Bob and his older boys butchered a
pig, Mack Moles came along at dusk and Bob called out to him to
take home a piece. When Mack came up he saw that Bob had
given all of it away except for a few pounds.

For generations, Buffalo people had parted from their friends
with the words "Go home with me"—which no one did. But
when the preacher said it, he meant it. Almost every time he
went home for dinner he had someone with him. And sure as
there was food left over from a meal, he'd gather it into a basket
for the next family he was visiting. Lelia had come to accept it.
He'd kiss her cheek and then turn to his children.

*Giles Harris loved dogs,
guns, and horses.*

"The Lord looks after us," he'd say. "And look—just to be sure, he sent us Mother!"

It was no idle jest. Lelia could make a meal out of next to nothing, and she put up food in huge amounts: ten bushels of peaches and more than that of green beans, fifteen gallons of apple butter at a time, plus pailfuls of huckleberries that Bob set the children to picking.

"The way your mother feeds us all is a modern-day miracle," he would say.

Bob continued to visit cabins, talking up the school, as well as

Sunday school and church. He bought two saddle horses and a team, and where there were no roads he went horseback. But wherever possible he used the T-Model. It never failed to bring men out of the house or in from the woods, where they might otherwise have hid out until his departure.

Men generally stood silent when he spoke. Then he'd begin to tell stories, pure corn, many of them, but they caused glum men to smile. Jokes on women they liked particularly.

"A woman's age," he said, "is her own business. Yes sir, and some have been in business a long time."

A man was out cutting wood, he said, when a neighbor came by, his eyes wild, and exclaimed, "Where's your woman?"

"Back in the house."

"Well get down thar quick. I just seen a wildcat jump inside the winder!"

The mountaineer kept on chopping. "He'll have to get out the best way he can," he said. "I guess next time he'll look whar he's a-jumpin'."

At first some folks were ashamed to let the preacher inside their one-room cabin that was living room, dining room, bedroom, and workshop all in one. Bob explained right off that the cabins he'd grown up in hadn't even had floors or windows.

Johnny White's cabin had twenty-six children. Johnny told Bob about the stranger who came at dinner time and all the children filed out on the porch. The stranger said to Johnny's wife, "I wanted to see Mr. White. I heard he lived here, but I see I'm wrong. I'm right sorry I broke up your school, ma'am."

At one home Bob inquired of the woman for her husband.

"I ain't got nary-un, and glad of it!" she said as her four children clustered around her. Bob learned later that five generations of women had dwelt in the same cabin without benefit of husbands. The Buffalo, though disapproving of promiscuity, didn't blame this family. It was a woman's own business what she did with herself, especially if she kept the family intact.

If Bob came a second time to visit a home, folks say they seldom worried over whether or not the dishes were washed, he was that common. Some fed him just because he seemed to make the house light up and warm up, and they wanted to keep him longer. Laughter was something that Buffalo Mountain didn't often hear, and it sounded so good!

A meal might be nothing but corn bread, fried cabbage, and buttermilk. But Bob was always enthusiastic, for he loved to eat.

"Nothing like johnny ashcake!" he said, and meant it. It was made without soda or salt or buttermilk or shortening—nothing but cornmeal and water poured onto hot coals with other coals heaped on top.

He sometimes took Lelia with him on his visits, but she could seldom spare that much time from the baby. She thought he shouldn't go to a cabin at mealtime, but he said, "Let a man feed you, and he becomes your friend."

Right near the school lived the most influential man on Buffalo Mountain, Bailey Goad, a big square ox of a man with eyes that danced like a mischievous schoolboy's. He was known to be even-tempered but a hard fighter when riled. He wore a knife and a gun. One night soon after Bob got to know him someone had broken into his smokehouse and stolen a ham—a giant of a ham, forty pounds it was. Bailey allowed he had a notion it must have been Willie Weaver, and asked Bob to go along to get the meat back. Willie was a likely suspect, already in trouble with the law.

"I hear tell you're a-sayin' that you can talk a man out of anythin'," he said, with what Bob hoped was a smile.

Willie met them at the door and Bailey spoke.

"Mr. Childress is here to help me get that ham-meat you gottened from me last night."

"No sir, Mr. Bailey," said Willie. "I don't have your ham-meat. I don't do things like that!"

Bob spoke. "Well, Willie, if you're not guilty, you won't mind putting your fingers on this doorknob so's we can compare your fingerprints with those on the padlock."

Willie began to whine. "Now wait a minute, Mr. Childress, wait a minute. You can sure get a man in trouble that way!"

He was as nervous, Bailey said, as a cat in a room full of rocking chairs.

He turned to his wife, who was still in bed.

"Elooadie," he said, "Mr. Goad came after that ham-meat I done borrowed the other night."

"Willie," she said, "I thought you told me you boughtened it." She reached under the covers beside her and pulled out the ham.

Bailey whipped out his knife. Bob froze. Bailey cut off a third of the ham and gave it to the woman, turned to Willie, and said, "Now, then, get out of the county!"

Bailey Goad was counted the "meanest" man on Buffalo Mountain. This was no term of contempt, but one of respect. It meant he was quick, decisive, a man of action not given to harangue or tongue-fights. Bailey's father, too, had been a leader. He was Butcher Knife Bob, the smithy who walked up and down the coves selling knives hung on a string around his neck, scaring children, rattling his knives and telling them he was a witch. Grown folks as well as children believed it. When the butter wouldn't come, women said that old Bob had it witched, and they whipped it with willow switches. And when a horse acted peculiar the men would say, "Old Bob's got it witched!" And that made him laugh. He'd ask folks to take hold of three mysterious little wax balls he carried. There weren't many who would.

His son Bailey married three of Dudey Gardner's daughters in turn—one died and one left him—and Dudey used to say to him, "I hope that third one lasts, because she's all I have left. But afore I'd leave you out of the family, I suppose I'd have to give you my wife Miney!"

Bailey was a powerful man. He could split four hundred chestnut rails a day and lay up a worm fence as fast as most men could put up a wire one. He was a just man, too, but he liked to fight. He was counted the toughest fighter on Buffalo Mountain. Once a man gets a reputation like that he is forever being needled into what mountaineers call a wrestle, or else a fist fight. Three eyewitnesses said that Bailey's biggest day was one Sunday at Mount Hebron Primitive Baptist church.

A little man had slipped inside to the bench beside Bailey.

"Jim Dickerson is out on the ridge and wants to talk to you," he whispered, so loud the whole congregation could hear. Now, Jim Dickerson was counted the stoutest man on Indian Ridge, which adjoined Buffalo to the north.

Bailey said, "Can't you see I've no time for that now?"

"He said you're a coward."

Bailey got up and went out. Half a dozen men followed.

"I have no quarrel with you," Bailey said to Dickerson.

"I didn't like what you said about me at meeting," said Dickerson.

"I never said a thing," said Bailey.

"You're a liar!"

And so they were at it, fist smashing fist, knee against groin, while those on the sidelines gasped and shouted.

Some say that Bailey started shooting, others that Dickerson got his knife out first. Anyway, Bailey shot the other man's cravat off, for Bailey was an excellent shot. Then Dickerson stabbed Bailey plumb to the hollow. Unshaken, Bailey took careful aim, held his revolver with both hands, and fired. He hit Dickerson what looked like square in the forehead. Blood was running into his eyes as he went down. But that Dickerson always did have a slanting forehead, folks said, and the bullet went up under the scalp and plowed a groove all the way to the back of his head. (An old Owlshead, folks said, you just couldn't tell what would happen with 'em.)

"Well Bailey, you've done killed him," an onlooker said. "You'd better clear out."

"Not yet," said Bailey. "I've got to get the little man who started all this." He started to walk off, but staggered and fell near Dickerson.

They dragged the men to two houses across the road from each other, and for three days they both lay near death. Dickerson prayed all three days, he said, first that Bailey was dead, and then, when he'd thought more about it, that Bailey would live. When he got well, to keep from getting killed he set out for the west, and stories came back that he eventually grew rich.

Bob Childress liked talking with Bailey Goad. He made a shortcut so he could walk across the meadow to his place.

"Bailey," Bob said one day, "whyn't you come to church?"

Bailey's eyes twinkled. "Oh, I reckon because I don't have much trouble with the devil."

"Bailey," said Bob, "if you don't have much trouble with the devil, I guess it's because the devil doesn't have much trouble with you!"

Bailey started coming to church, off and on. Now and then Bob would quote him in a sermon. It seemed Bailey was beginning to change his mind about some things. "Bailey Goad told me"—that was enough to capture every listener—"that he'd a whole lot rather be a coward for fifteen minutes than a dead man all his life. I told him I believed that was a right smart idea. I know I can run a good ways in fifteen minutes." And Bailey must have meant it, folks said, for he said "Amen," right out loud. Had the preacher made a coward out of Bailey? It didn't seem likely, though Bailey was sitting right there, nodding his head.

With the Harris brothers and Mack Moles and now Bailey Goad as his friends and churchgoers, Bob felt that he might be getting somewhere.

Softening the Hardshells

There were those who said Bob Childress wouldn't last the summer—if the bootleggers didn't run him off, the Hardshells would. Not that he had been heard to preach out strong against either of them, but it seemed sure he would someday.

Bob knew that before he did anything else, he must come to some sort of terms with the Primitive Baptist religion. In actual number of baptized members it was never large, yet its traditions and social customs set the pattern for the mountains. It was the force that dominated the Blue Ridge—even its politics and courts—and its emphasis on predestination partly excused men of brutality and bloodshed. He had come to feel it was a power more sinister than bootleggers and moonshiners. And yet its preachers, or elders, were good men, mostly, who had started preaching because there was no one else to do it, and because it didn't seem decent to lay away a loved one without someone saying a few words over him.

Most of the Hardshell preachers drank or approved of it. Some got drunk for services. Nearly all were illiterate, and they often warred with one another over doctrine. Some hollows taught that a child who died before he was six months old was bound to eternal torment; others denied it. There were fights over what heaven was like—now and then a member was even killed. One hollow would sprout a doctrine unlike that of the next, and defend it—to the death.

There was no avoiding a clash with Bob Childress. For, much as they argued and fought among themselves, the Hardshells agreed with a fervor on some things: Sunday schools were a curse; night services of any kind were against God; preachers must not accept pay; an educated preacher was a tool of the devil; and everything was predestined by God so that if a man had his rifle aimed at a neighbor and the Lord predestined him to pull the trigger, no power on earth could prevent it.

Bob Childress disagreed on every point. It especially rankled the Hardshells that he got paid. Bob figured he might arrange to trade off pulpits with one of the better Hardshell preachers, but it wasn't permitted. Only God's elect—chosen before the foundation of the world and properly baptized—could preach. Some churches didn't permit outsiders to enter the building, and one preacher was heard to say before he began a service, "I see some young folks and others who ain't been baptized. All you infidels get out!"

The Primitive Baptists saw in Bob the biggest threat to their supremacy ever to penetrate the mountains. He wasn't another of the saddlebag preachers who passed through once a summer, sang a little, prayed a little, and went on. Nor was he like city preachers, who sat on their laziness, folks said, and who, mainly out of curiosity, made a trip or two in summer when the roads were dry and the creeks easy to ford. This man meant to stay, to live and grow his family on Buffalo Mountain.

And Preacher Childress was a hard man to be against. He befriended nearly everybody soon after he arrived. And he didn't rile easily. He had already made friends with most of the strong, independent men on the Buffalo, and had completely won over the most prominent Primitive Baptist preacher in the lower Blue Ridge—Joel Marshall.

As a young man, Elder Marshall had had a stammer so bad folks could hardly understand anything he said. But he had kept praying that the Lord would clear his tongue of its affliction so that he could fulfill his dream to preach. One day in the woods, as he buried his face in the fallen leaves to pray, he felt sure he had an answer. Praise be, that day when he got up to speak in church his words came as easily as spring rain—for the first time in his life! When he finished and sat down, folks rushed up to greet him, to glory in his triumph—but his tongue was suddenly as afflicted as ever. From that day on, though out of the pulpit he stammered so hard he shook, he could preach without a hint of trouble. In seventy-two years of the ministry he preached at more than four thousand funerals.

Bob loved him from the moment they met.

Joel Marshall's stammer lifted,
and he preached for seventy years.

"You know, Joel," he said, "one day I found a ten dollar bill in the collection plate. I hustled back to my deacon to find who dropped it, and the deacon said it was a stranger. 'Follow him and find out who he is,' I said, 'for we need a man like that.' A week later my deacon reported. He still didn't know who the man was, except that he sang like a Presbyterian and shouted like a Methodist, but his breath was Primitive Baptist."

Elder Marshall had a rejoinder. "Bob, you Presbyterians don't baptize, you dry clean!" In a serious moment he said, "I guess you want us to fret less about our differences. I guess you're right." And he told his friends, "I love that man."

There were other friendly Hardshell preachers, but many feared the inroads he was making—schools, Sunday schools, night services, and sprinkling. He didn't believe in their kind of

predestination, and he obviously didn't drink. It was easy enough
for a Hardshell preacher to stir up those whose life's work was
stilling or bootlegging, to tell them that here was a man who
probably was out to bring in more revenuers and eventually
smash every still in the Blue Ridge.

He was making real headway, too, going visiting in people's
homes, something no Primitive Baptist elder did. And folks were
feeding him, too. And once they did that, it seemed he had them.
Every excuse they offered for not going to his church, he had an
answer for. Not good enough clothes? Well, you just come on over
to the store-house we're setting up and pick out some. No way
of getting to church? I'll be along at a quarter to eleven. You're
sick? I'll be over to your house and have services. No, there
wasn't any way of getting out of churchgoing, save just telling
him you didn't want to go, and that wasn't easy. And with
children he seemed to cast a spell. It was strange how the shyest
of them warmed to such a big, boisterous, forbidding-looking
man.

From the start, Bob tried to calm the Hardshells with humor.

"Some Baptists are so hard you can't crack their shells. Some
Presbyterians are so mean you smell the brimstone behind them,"
he said, and smiled. "But that's no reason for all Baptists to fight
all Presbyterians." Again, "Some Baptist children were dipping a
family of kittens in a pail of water to baptize them. When they
tried to dunk the mother cat, she ran off. There was no way of
catching her. Finally one child said in disgust, 'Let's just sprinkle
her as she runs by and let her go to hell!' "

A lot of people got pretty sore about it. What kind of a
preacher was this, making jokes about their beliefs!

A Hardshell preacher stopped Bob in a roadside store-house,
determined to do verbal battle.

"Look here," the man started, "education ain't religion!"

"Neither is ignorance," said Bob, and went on with his
purchases.

A few days later another asked him, "Man, don't you believe
what will be, will be?"

"Well—I don't believe what won't be, will be." Bob laughed

and turned to the counter. The man tried again, but all he could get Bob to say was this: "The Lord promises us a good harvest of beans and corn by sending us the sun and rain, but that doesn't mean we'll get a crop if we don't keep the weeds out. If everything is foreordained, why bother about studying the Bible, why hold revivals, why preach at all?"

Try as he might, Bob couldn't avoid argument, with the Little Flock church and its giant following no more than five miles away. Often it seemed that the nonmembers who frequented the grounds outside church were its staunchest defenders.

Little Flock Primitive Baptist Church.
Hundreds, sometimes thousands,
gathered for August meetings.

Bob wouldn't permit anyone to loiter outside his services. From the first, he took to herding everyone inside before he began. Any who wouldn't enter he asked to go home. Nor did he permit them to wander in and out throughout the hour as they had done in the Hardshell church for as long as anyone could remember. Occasionally he would stop a service to go outside and shoo a few inside. Still, boys would walk past the windows or peer in, motioning their girls to leave, sometimes blowing the horn of Bob's car for emphasis.

Bob would explode. "Any boy who hasn't the gumption to ask for a girl at home isn't fit to be seen with at a dog frolic!"

After that, no girl stirred. Many young men began to resent the new preacher, and Bob found it hard to hold a service after dark. Boys would pelt the meeting place with rocks. Bob was long used to the practice. It was perhaps the commonest kind of excitement for young boys in the Blue Ridge. In fact, it was disturbing a church service that had brought the two young Allens up against the law in the first place and set off the whole Hillsville shooting years before.

Bob couldn't be sure how much of the disturbance was natural deviltry and how much an outright campaign to scare him off the mountain. There was hardly a service that wasn't rocked. He felt sure that sometimes a stiller took part, justifying his action in the name of the Primitive Baptists.

When a man came to ask Bob to preach at a Hardshell funeral for his wife, Bob was stunned but quickly accepted. He only said a few words, but the other preachers went on for hours until you could hear the cows bawling, impatient to be milked, and even the husband of the deceased left the services to begin chores. Bob followed him out. It surprised him that nobody seemed to have objected to his being there. He was even more surprised when, a short while later, he was asked to come to another funeral. This time while Bob waited to preach the sun grew so hot, folks said, the shadows of the elms kept getting up and looking for a cooler place to lie down. Eventually the rain fell in torrents, and since there were still three other speakers to come, the funeral was postponed till the next day. The attendance was just about as good the second time.

The size of the crowds at Hardshell meetings was a contrast to Bob's own services. Now that the novelty had worn off, there was a small and slowly growing group of families who kept coming regularly, but nothing to compare with most Hardshell gatherings. It was partly the problem of new ideas coming up against entrenched beliefs. And partly it was just hard for anyone brought up among Primitive Baptists to be impressed with a preacher who didn't shout or chant for hours.

"Oh, he talks good enough," said one mountaineer, "but you can't call it preachin'."

For another thing, the big crowds went to the Hardshell services because there was excitement. Besides the loud and emotional preaching, there was drama whenever someone asked to join. Before admission, a candidate had to stand up before the whole congregation and testify to the dream or vision or experience that demonstrated that the Lord had indeed given sanction.

Will Goins, a big, surly man given to violent attacks of temper, joined on the basis of an experience. "I was a-ridin' my ol' mule Press along a branch," he told the congregation, "when I gottened a turrible borin'-down feelin' on my bosom. I got down off the mule, 'cause somethin' told me to, and ate some muscadines, 'cause somethin' told me to. And don't you know that borin'-down feelin' left my bosom and I loved everybody?"

The preacher was incredulous. "You loved everybody?"

"Well no," said Will, realizing how well his audience knew him. "Everybody but that man who cheated me out of my other mule. But I loved everybody else."

That was more convincing. Will was baptized into the elect.

The congregation, sitting as a jury, excommunicated members too, as they did Molly Spence and Sally Sutphin after they had had a fight. Women weren't supposed to brawl. Sally was readmitted after a vision, and later Molly testified too. "I dreamed I died," she told the congregation, "and went to torment and saw the devil and all his angels."

She paused and the preacher asked, "Sister Spence, how did the devil look?"

Her eyes hardened. "As much like Sally Sutphin over there as two black-eyed peas!"

Molly Spence had to wait for another vision.

The congregation sometimes sat as a jury on more personal matters. Two couples lived on opposite sides of a stream that went down past the Pinnacles. It wasn't much of a stream normally, only about ten steps across, bridged by chestnut foot-logs. The womenfolk were good friends. One day they had gone to visit each other, using different foot-logs, when a storm came up, and the creek rose high above the bridges.

It was a real predicament. Each was caught on the wrong side with the wrong husband. One man hollered across the river, "You've got my wife!"

"Yes, and you got mine!"

They figured awhile.

"We ain't had nothin' to do with it," one hollered. "It's bound to be predestined that way!"

"No, we didn't plan it, and our women didn't plan it!" cried the other.

"Well, it's gettin' late, awful late, and somethin'll have to be done," said the first. "Since we're in this terrible fix, would you want to swap?"

"Well now, mine's younger'n your'n!" He studied. "I'll swap for two bushels of buckwheat."

"I'll give it!" shouted the other.

So they traded, and it worked so well that the wives stayed

Primitive Baptists gather for a river baptism.

put until the next summer, when the Primitive Baptist church heard about it and had them up for trial before the congregation. The couples told their story and how they hadn't meant any wrong. But the preacher and the congregation decided they'd have to swap back, that it wasn't right.

"How about my two bushels of buckwheat?" said the one man.

The preacher said, "You'll have to pay them back."

Everything about a Presbyterian service seemed placid and dull by comparison.

As the summer went on, Bob and Lelia grew anxious, for their boy Conduff was twelve and hankered to go to August meetings. He had been watching preparations at the Little Flock church. Whole casks of liquor were being brought and stored under one end of the building.

August meetings were the gala social event of the southern mountains, as well as the climax of the Primitive Baptist year. As early as eight on Saturday morning there was preaching and baptizing in the river as just about everybody in the mountains came to watch. Often there were crowds of two and three thousand, and at noon so many baskets of food that it sometimes took a hundred feet of table to hold them all. After dinner there would be Holy Communion and foot-washing, when communicants traded off washing feet and drying them on a towel draped about the waist. Since Communion and foot-washing were for baptized members only, the big crowds stayed outside church, strolling up and down the roads in their finest clothes, store-bought for the occasion, or sitting under the trees talking, or buying soda pop, chewing gum, and trinkets from merchants who set up stands on the grounds.

Love bloomed at August meetings. Friendships began and ended. By Saturday evening when the shadows turned deep blue along the ridges, the crowds outside grew noisier than the preaching inside. Quarrels started, as liquor quickened them, and sometimes shooting followed, and sometimes death. Then next day everyone would go on to another church, the merchants packing their tents and following. And so it went every Saturday and

Sunday during August at a different church up and down the Blue Ridge.

Bob told his son, "Boy, if you go, see that you stay inside and worship, and don't mosey along the roads." Conduff tired after three days of listening to the day-long preaching.

But a little later a merchant, seeing the crowd at a cabin where Bob was about to preach, set up his stand. Conduff was with his father as he strode towards the man.

"Who gave you permission?" asked Bob.

There was no answer.

"There's no selling on these grounds!" Bob thundered.

The merchant whispered that they could split profits. "Papa like to exploded," Conduff told his mother later. "He slung cases of soda pop onto the man's pickup and tossed plaster dolls on after them, while the drummer hopped on one foot and then the other, crying."

With all the changes Bob was making, it wasn't strange that folks were getting more resentful. On the way back from Floyd, where he had tried again to interest a sawmill owner to begin operations, Bob picked up an old woman he'd never seen before. She started talking to him about the new minister at Buffalo Mountain.

"Our church is out to get him," she said, as she dipped at her snuffbox, "but I been a-tellin' 'em not to stir him up, for from what I hear tell, he's like a hornet's nest, and if they rile him, he's plumb likely to take over the whole country!"

When Bob introduced himself, she only nodded her head and repeated, "I say, don't stir him up!"

For a while, Bob avoided any open clash with either Hardshells or liquor dealers. He hoped it wouldn't be necessary. But in his heart was a foreboding, for the Primitive Baptists had been taunting him more than ever.

Two seventeen-year-old boys Bob knew slightly were both courting the same young widow. After a drinking bout, one stabbed the other to death, not three miles from the school. The dead boy's father rode over to ask Bob to take the funeral. This time he would be the only preacher. Bob agreed to go, but wondered about his decision that afternoon after Mack Moles came over.

"Bob," he said grimly, "I've heard as how there'll be a crowd, and bootleggers are comin' with guns, waitin' for what you're a-goin' to say. They say that a Hardshell preacher put 'em up to it, but I think they just want to git you."

That night Bob lay sleepless, pondering what to say. Was this the time for him to come right out with everything he felt? He listened to Lelia's soft breathing beside him. From the other room came the night sounds of the children. There was more than his own safety to consider.

All Buffalo Mountain, it seemed, was at the funeral the next day, hundreds standing or sitting on the grass outside the dead boy's home. When Bob mounted the front porch beside the coffin, women dug sweetcakes out of "ridicules" to pacify their babies. The crowd hushed. You could hear the crickets chirping.

He started slowly, talking about the boys and how sad the loss of a young man was. It wasn't long before he was saying things few had ever before heard.

"Now, how do we figure what happened? Well, I say you can't go blaming God for what happened." He looked out fiercely over the crowd. "We mortals are to blame, especially we older ones. Our young'uns just don't know any better. We didn't train them. They learned from us, and we don't do anything but fight and drink. We can't lay the blame on God!"

There was a rustle in the crowd. People sitting down got to their feet for a better look.

"These poor boys didn't have a thing against one another," he went on. "Now, you know I was born over back of Granny Puckett's and know what I'm talking about, and I say we older people are responsible for what happened."

He paused for what seemed like an age, then said slowly, underlining every word: "The man who sold those boys the liquor is as much to blame as the boy who did the stabbing."

All eyes turned to the liquor dealers interspersed in the crowd, where some of them had even been making sales. Mack Moles

*Hardshell elders wait their turn to preach
at an all-day funeral.*

was sure, he said, that the preacher's body would be the next corpse they'd mourn over. But the men seemed stunned. They too listened as Bob told the people of Buffalo Mountain that they were ignorant, silly fools who needed the grace of God to civilize them. It got so quiet among the hundreds of people that you could hear a lamb bleat on the opposite hillside.

"Try spending a quarter for candy for your young'uns. It will make you happier than liquor will."

Then he pointed to the casket. "Sin is the cause of all this. It's sin—"

The door of the house flew open and out burst the young widow, screaming in his face that he was defaming her and must apologize. Then before anyone knew it, a tiny wisp of a woman, Josephine Mayberry, hopped up on the porch and shook the preacher's hand. In a small voice that carried to the farthest fringe of the crowd, she said, "Brother Childress, you done told us what we needed to be told. God bless you for it."

The storm was suddenly over. The dead boy's mother embraced the new preacher and wept. So, too, the slayer's mother. Dozens came up to shake his hand. The rest started hitching up and leaving. There would be no shooting today.

Bob Childress had survived his first big test with Buffalo Mountain. It would not be his last.

The week after the funeral Bob was riding horseback to a night service when two men stepped out of the darkness and grabbed his bridle reins. The horse reared. Bob could only guess who it was. He sang out their names, loud and cheerful, and said, "Glad to see you're up and about. Come along to church with me."

The men dropped the bridle and disappeared into the darkness. Bob had guessed right: they were two liquor dealers from down the mountain. And stripped of the courage that comes from anonymity, they had backed down from whatever they had had in mind. Bob shivered a little, then went on. He wondered if it would always work out that way.

He was driving a visiting pastor and his elder down the mountain in his T-Model the following week when a man stepped out from the bushes into the center of the road. He was big and stoop-shouldered, with a black felt hat, black coat and pants.

Bob stopped the car. The man made no move. He eyed them steadily. Bob lifted himself out and approached him.

"We're in a hurry, brother," he said quietly, "but let's hear what you want." The man studied him out of black, beady eyes, then looked at the others in the car.

"What I've got to say to you is private," he said, tense with emotion. "Come down thar in the woods with me."

Bob hesitated. Trying not to let his eyes betray him, he looked for the bulge that might mean a sidearm, then followed as the man walked down the hill to a patch of water oak.

Once inside the dark of the trees, the man turned. Bob felt his heart pound like a hammer.

The man fixed his eyes on him.

"I was at that thar funeral the other day. I heared every word you done said. I was thar with a load of liquor."

His eyes dropped.

"I've been a-thinkin' ever since of what you said." His voice broke. "I've been that worried that when I heared your T-Model a-comin' I just had to ask you to come here and pray for me."

They knelt together in prayer, and whether or not the man was blessed by God nobody knows, for Bob never saw him again.

The lines were drawn, it seemed. Some would want to take a gun to him now, but maybe there'd be others like this man, folks who would listen and take the hand he stretched towards them.

Brewing and Bridges

Bob's plans for Buffalo Mountain made sense, the Presbytery officials at Roanoke agreed. He would open school with three mission teachers that fall. A little later he'd send out buses to haul pupils from greater distances, and add more teachers. He would hold services at the school and in a cabin at Indian Ridge, at two cabins to the south, and at as many more as he could set up. He'd try to bring in all the outside influences he could induce to come to the mountains. And he'd look for ways besides stilling for people to spend their time and make a living.

Big plans—Bob chuckled to himself—pretty big plans for a body who can't even get out of the water. It was midnight and he was marooned in the middle of Burk's Fork in his T-Model, the waters of the swollen creek gurgling around the tires. Before he did anything on Buffalo Mountain, he'd have to get back there. But it was hard to depend on anything—roads or streams any more than people. Maybe the Lord wants me to recollect who's in charge, he thought wryly as he curled his big body up on the cushions and tried to sleep.

He had told Lelia not to expect him back home unless it be late. On the way up Bent Mountain it had started to rain, and as he had stopped to put up the top he had wondered whether he should try going in by Willis, fording Burk's Fork at Little Flock, or by way of Laurel Fork. There was only one other way, and that was from the west, up from Hillsville, and this too required making a crossing of the churning stream. All of the crossings were likely to be hard to ford. He had settled on the shortest way, through Willis. The rain had stopped as he had begun the climb across hills and hogbacks, and the moon had come out so full and bright that it had made his headlights seem feeble. He could see the glint on the water as he had started the descent into the valley. The stream was high, higher than he had ever seen it. He hadn't known how deep, but he had decided to plunge the little car in. If nothing else, the momentum might carry him across. But halfway through the car had hit a rock, stopped still, sputtered, and died. He was still five miles from home. There was nothing to do but wait until morning to be fished out.

He thought now how cut off the Buffalo was—a rain made it a world apart, a fortress encircled by a moat of churning water. Even small creeks turned into torrents that tore out bridges. There was no way of getting in without fording.

He couldn't seem to interest anyone in bridges. "They'll save time," he had said. But time—what was that to a mountaineer? Some didn't have a clock in the house. What need, if a man had a good-crowing rooster? If the creek was too high today, there was no harm in waiting till tomorrow or the next day. So, many just didn't care one way or the other. But as Bob tried to sleep, alternately cradling his head on the steering wheel and then turning end for end with his feet on it, he puzzled why some men at the Buffalo were actually fighting the idea of roads and bridges.

The morning was beautiful, and Bob felt buoyed up as the sun began to light the valley. On both sides of the gentle valley were rich green meadows. Upstream was a white frame house, and just across from him at the edge of the meadow was a sparkling white church under a spreading tree. This was the Little Flock church. Beside it were a store and a little frame schoolhouse. The whole scene was like something out of a picture book, Bob thought, like a valley in Switzerland.

Coming towards him along the south bank was a man with a team of grays. It turned out to be Kyle Bolt, who lived in the white house. Bob waved his arms and called to him and, as Kyle came and urged his team into the swift water, he shouted above the noise of the current, "I only hope I can find you in this fix sometime so I can return the favor!" Kyle smiled. With a rope lashed to an axle he pulled the car out, then towed it until it started. Bob vowed not to give up the fight for bridges, even if he had to put it off awhile.

With all the driving he had to do, Bob began learning how to ford the creek at Little Flock and at Laurel Fork and farther downstream near Herman Kemp's place, on the way in from Hillsville. At all of them, the streams were narrow but treacherous. Often storms cut a deep channel; sometimes they brought down boulders. The waters would recede as fast as they rose, and usually Bob would wait for the level to fall. Then he'd disconnect the fan belt, plug the oil breather pipe, take off his shoes and socks, roll up his pants legs, and let the car plunge in. Sometimes the water might swirl up to the headlights and over, and the back seat cushions might even float. But if the condenser stayed dry, and if the car didn't hit a rock, he would make it.

September came, and it was time for school to open. Previously, the only school nearby had been the one at Little Flock, which was open barely four months a year, with a teacher who hadn't finished eighth grade. The new Buffalo school would be nine months, with three teachers, all college graduates. On his own, Bob persuaded a music teacher from Mount Airy to come live in their home and teach Buffalo girls to play the piano. This much of the plan was working.

Children came in waves. Bob's visits seemed to have done something. Every cove poured forth half a dozen. Getting them registered was a chore. Sometimes parents of a dozen or more had run out of names or simply forgotten to name their youngest ones, who became just Boy or Babe. Others were simply Champ or General or Doc. Bob could only guess at the spelling of still others. They sounded to him like Jude Idey, Nicktie, Icy, Julita, and Elodia.

A little girl stood before Bob. "My name is Gentle Dove."

"That's very pretty, but now tell me your real name."

"It's Gentle Dove," she repeated, her lower lip trembling.

"That's my onliest name." He patted her on the head reassuringly.

"And this is your little brother?" he asked.

"Yes sir," she said brightly, "and his only name is Jesus Christ."

The two children became Dovey and Jacky.

Bob's T-Model, his "mountain Cadillac,"
was often stuck in mud or snow.

In October the church house that had been started that summer was finished, and the Childresses moved in. It was built no more than a stone's throw from the school on the side of a gentle hill. At the foot was a springhead that would serve both house and school. Mountaineers had come all summer to watch the manse take shape. Except for the Lee house, it was the biggest on the mountain. The Childresses invited everyone in to look it over. The first floor had a living room, a dining room, and a kitchen with a big, wood-burning range. Upstairs were four bedrooms. One big fireplace heated the house, and though the floors upstairs would nip the toes in winter, the living room would always be cozy.

When the first snow fell on the mountains, Bob saw that it would mean the end of his driving. It came in smothering layers as it never had down in The Hollow, and the wind piled it into sudden, unexpected drifts. When he tried going up the hill past Alice Sutphin's on the way home from getting his mail at Willis, the ruts turned to ice and he slipped down backwards. He realized he had made his last trip to town. It was a shame, too, because people were starting to go in with him to let Doc Burnett treat the agues and other afflictions they had used to suffer through with their own mountain remedies. Two people had even gone to the hospital at Christiansburg, fifty miles away.

In some ways, Bob and Lelia dreaded the approach of Christmas. There had been signs of trouble that fall. One evening someone sent a rock crashing through the window of a cabin where Bob was holding services. Bob sprang to the window and looked out. No one was in sight. The next time a window broke, Giles Harris leaped to his feet, raced outside, and arrested the man. Bob asked that the man be jailed. On the day of the trial a minister from Roanoke, Robert Zehmer, and a friend came to go squirrel hunting with Bob.

"First, I've got a little trial to attend to," he said. "Come along, and we'll set out from there." It was only two miles up the road toward Willis, at the Starr store, that the justice of the peace was hearing the case. When the three arrived, thirty men were outside, most of them armed.

"Better not come in," Bob whispered. "These folks are right unpredictable."

So the two men waited outside in their hunting jackets, cartridge belts slung around their middles. The mountain men looked them over intently and then went inside. The accused directly got up and pleaded guilty, and was fined. But folks say that as he was walking home afterwards he showed them the .38 Owlshead he'd brought in his pocket, intending to settle the case himself if it hadn't been for the lawmen standing outside. Bob never did find out just why the man was so bitter against him, but he had another enemy.

There were reasons to feel uneasy as Christmas neared. Mountain Christmases were always noisy, but at the Buffalo they were often wild. Friends would gather at someone's house for the day, lighting firecrackers, and in the evening, after a giant feast, the men played poker and started drinking. About midnight more firecrackers were set off in volleys, men fired their pistols and shotguns, and the prize of the evening, a tremendous charge of dynamite, was lit. Folks as far away as Rich Hill, Hoot Owl Holler, Hickory Ridge, and Shooting Creek would answer with their dynamite blasts. A Laurel Fork woman says: "About Christmas time my whiskey-drinking aunt and uncle began to hate each other out loud, threatening to shoot each other and daring each other to do it. That was Christmas for us, and I had to go to school before I found that Christ was the real reason."

It was at Christmas two years before, in an argument over a bottle of whiskey, that a man had gotten the end of his nose cut off, one ear part cut and the other hanging, and a knife wound in his back. Steve Kemp, a man of peace, tried to stop the fight but was too late. He ran into the house, where he had a phone (he lived near enough to Laurel Fork), and called Doc Burnett at Willis.

"Doc, there's been a fracas," he said.

"Cutting or shooting?" Doc asked.

"Cuttin'."

"I'll be right out. Where will I find him?"

"He's here now, but I'm a-sendin' him up the hill to his daddy's place."

"Blood was still runnin' down him and puddlin' on the floor," Steve told Bob, "but I couldn't let him stay. You see, we try not to be witnesses. It's no good to testify for or against your neighbor or kinfolk." Then he brightened. "Well sir, Doc came and tied up that ear, and it grew back on just as nice as you please."

At a Christmas party the following year, two brothers had called a young husband outside the house and shot and killed him, and no one knew why. Once, just for excitement, men on horseback had ridden right inside the Little Flock school and carried out the Christmas tree. And when a city congregation had sent out a load of presents shooting broke out between two fathers over which family should get the better presents. The visiting Santa Claus was so scared he crawled under the Christmas tree and hid. Most folks at the Buffalo had never heard of Santa Claus. The Roanoke lay worker had come one Christmas and for fun had dressed up Arthur Burwell, the nephew of Robert E. Lee, as Santa and had taken him down the road in a buggy. As they approached the very first house someone inside began screaming. The lay preacher ran for the house just as a mountaineer came loping in from the woods and hurried inside. Presently the screaming stopped. A few minutes later the man came out and looked towards the buggy.

"What's that?" he asked.

"Why, that's Arthur Burwell dressed up like Santa Claus," the Roanoke man said. As he explained about Santa Claus the man eased up.

"You know," he said, "my wife thought it was the ghost of her first husband come to ha'nt her. He was killed on top of the Buffalo a few years back."

Santa Claus went no farther.

The week before Christmas Bob and Lelia took small presents to every family they could reach around the Buffalo. And at Sunday school they heaped the gifts sent by presbytery into a pile and distributed them without regard to age or sex of child, or suitability. And when it was January an old mountain woman told Lelia: "This is the best Christmas we'uns have ever had."

"How's that?" asked Lelia.

"They's not been a single person killed or even cut up a bit."

By April, when spring greened the coves, Bob's spirits lifted even more. The school was pulling children from almost every cabin he'd been able to visit. Not too many people were coming to church, but those that did were regular. And he began to get friendly greetings when he passed by in his car. Could it be that better days were ahead, or was he just lulled by the fresh smells of spring, so full of promise? Maybe it was that Lelia had just had her sixth child, Robert, making eight children in the manse, the oldest thirteen. Bob was thankful it had turned warm early so the roads were just good enough to take her to the hospital at Christiansburg for the delivery.

There were signs that the mountain might be changing. When a young man named Lindbergh flew his plane across the ocean, a crowd at the Buffalo listened in over a battery radio at the manse. A railroad was laid in to Sylvatus, forty miles away, and a boy walked all the way over to see it. His father jawed him on his return, for his mother had worried over his sudden disappearance. But the boy said, "I'm seventeen, Pa, and a man sure ought to see a train by the time he's that old!" There seemed to be spunk in the young folks. Maybe they'd break out of the old ways. They'd be interested in roads for sure.

All winter Bob had felt hog-tied by the snows and cold and isolation. If roads and bridges didn't come, there was no real hope for people sealed off from the civilization developing beyond the mountains.

Whenever he talked to the mountaineers about roads and all-season bridges, he was met with shrugs and grunts. What need was there? They had their own remedies for aches and pains and wheezes, and Doc Burnett would come if needed. They had Doc Vaughn, a three-hundred-pound, self-trained dentist, to pull teeth for a quarter apiece and make plates, ten dollars an upper and eight a lower, and he was so good that a dentist who had seen his work came up and spent the summer learning his techniques.

Folks set their own broken bones, too. The only time they needed to leave the mountain was to take hogs or chestnuts to market, and wagons would do for that.

Without roads, lumbermen in Roanoke weren't interested in the oak and poplar and chestnuts that covered the slopes. Bob told presbytery about it, and how vital a sawmill was to overcome the idleness and boredom. When he told them he was thinking of starting his own they urged him not to; it wouldn't do, it wasn't wise to have a minister involved in a business. Bob nodded, unconvinced.

"If I'd done the wise thing," he said with a chuckle, "I s'pose I'd never have gone to the mountains in the first place."

More and more Bob realized that the stillers and retailers were responsible for the resistance to roads and bridges. He should have anticipated it, he thought, practically from the day he had come. The man who ran the store right alongside the school was selling white lightning, Bob learned.

Bob had gone to him directly and spoken to him softly, inches away.

"This is going to be embarrassing," he said, confidingly, "to have me preaching against liquor on one side of the road and you selling it on the other."

The man studied him awhile but said nothing.

"You know, one of us ought to buy the other one out, and I'm afraid it would take too much money to buy me. How much will you take for your store-house?"

That started the man talking right off, and it wasn't long until they made a deal. Bob was surprised, until the man dropped a hint during the dickering that Bob was causing such a stir and so much traffic thereabout he couldn't feel safe doing business, so he was willing to clear out. Bob had the store-house moved back of the manse to keep secondhand clothing sent by presbytery for mountain people.

Bob had known there was moonshining, but he hadn't known how much. One time Hasten had driven over from The Hollow and gotten Bob to go out squirrel hunting. They set out down the hill from the school and within minutes stumbled onto a copper kettle and coils, with two sacks of sugar waiting to be emptied. The brothers hesitated only a moment, then went past, pretending not to have seen. But they felt eyes on them. Next day from a distance they saw that the still was gone. Not a trace left. Bob realized that the mountain wasn't ready to trust the new preacher.

A week later the sheriff stopped by.

"Brother Childress, is that man Spence making liquor?"

Only smoke and the smell of mash
betrayed stills hidden in the woods.

"Friend," said Bob, "he's been accused of it, but I can't say yes or no."

After the law was gone, Spence, who unbeknownst to Bob was in the clothing store-house within earshot, came out and extended his hand.

"I sure 'preciate what you said. I'm guilty, but I'm a-goin' to quit it, soon as I can."

"Brother," said Bob, "I'm right relieved to hear that." Then he went on with an explanation that he would use time and time again with stillers. "I've always thought that any man who worked half as hard at anything else would make a better living. All that night work in the cold, and working all day too—that's hard on a man."

Spence moved away soon after, and no one knows for sure whether he found a new trade.

Stilling was more profitable than Bob had realized. Even a small still that cost no more than fifty dollars for copper coils and kettles could bring in that much in a week—and that was a mint to Buffalo people. An occasional sack of sugar was all they needed to buy. They had plenty of corn and apples and firewood.

The big profits, though, went to the bootleggers who bought the liquor from mountaineers and diluted it half and half with water, adding wild ginger root and cayenne pepper to make it taste as strong as ever, and a touch of old Red Devil lye to "give it a bead"—make it bubble. Some bootleggers came to the Buffalo to buy. More of them waited at Floyd for delivery. Folks said they made a thousand dollars a week.

No wonder the mountain feared better roads and bridges, Bob thought. The law could get in that much easier. When revenue officers converged on Buffalo Mountain that summer, some of Bob's nearest neighbors, who were in the business, were sure he was in league with them. He could tell from the way they scorned him. Revenuers were despised, often for good reason. Many took bribes from more prosperous stillers below the mountains who had learned to expect them to come galloping up, sit down to a rich table and drink their host's best liquor, and end up roaring drunk, at which time they'd publicly announce their next raid, to assure a friendly reception. Buffalo men hadn't learned the civilized arts of entertaining and bribery, and felt resentful when their stills were cut down and their mash emptied. So they hated, and they fought back.

One church member told Bob that a young revenuer had stopped a Buffalo man with a yoke of oxen and a wagon outside the school.

"What you loaded with?" asked the officer.

"Manhood and moonshine," said the mountaineer. The two looked at each other silently. The officer left.

The story was told, too—though Bob couldn't be sure it was true—that the same young revenuer came to search a mountaineer's barn with a warrant that he read aloud. When he was done, the mountain man spoke.

"Stranger, that thar paper says you've got a right to go in, but hit don't say nothin' 'bout you comin' out agin, now do it?"

The officer hurried off.

Bob tried not to see any lawman if he could help it. He hated liquor and what it could make men do, but he still believed the law couldn't stop it, the way the law was carried out.

There were arrests all over Buffalo Mountain and the surrounding area that year. The records show that, in Floyd County alone, fifty-two were indicted for liquor violations at the January session of court, twenty-three at the March term, sixteen at the May term, and twenty in July. Indicted too was "one gray horse, for transportation of ardent spirits." Three times, when revenuers had swooped down to make a raid, all they had found to greet them was the same old mare, and each time, though they gave the forlorn animal her freedom, she had refused to lead them home to her owner. So they had locked her up in the local livery stable. Also indicted were guilty vehicles, caught in the mud after a chase or with a blowout, while their operators took to the woods.

Bob preached against liquor, but more often he talked to stillers privately when the time seemed right. He would never inform on them. He knew from experience that the law might halt—but it wouldn't end—a man's stilling. The profits were too good. The only way was to change his mind, to persuade him that it was wrong, for one thing, and that there were safer ways of making a living.

Most people had already met up with the idea that liquor was wrong, even though the Primitive Baptists for generations had allowed liquor on church grounds. In fact, the right to sell it there was generally conceded to be part of the rewards of preaching. But every other denomination considered it a sin, and folks knew it.

People were coming to Bob's services in growing numbers, but few were joining, and Bob knew why. Mountain people took their vows seriously, and weren't about to give up their old ways and serve the Lord unless they meant it. So the decision to join was often a momentous one.

In June when Bob's classmate, Sam Query, came up from his church in the lowlands with one of his elders to hold a revival, one young mountaineer professed his faith and then ran out of the room crying. At the end of the week, Mr. Query and his elder took supper with the new convert and his father-in-law while the women waited table. The timid young man was telling that he hadn't touched a drop of liquor all week.

He turned to Query's elder. "How long since you were converted?" The elder told him.

"Does it still trouble you?"

The elder didn't understand.

"Doesn't the thirst of whiskey still ha'nt you now and then?"

The elder said he had never tasted liquor in his life.

The young man looked at him unbelieving. Then he turned to his father-in-law.

"Dad," he said, "here's a man who's been a Christian all the days of his life!"

The elder dropped his head, embarrassed, and protested. But the young man didn't hear him. What reason was there for repentance other than drinking?

Bob knew the agony that the young man felt. Even now, after all the years without liquor, there was scarcely a week went by but what it still called out to him strong.

IN RE:

 (GRAND JURY # Indictments

 The Regular Grand jury summoned, sworn, instructed and empanelled and sent to their room to consider of their presentments, on a former day of this term of Court, returned into court the following indictments as True Bills:

COMMONWEALTH	Vs.	Floyd Ayers, Adultery, Misdemeanor
Commonwealth	Vs.	Floyd Ayers, " "
Commonwealth	VS.	Anna Ayers, house of ill fame, Misdemeanor
Commonwealth	VS.	Alex Ayers, house of ill fame, Misdemeanor
Commonwealth	Vs.	Lon Allen, Adultery, Misdemeanor
Commonwealth	VS.	Pete Bedsaul, Violation prohibition law, Felony, manufacturing
Commonwealth	Vs.	Wayne Bedsaul, Violation prohibition law, Felony, manufacturing
Commonwealth	Vs.	George Brendle, Violation prohibition law, Misdemeanor, transporting
Commonwealth	Vs.	Earn Beasley, Violation prohibition law , Misdemeanor, transporting
Commonwealth	Vs.	George Brendle, Violation prohibition law, Felony Manufacturing
Commonwealth	Vs.	Elmer Boyd, Violation prohibition law, Misdemeahor, intoxication
Commonwealth	Vs.	Isaac Barker, Violation prohibition law, Felony, manufacturing
Commonwealth	Vs.	Jim Brown, Felony, Maiming
Commonwealth	Vs.	Robert Edwards, Misdemeanor,shooting along public road
Commonwealth	Vs.	Robert Edwards, Misdemeanor, abuse
Commonwealth	Vs.	Robert Edwards, Misdemeanor, carrying concealed weapon
Commonwealth	Vs.	Charlie Edwards, Misdemeanor carrying concealed weapon
Commonwealth	Vs.	George Edwards, Felony, kill a calf
Commonwealth	Vs.	Fielden Easter, Violation Prohibition law, Felony, storing for sale
Commonwealth	Vs.	Taylor Easter, Violation prohibition law, Felony, manufacture
Commonwealth	Vs.	Jerry Frazier, Felony, Manufacturing.
Commonwealth	Vs.	Jerry Frazier, Misdemeanor, transporring
Commonwealth	Vs.	Perry Flannigan, Violation prohibition law, Misdemeahor, transporti
Commonwealth	Vs.	Garney Guynn, Violation prohibition law, Misdemeanor, transporting
Commonwealth	Vs.	Garney Guynn, Violation prohibition law, Misdemeanor,offer for sale
Commonwealth	Vs.	Early Guynn, Felony, entering store building to commit laceny
Commonwealth	Vs.	Early Guynn, Violation prohibition law , transporting
Commonwealth	Vs.	Johnson Frazier, Violation prohibition law, Misdemeanor, intoxicati
Commonwealth	Vs.	Tom Guynn, Misdemeanor, carnal communication
Commonwealth	Vs.	Booker Harrold, Violation prohibition law, Felony, manufacturing
Commonwealth	Vs.	Booker Harrold, Violation prohibition law, Misdemeabor, intoxicati
Commonwealth	Vs.	Glenn Hanks, Misdemeanor, disturb public worship

The court docket of Carroll County on a typical day in 1928.

He knew now what he must say about drunkenness—that, bad as it was, there were other sins, many of them far worse. He said just that, the first Sunday after a revival meeting. It was on a day that was warm and fragrant and sparkling as only a day in June in the Blue Ridge can be.

Then he made an altar call. "Just come to the Lord and let the Lord cure your soul first. Then you can start to work on your drinking."

Giles Harris got to his feet. "We didn't know whether he was walking outside or coming forward," said his daughter. "He stood for a moment, and then started slowly walking up. I could hardly look, I was that excited, for you know what a reputation Dad had for his temper and those Easter Sunday shootings and the Bowman boy outside church. It got so quiet you could hear the redbirds singing. It was the happiest day in my life!"

Bob had tears in his eyes. This was the man that people at Willis and Hillsville and Floyd still called the most dangerous man on Buffalo Mountain.

"Giles, if it weren't for you," he said, "I could never keep my churches going."

Conviction came that day to fifteen others, and as they went up front, one after another, it seemed to Bob that all of the Buffalo might break loose and profess Christ. Claude Harris's family joined, and Mack Moles and his family.

Bob knew he couldn't change the Buffalo overnight. There were too many things to tackle all at the same time. So he preached and talked about killing and drinking and stilling every chance he got, just as he did about roads. But each day brought a hundred other needs too, and he just tried to meet whatever seemed the most urgent.

Folks said that Bob worked like a man either running from the devil, or after him. He'd leave home at breakfast and not re-appear until past dark, without even time for a noon meal. He kept a diary one winter at the request of Home Mission head-quarters:

Jan. 2   Car trouble, worked on car, helped get wood for school furnace, hung up on ice in Laurel Fork. Conducted chapel.

Jan. 3   Visited eight homes.

Jan. 4   Visited five homes. Took supplies to Mrs. Puckett. Bailey Goad went along.

Jan. 5   Visited three homes. Got snowbound. Spent night with S. Branscome.

Jan. 6   Visited five homes on horseback. Worked in office. Conducted night service. Text: "Depart from me for I am a sinful man."

Jan. 7   Sunday. Rev. 2: 13. "Know where thou dwellest." Text suggests it is harder to live a Christian in some places than in others. Text may disturb some, comfort others. Held three services but could not get to Slate Mountain. No more driving.

By late February he was back in his T-Model, going strong.

Feb. 29   Visited ten homes.

Mar. 1   Took Steve Goad to hospital. Conducted chapel.

Mar. 3   Spent the day mostly at home. Conducted chapel at night. "My people doth not consider." Visited bereaved family. Held song service.

Mar. 4   Attended Hillsville court. Dismissed case against four who disturbed church services. Had song services at hotel.

Mar. 5.   Attended road meeting. Made address at night.

Mar. 6   Late to Buffalo Knob service. Congregation had left me. Visited one home. Taught class at Buffalo in afternoon, preached afterward. Preached at Meadows of Dan on sincerity. Preached at Indian Valley.

Mar. 7   Built stage at school. Had cottage prayer service at Byrd Branscome's.

Mar. 8   Hung in mud and missed appointment at Sunnyside.

Mar. 9   Took Mr. and Mrs. Moles to doctor in Floyd in A.M. Took Mrs. Branscome to doctor in P.M.

Mar. 10   Took two to hospital at Christiansburg. Went on to road meeting at Roanoke.

Mar. 11   Friday night services. "Take the little foxes that destroy the vines." Solomon 2. Sin like a fox is a cunning thing, and a growing thing. Some little foxes: selfishness, indifference, moderate drinking. Missed services. Stuck in mud at Slate Mountain. Preached from Exodus: While delivered from the enemy, a man may still be threatened by them. Murmuring will not take the place of marching.

In the midst of Bob's work church headquarters asked him to take time out to travel around the country telling the story of mountain missions. On a visit to Tennessee he saw churches built with fieldstone, the most beautiful he'd ever seen. Folks told him they weren't too expensive to build, either, if you had plenty of rocks and manpower. Bob began then to dream of the church he hoped to build on the Buffalo. But there was plenty to do before then.

Sundays, of course, were the busiest. He'd start with services at some cabin or store-house at eight o'clock and again at ten o'clock. "Evening" services were around 2:30, and night meetings around 7:30. Generally he ate no food from early morning until after dark. Lelia seldom went along, being too occupied with Hattie and Robert, but several children from school, including his own, would go along to help conduct Sunday school. Often there might be a visiting pastor or lay worker, too.

Most folks would gather an hour or so before the service. They didn't want to miss being there when Bob pulled onto the grounds, clambered out of the car, and started visiting, shaking hands with every person there. He always had a joke to tell. One time it was on Rollie Phillips, who ran the Indian Valley store.

When Bob had stopped for gas one midnight, he had come out in his nightshirt with a pistol that he tried to hide when he saw it was the preacher. Fumbling with flashlight and pistol and gas pump, Rollie seemed comic to Bob. "Maybe I ought to equip my elders with pistols when they pass the plate. How about it, Rollie?" To a pastor traveling with Bob it seemed a trifle risky to poke fun at the men, as though carrying a gun was something childish, something to be ashamed of. But Rollie only reddened and smiled.

Inside, Sunday school would already have begun. In one pew might be Conduff or Evelyn and Marie, or any of half a dozen others from the Buffalo school. Between Sunday school and church services there would be fifteen minutes of singing, or what Bob caled relaxation. He'd summon half a dozen up front to form a choir to lead the others. After a couple of lines he might stop to call out to a young woman in back, "Clara Mac, just bring your big mouth up here!" After a verse he might stop. "Look here, I heard two or three of you back there who weren't a-singin'!"

Bob would explain to a visiting pastor, "I just can't stand to preach to gloomy people."

Visitors had a way of remembering Bob's sermons, simple as they always were.

One man recalls how he started off with a preface.

"I understand that last Sunday when I was gone our deacon, before introducing our visiting pastor, said, 'We are sad to miss the vacant face of our beloved pastor.' Well, here I am, vacant face and all."

Then followed a sermon on Job, spoken from a single note card that read: "A word spoken in due season—how good it is! It is wrong not to speak at times. We must not keep back words at these times—warning, encouragement, comfort."

The message was this. "Job's first tests were years of property, power, family, the love of friends. His faith didn't depend on home or health or worldly applause. The secret—the ability to see and the willingness to look for God's hands in everything. Do you see God's hand in the full corn-crib, the full smokehouse, strong bodies? And do you still look for his hand in the storm or in the sickbed, or when you lose something, or by an open grave or the side of a suffering friend, or in the hard breathing or the hot brow of a little child? If you are enjoying life's blessings, the hand of God is there. If you are feeling life's losses, his hand is still there."

The delivery was simple. A few times he thundered a point, but otherwise he was quiet and conversational. It was his examples and imagery that made the sermon vivid. Suddenly it would be over.

Bob couldn't stand long sermons, he said. His own were seldom longer than fifteen minutes. "Only three things I try to remember—just get up, speak up, and shut up."

The moment the service was over, Bob would usually hurry to the car without pausing to shake hands at the door, and start for the next church. Given his choice, Bob said, he'd much rather welcome people to services than tell them good-bye.

"Too many good-byes in this old world," he said.

At the next service, Bob might warm up his congregation by saying he had met a member on the way to church.

"How are you, Brother Lige?"

"No 'count. No 'count."

"I know that, Lige, but how about your health?"

If there was a latecomer during the service, even though the sermon had begun, Bob would greet the man warmly and say, "Look, there's still a seat up front here." Bob reasoned that the congregation was already disturbed, and might better have an authorized look rather than a furtive peek at the arrival.

Whenever he had a visitor, Bob would introduce him to the congregation and add: "I know if I didn't tell you who he was, you wouldn't listen to me all hour for wondering whether my friend was a revenuer." Then he would add, "I can tell you he's not, at least not for today." And though he laughed when he made the announcement, Bob knew that for many it was no joking matter.

Sometimes Bob would be invited to preach at a church down toward The Hollow, and whenever he could he tried to make a side trip up to Squirrel Creek to visit Aunt Lucy and Anderson Carter and his other friends. And sometimes he'd hold a service right then in their tiny chapel.

The whole cove was wild to see him. As he met one friend after another, his spirits soared. Later, he would sit down with the Carters to an impromptu meal of chittlins and hominy and salt pork.

"Conduff," Bob said once when his son was along, lapsing into mountain talk as he loved to do, "hit was Aunt Lucy who baked your mammy's wedding cake."

The tall, handsome woman beamed. "A good one, if I do say so. And afterwards your daddy carried me home in the surrey."

Bob turned to Anderson. "One day I want to drive you-all up to Buffalo Mountain to worship with us. I really mean to do that, first chancet I get."

Bob thought about it as he threaded the narrow trail that led up the valley to Squirrel Spur above. There was just no point in people being shut up in one cove. His folks needed to see his friends from Squirrel Creek. They needed to feel their friendly warmth, their honesty and kindness. Bringing them all together was something he was bound to do someday.

With all the trips to lead services, carry folks to town, and calling, Bob realized that he was seeing his family too briefly. He tried to make the most of breakfast, when they were sure to be together. As they gathered around the big oblong table in the dining room, Bob would ask a blessing. The children could feel how strongly their father meant his thanks. Lelia had told them how hungry he had been as a boy, and they never forgot it. Platters loaded with fried eggs and potatoes would come to the board, along with blackberry jam and steaming biscuits that Evelyn had made, and pitchers of cold milk. Afterward, Bob would offer a devotion, and they'd sing together. Before Bob left the house, he would give Hattie a walking lesson. Her progress was slow, and it hurt to see how hard she tried.

Now and then there'd be an evening when Bob could be home, and Lelia would say, "Bob, those children go crazy when they know you'll be here." They took their mother's gentle watch-fulness for granted, but they adored the attention their dad gave them. Without being told, the boys would hustle out to get the biggest logs in the woodpile, so they wouldn't need to budge from the fireplace while their dad, his lap crowded with chil-dren, told stories of the places he had seen on his trips or of his early life in The Hollow. Sometimes he recited poetry. Other times he read comic strips from the Sunday paper. He read with such drama that even Lelia would look up from her darning to listen. When it was near time to go to bed he'd ask someone to go down cellar for apples, a different child each time. They knew why—to help them lose their fear of the dark—a fear he had once known well.

As time came for school to open that September, Bob had to face a new crisis. The Little Flock school board decided to close its school and transport the children to the Buffalo. Giles Harris was chosen to drive the old bus they had picked up.

The board hadn't reckoned with Grant Massey, a man all the mountain feared. It was said he'd killed three men from another mountain, just because he didn't like the way they joked—dropping them in their tracks, one body on top of the other. But Grant had never been brought to court, because no one dared to testify against him. And now he was angry again, and nobody knew quite why, but it had something to do with the school closing and with Giles's being chosen to drive the bus.

Before breakfast one morning, a member of the church rode horseback up to the Childress door and warned Bob not to go driving that day, because several people had heard Massey threaten to kill the preacher if the bus began hauling children. He aimed to shoot Giles, too, the moment he saw him.

Bob got up from the table. He drove to Massey's home and stepped out of the car. The man met him at the door, glowering. Bob explained, through the screen door, that the decision to transport had been made by the board, and that Giles had made the lowest bid. Massey said nothing.

"Look, friend," said Bob, coming to the point at once. "What good will it do for you to shoot Giles, or me either? This killing has got to stop somewhere. All it takes is a man big enough, who thinks straight enough, to see that the bravest man is the one who will stop killing. We've got to find somebody to be the first one. Why isn't that somebody you?"

The man didn't answer, but it seemed from his face that a new idea was fermenting inside him.

He opened the door and came outside. A dog trotted up to them.

"There's a likely looking one," said Bob, brightening, "but, Grant, I'll wager he can't come up to my little black feist. Why, that dog can smell out where a bunny is going to, not just where he's been! He's spotted me a bunch of bunnies as far ahead as next Saturday. How about coming over and hunting with me?"

Massey smiled, even though he shook his head. So Bob reached out and grabbed his hand, then turned and walked off the porch.

Conduff and a friend at the Buffalo school.

He felt better after the visit, though he was still worried. But next day the school bus picked up the Little Flock children without incident.

Every spare moment, Bob was at the school, insisting that it be made a pleasure, for otherwise mountain children wouldn't come. When he found that one teacher was punishing children by standing them for an hour with their noses to the blackboard, he sent the teacher packing.

"There are better ways of handling a boy with a case of the smarts," he said.

Eight girls lived at the school. To keep them occupied, Bob arranged an activity for almost every evening—a spelldown, a ball game, or a party. Parties were a dangerous trial, but one of the teachers, a snappy redhaired little mountain woman named Clara Belle Smith, a sister of Bob's closest friend Roy Smith, knew mountain boys. She made it a rule that only boys especially invited by the girls could attend. She would meet them at the door, scrutinizing them as she shook hands. Then she passed them along to Miss Bennett Sturgeon, another teacher.

"My nose isn't good," she confided to Bob. "I can't tell if a boy's been drinking or whether he has plastered something on his hair. But Miss Sturgeon—there's a nose!"

At the Halloween party, boys were to come masked, but before they entered, they had to give Clara Belle and Miss Sturgeon a quick look and a sniff behind the mask.

Even so, there was trouble. A parcel of uninvited young men rocked the building, breaking windows, and threatening to come inside. They threw a rock at the preacher that barely missed his head. He took fifteen of them to court, and then when the justice was about to sentence them, he interceded.

"They're good boys, judge," he said. "They just don't behave." He asked that the case be dismissed. He knew what being locked up meant to a free and footloose mountain boy.

Fall passed swiftly into winter, and soon it was Christmas of their third year. And on Christmas morning there was a giant box of candy with a ribbon which bore in gold letters: "Packed especially for Lelia Childress."

"Hit's too expensive, Bob," she said, her eyes shining. Bob simply put his arms around her.

One of the children said, "What Mama really wanted was new linoleum for the kitchen." That came, too, a few days later.

As the year came to a close at the Buffalo, Bob and Lelia thanked the Lord that Christmas had again been quiet. Life didn't seem as uncertain, as dangerous, as they had thought it might be. Lelia was the surprising one: she had come to love the mountain as much as or more than Bob. "I guess you, or the Lord, or both of you, must have been right," she said.

And Bob answered, "Without you here, I would have been wrong, even if God was right."

As 1928 came to a close, Bob and Lelia were filled with hope. People were joining the church. The piano teacher who lived in the manse had taught half a dozen girls to play. They vied for the chance to travel from church to church.

People dared talk about the past as though it were over and done with. Folks laughed about the number in the congregation who had been hauled into court for murder or mayhem, as though it were something they had outgrown and left behind.

The Year the Chestnuts Died

Folks say that 1929 was a bewitched year, from the very start. For it was the year the chestnuts died. When Bob had first come, there had been a few brown limbs. The next year there had been more, and whole trees had begun dying. The year after that the blight had struck worse. But in 1929 not a chestnut was left alive. Trees in the yard that had been friends of a family since great-great-grandfather's time stood black as if fire had swept them. And all through the forests every chestnut was bare and ghostly, without a leaf to stir in the spring rain and sun. It was a visitation of the Lord, some said, for something evil. And a few hinted darkly that the new preacher might have had something to do with it.

He had made things that different. He was preaching regularly at half a dozen places besides the Buffalo school, and holding Sunday schools at even more, and it was a caution the way folks were beginning to flock to him. He had such a way with children it was as if he'd been born with special powers.

He'd go into a house and pat a child on the head and say, "Wouldn't you like to go with me to Sunday school?" And of course every one would. Then he'd turn to the daddy and say, "Whyn't you let this child go with me? I'll stop by at ten for him." He even got hold of a little bus and would go almost to Willis, twelve miles off, to pick them up.

He seemed about as persuasive with adults too. Sometimes an angry father would decide not to let the big jokey minister into the house, and would stand stolidly in the doorway. And don't you suppose that that would be the time he had brought half a

147

dozen sweaters for the children? Now and then, if a mother took the clothes she'd have to return them, for mountain men were proud.

After the children had gone to Sunday school a few times, generally the mother would start going too. Then Bob would ask the reluctant father, "How 'bout the whole family a-goin'?"

"I don't have clothes fitten."

"Ah, brother," he'd say with an arm around the man's shoulder, "don't let clothes keep you away. Men look at the clothes, but the Lord looks at the heart."

Next time he'd come by to drop off a suit of men's clothes.

How could you refuse a man like that?

One Buffalo mountaineer after another joined the church. Many remember exactly how it happened.

"He just came up to me," said Steve Kemp, "and put his arm around me and said, 'You're a sweet man. Why don't you join up?'" Steve, a big, lean mountaineer, grins as he recalls it. "Well, I got to studying the Bible," he continued. "I read it

Buffalo neighbors helped Bob (third from right)
put up a split-rail fence
the year before the church was built.

through twicet in one year, and all the time I was shuckin' corn I prayed God to give me the answer. It came to me then that I should join."

Roy Weddle was another. "We'd been talking about fox-hounds," said Roy, "and all at once he put his arm around my shoulder like this and said, 'Brother, you're my kind of man. Come on over to church.' " Soon Bob got him to singing solo in church, too, and took him along to services beyond Buffalo Mountain. His voice was like a French horn, big and mellow and stirring.

If a mountaineer wanted to join but felt uneasy about being baptized by sprinkling, the preacher took him out into the creek and immersed him.

Sometimes Giles Harris, an elder by then, went along with Bob on night services in cabins farther off where Bob was starting to preach and hold Sunday schools. Bob asked him to stand at the door and greet people as they entered. Folks listened when Giles spoke. And if men or boys started rocking the building to break up services, all Giles had to do was step out on the porch and they'd scramble into the woods.

Bailey Goad was an elder, too, and often went along from one service to the next. And when he would tell of his past misdeeds, the preacher would only say, "Brother, my sweetest friends and best Christians are those with humility. The man who knows sin is the man who knows forgiveness."

Once you got inside them, Bob often thought, his Buffalo friends were the kind of human beings he had been searching for all his life, people who cared as deeply as he about loyalty and friendship and love. They were people who liked you for yourself, and not just for the funny stories you could tell, or what you could do for them or bring them. They were the kind of brothers Jesus talked about. A dozen of them had come with scythes and cradles to put up hay for his cows and saddle horse and team. And again they had come with axes and saws to put up firewood. And just before Thanksgiving they had come—a long line of them on horseback led by Bailey Goad in a wagon, blowing a mellow blast on a long steer's horn—with a whole wagon-load of cattle chop and produce and cornmeal and hams and bacon. "My brothers," Bob had said, with happy tears in his eyes, "I reckon I don't deserve you."

It was time Buffalo Mountain had a real church. There was no longer room enough in the school, even when the partition between the two downstairs classrooms was pulled out and the two rooms made into one. Home Mission headquarters agreed. Now was the time, Bob thought. This would be the great year.

He met with bank directors at Willis.

"That gang of outlaws build a church?" said one.

"Too many bootleggers!" said another.

"There isn't a hundred dollars on all Buffalo Mountain," said still another.

Bob spoke up. "The Lord has given us the materials. We've got the stones, we've got the timber, we've got the manpower, we've got horses, mules, oxen, and a few trucks. We don't need much money."

"Just how much?" one asked.

Bob figured ten thousand.

The men snorted—all but Elbert Weeks, the cashier. "I haven't known this man long, but I never did see him start anything he didn't finish."

Weeks had a name as a cautious man. Now he spoke with an urgency the others had never before heard. When he concluded, notes were drawn up with Bob as first signer and all the men of the Buffalo church who could write as co-signers—a short list.

Bailey Goad suggested that the church go right on the spot above the school where long ago there had been a still and where men later took not just bottles of whiskey but kegs to drink, for they liked the view across the valley of the Buffalo. There had been several killings on the spot. Folks liked Bailey's idea. It was as if the church would blot out the past.

Bob suggested that it be built out of Buffalo Mountain itself, the jagged rocks men fought with. Bailey Goad objected. "I've cussed every rock in the county, trying to make a stalk of corn grow," he said. But most others took to the idea.

The summer started out with what seemed like the whole mountain joining in. Methodists and even Primitive Baptists came to help. One preacher from down the valley kicked up sand about that, but Bob sent word that any denomination would be welcome to use the church.

Since the building would belong to everybody, Bob suggested that folks cut down the trees on the boundaries of their places, the line trees that had started so many misunderstandings. Many of them, having stood for centuries, were of enormous size. Men skidded them out with oxen, sawed beams out of water oak, and made poplar logs into German siding. Gradually the basement and foundations took shape.

Soon it was time for the stones that would form the massive walls. Bob announced a contest: the person who brought the prettiest stone would be first to pass inside the building. Billy Goad—no kin to Bailey—brought a piece of solid quartz, and Mack Moles brought another, so clear you could mighty nigh see through it. And since a man felt a trifle foolish bringing just one stone, he generally brought in a load, with the prize stone entry among them.

Billy Goad's foot-long piece of pure crystal quartz was judged the prettiest, and Mack Moles's was next, for he had pricked it a bit when he was prizing it out of the ground. Johnny Sutphin was quick to learn how to put up rocks, and he became a sort of foreman. Billy Goad's piece was mortared into place in the front entrance. Gradually the walls went up, the same yellows and reds and browns as the oaks and maples and tulip trees that were starting to color the Buffalo and the mountains all around.

The last stone was mortared in place the very week that the stock market collapsed. But none of that seemed real or important on the Buffalo, where little of the news trickled in.

Yet it was just then that darkness of a kind different from that over the rest of America fell on the mountain, and no one could really tell why it started or why it got so bad. But they could mark it from the killing of Dorie Cutter.

Dorie was a sunny, beautiful girl of eighteen who had gone to

*The Buffalo Mountain church was rocksided
like the others Bob built.*

Bob's Sunday school. She and her sister Esther had been rooming
in Willis while they attended high school. Dorie had been keeping
company for more than a year with Van Strang, a boy who lived
on the other side of the Buffalo. One day in December Esther
returned home to tell her folks that Dorie and Van had gone
away to be married. But a few days later a neighbor told the
father, Stiles Cutter, that Van was back at work and Dorie
wasn't with him. So Stiles set off at once to find the boy, and
ran into him by chance on the street in Willis.

"Did you marry up with my Dorie?"

Van said no.

"Well, didn't you stolen her from her house?"

"No, I didn't."

"You're coming back with me." Stiles took Van into Floyd
and had him jailed.

A posse started hunting for Dorie, but found not a trace.
Days passed. Then Giles Harris went to the jail and talked with
Van.

"Van, you've got a lot of sense," he said. "Where would you

look for her? I mean, not that you did it. But where would you look?"

Van studied a minute. "They's lots of places, I s'pose." Then, softly: "Over on Bent Mountain."

And there they found her body. Van finally confessed. He had suspected Dorie of being unfaithful and, in a burst of rage, tried to push her over a cliff and couldn't, then hit her with a branch and dragged her up the mountain away from the road and left her for dead. But she had come to and pulled herself down the mountain almost to the road, where she lay in the freezing cold all day and most of the night, calling out for help. Van returned at two in the morning and found her still alive. She pleaded to be taken home, and he studied awhile, but told her if he did, he knew her father would kill him. So he choked her to death with a cord.

Dorie's murder was only the beginning. Stiles's neighbor was a man named Mason who ran a store-house. One day when he had been drinking, his wife took her daughters and went to her mother's, leaving Mason alone in the store with his two small sons.

Stiles Cutter walked with his sons, nine and twelve, over to the store and went inside and sat on a sack of cattle chop.

"I've come to settle up my account," he said.

Mason stooped down behind the counter and came up with his gun.

"All right," he said, "we'll settle it oncet and for good!"

The shot went through Stiles and stuck in the wall behind him. His sons each took one of Stiles's hands and started him to the door as Mason fired again and missed. They didn't get him more than three steps from the door when he fell. The older boy told his brother, "Stay with Pa, and I'll run for Ma."

Running home, he heard one more shot. When he got back with his mother, his father was dead, and the Mason boys came running out of the store.

"Papa shot himself dead!" they cried.

All Mrs. Cutter could think of was to send for Bob Childress, but he was somewhere down below the mountain where no one could find him. His boy Conduff came running back to tell them, and almost stumbled over the bodies. It was late night before both graves were filled.

Bob was shocked into numb silence. Just when it had seemed that the old mountain was changing, that the bitter memories of the past were being swallowed up in the building of the church and the growth of the school, sudden death had come again. And Bob knew that the violence could spread, for it had before. Was there to be no end to the hatred? He went to the church alone and prayed, and the words of David seemed to cry out his own anguish: "O Lord, how long wilt thou be angry against the prayer of my people? Thou feedest them with the bread of tears, and givest them tears to drink in great measure." He prayed this would be the end of the tears.

Madness of a Mountain

Conduff had gotten sick to his stomach when he returned from seeing the gore at the store-house. Bob tried to comfort him, but the boy wouldn't speak or respond.

In the days after that, the Buffalo was no longer a mountain. It was a volcano of hate and fear. Men fought at their stills, in the road, in the churchyard.

Bob felt helpless. It wasn't just his agony over the people, but the downright physical danger to his family. When people had asked how he dared take his family to Buffalo Mountain he had laughed. He had thought only of himself, that he wasn't afraid. Now it came home sharp that his family was as deeply involved as he. And it wasn't right. They hadn't asked to come. Maybe he should have settled in Willis or Floyd and served the Buffalo from there. His family at least would have been safe.

Presbytery had offered a simple suggestion. Just don't get so mixed up in people's lives. Let them solve their own problems. Keep your doors locked when you want a little peace and quiet. And remember, you're a minister—not a sheriff or attorney or judge.

Not much of a minister, either, Bob thought as he drove home from a visit to presbytery headquarters at Roanoke. After four years, the mountain was suddenly more troubled than it had been when he came. At home that night he couldn't sleep. He got up and lit the coal-oil lamp. Suddenly he remembered a remark made by a missionary who had addressed the students at seminary. "The man who civilizes the Blue Ridge will be one who lives among the mountaineers, and whose family will set a pattern for Christian love and decency every day of the week."

Bob thought the speaker was probably right. But was it possible? He knew that preaching and revivals and house calls and all the rest might not do much. It was the way a man lived, and the way his family lived, that counted. But now, just keeping them alive and safe—yes, and sane, too—that was struggle enough. There was no refuge to which they could escape, even for a few hours.

He recalled a knock at the door a few nights before, and a woman with her daughter begging to come in. She was wild-eyed and breathless. Her stepson had run them out.

"What can I do, Mr. Childress?"

"What can you do, woman? You can stay right here with us and help Lelia!" And she was still with them.

Another woman sometimes came over with letters to her son, asking that Bob mail them from some distant town where he might be speaking. Her boy had cut up his friend and, thinking he had killed him, lit out for the west. The woman would sob and carry on each time she came, while the Childress youngsters looked on silently.

Bob preached more vigorously than ever against drink.

"It is high time to awake out of sleep," he read from Romans, "for now is our salvation nearer than when we believed. The night is far spent, the day is at hand: let us therefore cast off the works of darkness, and let us put on the armour of light. Let us walk honestly, as in the day; not in rioting and drunkenness."

But there was madness on the mountain. A young boy, just sixteen, beat up a man he thought was his father's murderer and left him for dead, draping him over a rail fence the way folks displayed the hawks or owls they had shot.

Bob preached on brotherly love.

"If there be any other commandment," he read from Romans, "it is briefly comprehended in this saying, namely, Thou shalt love thy neighbour as thyself."

One member said, "We 'preciate those sermons on bein' brothers, but ain't you overdoin' it?"

Mountaineers carry a coffin
across a branch to the family burial plot.

"Brother," said Bob, "as long as you-all keep a-sulkin' and a-shootin', I reckon I'll keep on a-preachin' brotherly love."

The violence would break out unexpectedly from people who were the least likely to be infected by it. One man Bob had always been close to got up in church one morning and told him he was a liar. He wouldn't quiet down when Bob asked, so Bob had to come down from the pulpit and take him out to the churchyard, and there the man lunged at him with a knife. So Bob had him arrested and jailed. There didn't seem anything else to do. But Bob was sick at heart because he saw hate where he would have expected love, and he knew the man would always be an enemy.

Was there no way to end the plague?

It could break out anywhere. One afternoon there was a crowd of people outside the manse, beside the store-house where secondhand clothing was being auctioned off. Ferd Naylor's wife Tula had warned Bob there'd be trouble because Mary Wiley had been shortcutting across Ferd's corn patch. When he stopped her he said he'd have beaten her up if she'd been a man, but instead he'd get his wife to do it. He was right proud of how husky his Tula was. On that sale day one lady took sick, and Mary came in to ask Lelia if she could make her some coffee and pancakes. While Lelia was at the stove, Tula came in and straight off hit Mary in the face with her fist. Mary threw up her hands to protect herself, and the pancake knife she was holding cut Tula.

Lelia grabbed Tula, but, being unsteady on her feet, was flung off and almost fell. She turned toward the door to call her husband.

"Don't call the men," cried Tula, "or there'll be trouble!"

Lelia ran to the other room, where she saw Tula's sister-in-law. "Get in the kitchen, quick!" she cried.

Tula had Mary on the floor and was pounding her something terrible, says Lelia, before her sister-in-law could pull her off. Mary's eye and face were badly bruised and bleeding.

There was no keeping the hate and violence out of the manse itself.

Not long after that, Bob took Will Goins and his brother into Floyd. Will was a massive man with big sagging muscles who somehow always thought he was sick. But when he got to town he decided not to see the doctor. Bob left the two men in the car while he attended to business in the courthouse. When he returned he found that the two had gotten into a fearsome argument. Will's brother showed Bob his hand, which was spurting blood. "Look, Mist' Child'ss," he said, "he bitened my finger nearly off." Bob hurried him to the doctor to stop the bleeding. On the way home the men went on arguing. Bob tried to reason, but there was no stopping them. He let them off at the corner by the church and drove on home quickly. There were limits to what he could do, he thought. But he couldn't shut out the battle that easily, for his boys would report to him from the window as he sat in his chair in the living room trying to prepare the Sunday sermon.

"Will's got a pistol, Papa, and he's threatening to shoot!"

"Just let them alone," said Bob. Then he asked, "Are they on church property?"

"No, but they're on the road beside it."

The boys would race over to watch from behind trees and report back periodically. For three solid hours the men argued, Will brandishing his pistol and his brother daring him to shoot. Bob longed to rush out and grapple with them and send them on home, but he had schooled himself against physical violence. This was what he was preaching and praying against every day of the week. Yet his muscles ached from inaction.

It was another thing when men invaded the church grounds. One Sunday a man with a grudge against a member lay in wait outside the church. As services ended he raced up to where the member was getting in the car and pulled him out. To Bill Joe, who was ten, the man seemed big as a giant. He screamed as his father rushed alongside the men and grabbed the attacker by the collar. Bill Joe was too terrified to look, but he could hear the big man shouting.

His dad's interruption was a roar. "What's between you and him is your own business, but when two men start feuding on the Lord's ground, then it's my business!"

When Bill Joe looked again it seemed as if his father was the giant. The other men walked away.

Bob took his son by the hand and started down the hill toward home.

"I'm sorry, Bill Joe," he said. "That's no way for a man to act, and a preacher especially, I suppose. But seems to me that church grounds are sort of sacred."

Bob felt hot with humiliation and spent anger. At the door Little Hattie was waiting. She looked up at her father.

"Why is my Papa wearing his everyday face?" she asked. Bob felt his spirits soar.

"There, that's better," she said. "Now he's put on his Sunday face."

Bob swept her into his arms and held her close. He had already forgotten why he was downcast.

In the whirlwind that raged outside the home, it was Hattie, more than anyone else, who kept the family peaceful. She could walk now, but with her head too big for her frail body she was unsteady and would often fall. Once in a while for no apparent reason she would suddenly grow rigid and speechless, and Bob or Lelia or one of the older children would massage her limbs to restore circulation until she came to.

And yet, with all her handicaps, she was a radiantly happy child and somehow the center of affection and fun. On somebody's birthday, following mountain tradition, she would slip up behind him with a speck of butter on her finger and try to smear his nose. And when she laughed, everyone laughed, for the sound was like music.

She liked teasing her father. She was only four when Giles Harris came to pick up a bird dog for which he'd paid Bob a good price. She said, good and loud, "I'm sure glad to see that eggsucker go!"

"Why, Hattie, that dog doesn't suck eggs," said her father.

"No, he just swallows them whole," she said, laughing at her father's discomfiture.

There was a special bond between the two. One Father's Day she had composed a poem for him that she called "To the Dearest Dad on Earth." The last stanza went:

> I love you of course you know,
> Although I seldom tell you so.
> It is for you each day I pray,
> And in secret these words I say,
> "God, bless my father and ever be
> Close to his side, while he liveth for Thee."

As tender and understanding as he was with all children, Bob could be firm with his own. His love for them made him want to make life joyful, but he also wanted to protect them from the worst of the mountain's ways. He couldn't abide gossip. He'd stop them when they began a tale. "Don't believe a word of it. That boy's mouth is no prayer book." To a noisy, biggety child he might say, "What sort of tongue-oil are you using?" Somewhat firmer when occasion demanded was: "Not so much backjaw, old boy." The final warning, spoken with quiet conviction, generally cooled all ardor: "Maybe you need a little strap-oil!"

*The gentle spirit of little Hattie (left,
shown with Lelia and brother Robert)
brought peace to the Childress home during days of violence.*

Across the road and up the hill a stone's throw was a log cabin belonging to the church. To it came what seemed like a continuous stream of refugees and transients that Bob brought home with him. Among the first inhabitants were Bob's sister Netta and her husband Bill who came one night dripping with rain after the law had taken their still and their money and had run them out of the cabin they'd been renting. Netta was resentful. "That old law never does bother about us when they know we're broke. They wait until we get a little ahead." Bill still owed on the fine and was working out the remainder with the convict road gang until Bob got him released, assuring the judge he would look after him. The judge insisted Bill go to church every Sunday. That was on a Saturday. Next day, halfway through the sermon Bill began squirming and finally got up and left. Outside after services he spoke to Bob.

"You busy tomorrow?"

"Not 'specially. What do you have in mind?"

"Reckon you could take me back to the road gang?"

The man was joking of course, Bob thought, and he chuckled. But Bill was dead serious. Bob hauled him back. Lelia was up when he came home.

"Are my sermons that bad, Lelia?" he asked with a half-hearted laugh. "I just can't understand it."

Lelia tried to smother her mirth. "Not that bad," she said, "it's just that Bill could never sit still that long." Then she flinched as she realized her unwitting joke. "I mean he's just so nervous he fidgets after five minutes."

The Childress home was a beehive of activity. Sometimes there'd be a seminary friend visiting, or someone from presbytery. Besides the family there were the piano teacher and the woman and her daughter who had taken refuge there. Bob brought back rabbits and squirrels and quail and grouse from his hunting to help out on food, and church members made occasional gifts of food. Bob bought most staples like sugar and beans and cornmeal by the sack. As a treat he'd bring home a whole stalk of bananas—to Lelia's dismay, for she knew that generally all the money they owned was in Bob's pocket. The refugee woman brought her cow to the Childress pasture to help out on her keep, but the stepson swore out a warrant and had the cow returned. The woman and her daughter lived with the Childresses a year until she found work in a neighboring town and went there to live.

Nobody could quite understand how the preacher could do all he did on a salary of ninety dollars a month. Bob himself didn't know, except that extra money would come in, sometimes just as he had need for it. Anybody who heard him tell about his work just didn't seem to forget him. Hasten says, "The fight that he was makin', people saw was unselfish. That was the force that brought in the money." A Mount Airy insurance man had told Bob, "Use me as your ace-in-the-hole. When you just don't know where else to get it, call on me." And that's what Bob sometimes did, though he tried never to abuse the arrangement.

Bob got a check for three hundred dollars marked for his personal use from someone in North Carolina who had heard him speak, and with it he made the down payment on two hundred acres of fields and timberland near the manse. He set the boys to planting beans and corn and repairing the rail fences of the pastureland. The family needed the food; the boys needed something to keep them occupied. Discipline and hard work were what the mountaineers needed, Bob thought. As a child he had known no restraints. His children would.

There were some mountain ways Bob wished were not so close to his home—for one thing, the trickery that was a tradition with some mountaineers. Bob had hired Posey Teller to cut firewood to stoke the school stoves. Folks said Posey wasn't exactly what you'd call a stealing man, he just liked ham. His nostrils quivered at the thought of it. He struck a deal with Ab McGrady to raise a pig on halves if Ab supplied the pig. On the day set to butcher, Ab came over to discover that Posey had butchered the day before.

"Hit were such a fine sunshiny day," Posey said, "that I reckoned to take chances, so I killed the pig myself."

He hesitated a moment and then went on.

"A funny thing happened, Mr. McGrady," he said. "I cut up that hog and hung him in the smokehouse, just as nice as you please, hung your side on the left of the door and my side on the right, so's not to get 'em mixed. And then last night, what do you s'pose happened? Someone came in and stole your half. There's not a hair left!"

Bob laughed when he heard the story, but he found himself wishing his boys wouldn't join in so heartily.

One night while their dad was away, the boys heard the dog barking over toward the store-house. Bill Joe tried hushing him, without success. It was probably a skunk, a possum, or a coon, he thought. He took down his new shotgun and fired a few blasts in that direction. The dog chased out after something in the distance.

Next morning Bill Joe looked for tracks. There wasn't a sign. But on a laurel branch hung a dress. Someone had been raiding the store-house. And at Goad's store that afternoon, so Everett Goad said, Willie Weaver was stiff and sore as a mine mule. He pulled up his pant leg to scratch his shins, and don't you know that birdshot—from his leg or his pants, Everett couldn't say which—dropped onto the floor and rolled across it. Willie could have had the clothes free. But stealing was a game to him.

Bob laid down the law that there would be no more shooting at sounds in the dark. The boys knew he meant it.

A little later in the fall, when squirrels were cutting in the oaks and folks had their corn shucked and lying in golden piles, Willie was riled up to find that someone had been stealing *his* corn—someone with tracks so big he couldn't believe his eyes. He marked a stick with notches to show folks how long the tracks were. But people only laughed when he tried getting them to come see the tracks for themselves. There was something comic, anyway, about anyone stealing from Willie.

The mystery was solved when the Childress boys were out hunting and came upon a deserted log cabin where Posey Teller had once lived. They climbed the log ends into the loft, and found a pair of shoes the like of which they'd never seen: pieces of board shaped like shoesoles, hinged at the middle with pieces of inner tube, with tire casings to fasten them to the feet. They were Posey's stealing shoes. Another pair was shaped like women's shoes, and still another like mule's feet. The boys took them home, and showed them to Posey when he came into the store-house. "Oh, they's play-pretties I done made for my young'uns," he said.

Bob wondered as he listened to his boys' merriment if they weren't coming to look on lying and thieving as little more than a joke. It was a worry he kept to himself. He didn't want to upset Lelia.

Even their own relatives could be a threat. That winter Bill and Netta came to borrow the Childress car because theirs was out of kilter. They returned it the same night and, while the boys were watching, opened the trunk and proudly explained how they had hid several cases of liquor that they hauled past a revenuer.

The children had never before seen their father so mad—"his neck veins were a-pumpin' and sweat balls came a-poppin' out."

"Get out," he shouted, "and stay out!"

The boys snickered. Their dad glared at them. They couldn't help it, they said, even though they knew that if their dad's car had been found full of liquor he might well have been ruined.

Bob awoke that night tormented by a dark conviction. His sons had come to laugh at the law. They found wrongdoing something amusing. A sudden fear seared across his mind. Could they already be drinking? He might be the last one to know it, just as one of the teachers had a son of fifteen who was drinking hard, and all but the father seemed to know. He felt it was somehow wrong for him to do, but he stole into his sons' rooms and bent over them, smelling their breath. Even as he did, he knew that they hadn't.

And yet, he thought as he lay awake afterward, how could his boys help but accept fists and weapons as the real forces of life? They didn't pick fights, but sometimes they were hard pressed not to strike back. Conduff had been walking home from seeing a girl across the valley when a gang of six started throwing rocks.

"They would have killed me, Pa" he said, "so I rocked them right back."

Conduff was a strapping, handsome boy. The other mountain boys liked him, but they also liked to test his mettle. Five of them jumped him one time and tried to force him to take a drink of whiskey from a bottle. He made out as though he was going to, then poured it out fast and quickly thrust his hand into his pocket as if he had a gun.

"They backed off, Papa. They were scared, all right. They tried to pass it off for a joke."

It very likely helped that Conduff was built like a wrestler, with his dad's wide shoulders and thick arms, and that he could sound mean if he was pushed. He could usually curb his impulse to fight, though; he had his mother's gentle disposition. But it was hard to stand by sometimes when his father was in trouble.

Big Will Goins seemed to be just spoiling for a fight the day he stepped up to Bob, who was cranking a balky car in the churchyard, and pushed him aside.

"Let a man get hold of that thar thing!" he said.

Bob reddened suddenly but tried to make a joke. "Whereabouts do I find one?"

Will flared up and let out a string of curses. Bob jumped toward him and roared: "What did you say?"

Will edged backwards. "Just that I think you're a pretty good man."

The car never did start, and Bob and Conduff walked home in silence. Bob was ashamed for having given way to his temper once again, and especially in front of his son. He tried to say how much he hated the fighting and how he tried to keep control, and hoped his son would too. Conduff nodded.

There didn't seem to be much Bob could do about the violence but just go on—preaching, teaching, visiting, holding prayer services wherever people asked for them, driving people to and from the doctor and hospital.

Girls began coming to Sunday school and church in growing numbers. It was a place where they could meet and socialize a little and feel safe. "Most everywhere else we were scared to death half the time," one woman recalls.

"Go get your boyfriends," Bob told the girls, "and bring them inside."

He told the young men, "Church is a fine place for sweethearting." But they resented the way girls were always at church. It seemed that was the only place they could find them anymore.

And they resented that they couldn't wander in and out, eyeing the crowd, as they could at Primitive Baptist services.

So they hid in the shrubbery until services began, then kept up a stream of mischief. Sometimes they lit firecrackers to simulate a shooting. It was a rare service when rocks didn't hit the church. Once they dropped a two-inch firecracker in the vestibule as people were coming out, and got away before Giles Harris could catch up.

At commencement exercises in the school, they pelted the building with rocks. Bob stopped and went outside and called them down, but they only began again. When he went out a second time, someone threw a rock that just missed his head and slammed against the wall. It was jagged as a piece of shrapnel, and could have killed him. Giles Harris came running out, and the boys scrambled into the woods. They knew how he loved Bob. Folks say he would have fought a circle saw for him.

Bob knew mountain boys too well to stay angry long. Almost every day at Buffalo Mountain was "a nothin'-doin' sort of day," and young bloods had to create their own excitement.

The worst offenders were the Childresses' near neighbors, the six lanky Lorimer boys, friendly but unpredictable, who lived just hollering distance away and sometimes went hunting with Conduff and Paul. They would ride past church on horseback, shouting "Wild hog! Wild bear!" Sometimes they'd hurl a rock through the door. It was hard for any man to keep calm, even one without a quick temper. Finally Bob had them thrown in jail. That, he figured, had to stop them. But when he saw them behind bars he went to the judge and pleaded.

"These boys aren't really bad. I guess you'd say they just misbehaved. I'd like to take them home with me."

The judge agreed, provided they attend church service for the rest of the year. They didn't. Instead they would gallop past church singing a new refrain: "I want to go home but it ain't no use, the old black bear won't turn me loose."

Bob hauled them to court again to ask they be fined. They had no money. They never did.

"He was the beatin'est man," says one Lorimer. "He'd carry

us into court and carry us back home the same day. He'd have us work out the price of the fine, but I reckon it weren't much help he got out of us."

Bob didn't want them working on the farm with his sons. So he assigned them yard work. A visiting minister twitted him about having his own gardeners. But it wasn't funny to Bob. "They misbehaved at church," he would say, "and didn't have money for the fines."

It happened so often that the commonwealth attorney at Floyd said, "Look, Childress, I'm sick and tired of your hauling these folks in and then paying their fines. Folks say I'm not prosecuting those hillbillies, and it's giving me a bad name. Take them somewhere else. Don't bring them here!"

One Sunday just before Christmas, when the bus was loaded with children, a rock crashed through the window, scattering glass and cutting one of the small boys. Bob was out of the bus in a flash. He could feel the blood pumping through the veins in his neck. He demanded to know who had done it. Conduff, who had been standing outside, knew. For a second he thought of telling, but his dad looked furious enough to fight. So Conduff kept silent.

As a minister, Bob had never struck a man, but this time, he told Lelia, he was sure he would have. He just couldn't keep his temper, he said, though he prayed to God he could.

Lelia said, "Hit's not all handicap, Bob. Folks say it bluffs out many people who'd like to run you off."

It was in June after school was out that Will Goins's wife came bursting into the Childress home late at night, dragging her two children. She was terrified. Her husband, wild with drink, was out after her with an ax. Bob rushed the woman and her children outside and down the hill to the school. He unlocked the door quickly and, by the light from a faint moon showing through the windows, led them up three flights to the attic. There he told them to crouch under the eaves. As he stole downstairs he remembered the advice from presbytery: "Don't get so mixed up in people's affairs!" And he could almost hear Hasten's disapproval: "There you go again, thinking with your feelings.

You don't have to be foolish to be a good minister." But what could he do? Outside the door, he felt his heart jump at the sudden movement of a shadow. It was Lelia with bedding for the refugees.

In the morning Will Goins rode up on horseback and asked to come inside to talk to Bob—about bird dogs, he said. It was clear he was trying to catch sounds of his family, and hearing none he soon left.

There was tension in the manse. Would Will return, next time with an ax? Each time Lelia stole over to the school with food, the children watched from the window.

After two days Bob talked to Will, who was feeling pretty lonely now. He made him promise to come to him first if he ever got so drunk or mad he felt like swinging an ax. In the afternoon Mrs. Goins left the school attic and went home with her children.

That evening Hattie had a poem for the whole family. "It's about spring," she said, and she read it at the supper table in her strong clear voice. The children clapped. Tears came to Lelia's eyes. Bob tried to talk, to tell little Hattie that it was she who kept them sane and happy in a shaking world. But he could only swallow and smile. It seemed to him then that he must be destined forever to be torn between two worlds, one of fear and hate and the other of gentleness and love, without knowing which would win out.

Salvation by Laughter

Late one night in Bob's fourth year at Buffalo Mountain he answered a knock at the door and found outside an old man whom he recognized as B. B. Franklin. He was a storekeeper and farmer who had induced the Presbyterians to send mission workers to Indian Valley, just nine miles off as the crow flies but more than double that far by horseback. No one was working there now.

"We have bad need of you," Franklin said when he had come in. "It's gotten worse."

The people of Indian Valley had a sickness of spirit that seemed to be contagious as any flu bug. They killed not each other but themselves. And it was the upright, good people who took their own lives, people who had never been in trouble with the law or with their neighbors.

Lord knows there's plenty to do right here, Bob thought, but dignified Mr. Franklin was so despondent and insistent that he decided he could at least go over and visit. He knew that if he didn't it would just never leave his conscience. Besides, he had been so upset with the turn events had taken at the Buffalo that he was tempted by the problems of a different place. And he knew the little church there needed someone.

From the treeless hill behind the Indian Valley post office the next day, Franklin pointed out to Bob the places where twenty-five people had taken their lives. Hardly a year passed without a suicide—for no reason that anyone could see. Even a few children had tried to kill themselves, Franklin said. One young father left a note and walked off into the mountains to die.

People searched all night by lantern light for him, the mountain-side lit like a meadow of fireflies, said the old man, and they found him at last hanging from a tree. Another time a father, son, and grandson—two of them Hardshell preachers—took their lives. One of them had just finished preaching that since destiny is fixed before the foundation of the world, why suffer torture? What was to hold a man if he was one of God's elect destined for heaven. Still another minister left his last words: "I'm going to glory a trifle early."

Sometimes drinking seemed to be the cause, but more often it was just a deep sadness that came over a body.

Bob interrupted the old man. "What this place needs is a little fun, so that staying alive is more exciting than dying."

"Well, I heard what you're doing on the Buffalo, and I'd sure like to have you come preach to these poor sinners." Franklin had felt his own spirits dragged down by the valley. They started down the hill to the store-house, where Bob bought them each a soda pop. As they were drinking it, a grizzled old mountaineer began telling the preacher his troubles.

"My wife is wrong with me," he began.

"How's that?" asked Bob.

"All I asked her to do was lie down and be fitted for a casket. I only wanted her to see what a fine one I meant to build her."

Bob's laugh burst out so strong that three men in the store-house wheeled around, almost in fear. It was a strange sound to Indian Valley.

The directness of Bob's first sermon surprised them even more.

"If you want a little excitement, try serving the Lord. Now, over at the Buffalo we've got excitement, and I guess you-all know about it. I don't recommend that kind. But at least we don't have suicides—nobody lives that long!"

In the congregation was big, red-faced Blaine Quesenberry and his drinking buddy, a crusty old farmer named Wyatt Hylton. Afterward, on the steps outside, Wyatt smiled.

"Blaine, he's a whale of a preacher! Why, he makes it real entertainin'!" The two had a drink on it. Bob began preaching every Sunday night at Indian Valley.

Wyatt was a follower of Bob Childress, he says, from the first service. "I walked plumb into Willis, fifteen miles, when I heared he was goin' to be there. After that, lots of times I walked again to where he was. I never had to walk back, though, for he or his boys would always carry me. He never once forgot about me, either. He'd always look to see if I needed a ride or anythin'."

Wyatt Hylton built his store-house
at the age of seventy.

One night Wyatt stopped the preacher after a prayer meeting. "Bob," he said, "I ain't a-goin' home till I accept Christ as my Savior." He went along with Bob to Blaine's house for supper, and something moved Blaine to profess too, and at midnight both of them were baptized.

Blaine was a tall, hearty, chest-out man who stood six foot two and weighed 220 pounds, and was married to big, outgoing Cora. Bob was drawn to them both. But Blaine told Bob he was a boozehound. He just couldn't help himself.

"Blaine, you'll just have to start spending your time learning some better habits, like going to church and teaching Sunday school and working longer hours in the field. You stop your bad habits by keeping so busy with good ones that there's no more time for them. Nature hates a vacuum, they say."

Bob started lambasting liquor from the pulpit, right off. Making jokes about it, too.

"If a rabbit could drink the way you men do," he'd say, "he'd whip every dog in the county."

Blaine wasn't ready to give up liquor, but he swore his little girl Muriel would never see her daddy drunk.

Bob brought over a few of the men from the Buffalo who had sworn off, and they talked about drink in meetings, making it something to laugh about, something childish, like mumblety-peg, that a man outgrows. Bailey Goad would get up and say, "Cornlicker and the devil has run this country long enough."

Bob laughed inwardly. Here was the old Buffalo doing missionary work!

Steve Kemp would tell about his boyhood at the Buffalo, when folks would bring back a gallon of brandy for each eight bushels of apples they brought to the still.

"I do believe people didn't drink so much then," said Steve, "because it was so plentiful. My daddy would take a jug to the fields and say, 'Boys, drink all you want, but don't never get drunk.'" He continued "I'll bet that if every branch ran nothing but brandy, people would shun it. For it ain't fitten to drink. But like the Bible says about forbidden fruit tasting sweet, the same with liquor."

There was no single formula for the way Bob helped Indian Valley drinkers back to their feet. It differed from person to person.

One will tell you: "He found me drunk along the road and said to me, 'Say, brother, but you're mighty sick.' And I was, sicker than a colicky colt. He takened me into town for medicine and carried me on home, a-laughin' and a-carryin' on, and never once mentioned my drinkin'."

Or he might stop at some man's home with a shotgun.

"How about some squirrel huntin'?" he'd say. On parting maybe he'd ask, "How about comin' Sunday to hear me preach?"

To another he'd say, "I'm not a-feelin' so well today. How about you drivin' for me?" Or, "I sure do need you. I'm goin' to Roanoke and wish you'd drive." He'd brag on them, pat them on the shoulder, ask them to help, and make them want to be sober so they could.

Finally Blaine decided to quit, and Bob came over often to talk and work side by side with him while he fought the urge. But it was Blaine's younger brother Hobert who put up the most heroic battle against liquor of anyone in Indian Valley. There wasn't a finer young man in the Valley, or anyone better to his family. But Hobert was marked with liquor before he was born, folks said, and that was why he could never throw it off.

The way Hobert tells the story, it was a war between his thirst and Bob Childress's determination.

He and his wife and four children were living on a farm that belonged to his father-in-law, Wyatt Hylton. Wyatt had a buyer for the place who wanted immediate occupancy, so they had to get out. Hobert didn't have the first penny to his name, he was drinking that bad, and gambling too. He had started drinking same as everybody else, but pretty soon he couldn't stop. He tried, tried for six months, and then a year, and then two years, but he couldn't. He was thirty-seven.

"It's terrible when you drink," he says. "You say things you don't mean, and start losing your friends. Then you lose your job and your credit, and for a poor man that's terrible. Why, there wasn't a one of my brothers and sisters—there were a dozen of us—who would help me. I knew without asking. They were poor, of course, but down in my heart I knowed they thought of me as a drunkard and no 'count. We had our garden all planted and nowhere to go."

The day came when they had to move out. And that's the very day Bob Childress came along. Hobert still doesn't know how he knew about the trouble, but there he was. He didn't ask why Hobert's brothers didn't help. He just said, "Let's go over to your daddy-in-law's."

"It's no use, Bob," said Hobert. "Wyatt's got to have the money right now. Five hundred dollars."

And all he said was, "Anyone who can shoot squirrels the way you can ought to be good for five hundred dollars. Let's go!"

They picked up Wyatt and hauled into town.

"How much money do I have in here?" Bob asked the lady cashier.

She told him thirty-five dollars.

"Do you s'pose I could write out a check for five hundred dollars?"

The lady grinned at him. "Reckon you can." So the money

Hobert Quesenberry, a good family man
who just couldn't stop drinking—
until Bob Childress came to Indian Valley.

was drawn out, and Bob signed the note with his big, jagged signature across the bottom of it.

They drove back home, and when the house loomed ahead on a hilltop, Hobert asked Bob to stop. "Hit's not so much to anyone else, but to me it looks like paradise."

Hobert started fighting liquor in earnest. He got a job tending boiler for a dollar a day. But he kept sliding back. "I couldn't stop. I felt I was letting down the only man in the world who had faith in me, and I drank all the harder. It went on that way for years. No one knows how terrible it was."

Bob stopped by often. He came in late one moonless winter night, his black bearskin gloves white with frost, and told how he had got stuck in the snow and walked for help, and how a man hitched a horse to his car and pulled him along for a quarter-mile. The horse did such a powerful job that Bob bought him on the spot, out of gratitude.

He stayed the night, and next morning Hobert went along to see the horse. It was old and battered, and looked as if it needed a pair of rails to prop it.

"Reckon I got stuck twicet!" Bob said, and laughed.

Bob seemed not just to stop in when he was in the Valley for some other reason; Hobert got the feeling he made some special trips. "And I puzzled why he should give a hang anyway. He kept a-stoppin' in to hunt. I had a little old red poppy-eyed feist that treed a squirrel for him to shoot, then picked it up and wouldn't give it to me but went over and laid it at Bob's feet."

" 'Hobert,' he said, 'how about swapping for that dog? I'll trade you my white beagle, even up.' "

And so they swapped.

Another day Bob would stop just to tell a story. He once had a mighty fine dog, but so old his legs were no 'count. Well sir, Bob said, he rolled him out in a wheelbarrow one night, and that old dog treed five coons!

"Hobert, how about helping shoot rabbits for the Lynchburg orphanage?" he said as he drove in one day. But Hobert was too drunk.

The harder the man tried to quit, the worse it got. It got so bad his wife took the children and went to live with the Childresses for a few days.

"Then one evening," Hobert says, "I was a-lyin' there on that couch when all of a sudden it came to me. I had to see the preacher. Seemed I couldn't get to him fast enough. I told Bertha I had to join the church. She gottened a neighbor to take me to him. I could barely whisper, but I had to talk with him." That night, at a prayer meeting in his own house, he was baptized, with the whole neighborhood watching, so glad they were to see him join.

"Afterward, it seemed every man I met on the road offered me a drink, but I never touched it, and haven't since. A man at the mill where I worked pushed me to have one to warm me up after I was rained on and cold, and I was sore tempted. But I said, 'The Bible says, Woe unto him that giveth his neighbor drink.' The man never bothered me again. Bertha and I started gnawing away at the debt, five dollars at a time. The more we paid back, the easier it gottened."

Neither Hobert nor Bob knew just why he had made the decision just then and stuck to it. But there was a footnote: down the road lived a young woman, Mrs. Thurman Harris, who also cared what happened to Hobert. "There wasn't a day but what I prayed for him," she says. "I'd known him from school days on up, and for years he was the first one in my prayers. One day he came over, drunk as a barred owl. I'll never forget it. He was weaving down the road, his head on his chest, his shoes untied, and stumbling over the laces, and it hit me, 'What's the use of praying for a man like that all these years?' But right away it seemed I had a strong answer, that something would happen. I don't like to tell about it much; when I hear people say these things I feel sort of embarrassed for them. Anyway, I told my husband that I thought Hobert was going to get well. It wasn't but a few hours till the news came."

Even in his casual meetings the preacher seemed to win people over. On the way to services at Indian Valley one evening Bob stopped to pick up an old, bearded mountaineer.

"Come along with me to church," said Bob.

The mountaineer spat. "Nope," he said. Then after a pause. "Too many hypocrites."

"Aw, come on," said Bob, laughing. "There's always room for one more!"

The man studied awhile, then started laughing too. He got in the car still chuckling, and directed Bob to his home, where his wife met him on the porch.

"Quick, Ma, find me my pants. I'm a-goin' with the preacher."

People began flocking to services. The whole of Indian Valley seemed to be changing. There was laughter at Rollie Phillips's store as folks began telling and retelling the stories Bob Childress brought them, or stories about him, as well as some they remembered or began making up themselves. Kate Morgan, the cashier in the bank at Floyd, liked best what he said the day he came in to take out another loan.

"Well, Kate, I'm even with the world."

"That's fine," said Kate, knowing how all his life he'd been in debt.

"Yes, ma'am," said Bob, "I owe as many people now as I don't owe."

At the diner in Hillsville he had asked to cash a check. The proprietor found him a blank one without a bank designation.

The man asked, "What bank shall I fill in?"

"Makes no difference," said Bob. "They all got money."

And when the preacher lost his false teeth he decided he must have sent them to the cleaners with some pressing. He went there to look.

"You come for your teeth?" they said, teasing.

"Yes. You cleaned 'em yit?"

And over at the restaurant at Fancy Gap when Andy Howlett brought the coffee he said, "Looks a lot like rain."

And Bob said, "Sure does, but it smells a heap like coffee."

It wasn't just the jokes and laughter, though. It was the way he made everybody feel important. Bob always seemed to seek out lonely, forgotten people. They weren't hard to find.

Ferry Hylton was one of many who say the preacher just never forgot or gave up on them. Ferry, tall and strong, and his black-eyed wife Odell farmed a few scrawny acres on the very flank of Buffalo Mountain. There were nine children in the house, in just two rooms and a loft. It was no fit way to live, but it seemed the harder they worked, the poorer they got.

Up the fork a piece was a farm Ferry longed to buy. It had a big house on it, with five bedrooms and a living room that faced some of the prettiest bottomland God ever made, and a forest behind that rose on up to the Buffalo. It seemed made for a big, hardworking family to own and love. It was an idle dream, Ferry knew, for there was nowhere he could scare up enough for a down payment.

He and Odell were regular churchgoers, but he wasn't one to jaw about his troubles, and he didn't remember telling Bob Childress about the farm. But one day the preacher told him to go into Floyd and fill out a loan application.

"Mist' Child'ss, there's no use. I've got but two cows and a horse, and not a penny to my name. Those federal loans mostly ask you to have a third of the price. I can't ever get it."

" 'Course you can. You can buy it, and you can get cattle on it. Now you take your feet in your hand and get into town on Tuesday."

"Mist' Child'ss, there's not a man who'd recommend me. Everyone knows I've been poor as a bird all my life."

"Just you go in anyhow—or I'll set yore heels on fire."

So he went, and when he got to the loan office, the people seemed to be expecting him. He told them right off that he didn't have the next meal paid for, but they had him fill out a form.

"You've already been recommended," they said.

Ferry was bewildered. He didn't think to ask who it was. He was too excited. A few days later he got a notice to return to sign papers, that the down payment had been waived. The farm could be theirs, with enough of a loan to stock it with cattle. Ferry and Odell nearly ran all the way to town to sign.

"Who was it," they asked, "would vouch for us?"

"Why Preacher Childress, of course. He talked so big of you both, the committee figured you must be worth it."

Nine years—and five babies—later, the farm was paid for. Years of laughter mixed sometimes with pain. Years of meeting Bob Childress at the corner to go to prayer meeting, revivals, Sunday school picnics. Anxious trips with him to the doctor in -Charlottesville, nearly two hundred miles away, with their eleventh child, a boy whose brain injury at birth had left him helpless. And that final trip when they had to leave the boy at Lynchburg, a trip that somehow wasn't as bad as they had feared, for the preacher kept their hearts light.

As Ferry looks out on his pastures of cattle and rich bottom-land his eyes are moist. "We wouldn't have this, any of this, except for him. He must have seen something in us that no one else, not even our brothers, not even us, believed was there."

Another minister, known to Bob from his childhood, began to serve Indian Valley two years after Bob had started there. He was Joe Williams, son of the distiller whose wagons had gone past the Childress cabin twice a week. Preacher Joe was the only one of eighteen sons who didn't follow his father's vocation, and the only one who left home to be educated—starting first grade when he was eighteen, and going on through seminary to become an ordained Presbyterian minister.

Bob lost touch with Indian Valley at intervals, and it was when Preacher Williams had left the Valley that Bob got word that the bank had foreclosed on B. B. Franklin. Bob drove over at once, to find the old man and his wife without so much as a scoop of cornmeal, and so worried they were sick in bed.

"What you worried 'bout?" Bob asked. "You've got a home as long as you live!" He helped them pack some of their belongings and then carried the little woman out to the car. He returned to the house for a favorite rocking chair and set out for Buffalo Mountain.

"We've got a little honeymoon cabin for you," he said, "right across from our house." The couple were silent as the car took them over roads Bob knew they must have walked and ridden for nearly fifty years. He tried conversation, but there was almost no answer. Then, after they had crossed the first divide and started up the mountain over the rocks and ledges that led to the Buffalo, the old people seemed to revive. They appeared to enjoy the punishing bumps, the winding trail through the tulip trees of the coves, and the climb up the next crest. Bob worried about their first look at the cabin, but he needn't have.

"Why, hit's beautiful!" said Mrs. Franklin.

The little cabin warmed with laughter and fun as Lelia and the girls brought over hot supper, lit the lamp, plumped the feather tick, and started a fire in the fireplace.

Bob hired a girl to care for them, to spare Lelia, whose ankle was bothering her considerably.

That year in the cabin for the Franklins was a happy one. In church they were everybody's favorites, sitting up front so they could hear, with Mr. Franklin in a rocking chair to comfort his back. It was nice, folks said, that when the old lady died, her husband died the very next day after she was put away.

B. B. Franklin and his wife outside
their cabin near the Childress home.

So sensitive to what people needed, and so quick to respond, Bob sometimes found himself too involved in too many lives. When people came to him for help he always listened, tried to make fair decisions and to act.

Perhaps he shouldn't get so entangled. But who else on earth could watch out for them, who else would show an affection that never wavered, no matter how much they seemed sometimes to try to test it.

An elder's son asked Bob's help in getting his parents' approval of a girl he loved and wanted to marry, and Bob was glad to try, for he knew the girl and liked her. But the parents were set against her. Later, when the girl was pregnant, Bob went again to ask them to reconsider. They were furious and quit the church.

The more involved a minister becomes, he knew, the greater the danger. And here he was, sometimes acting as judge, sometimes keeper of the peace, and occasionally the man to whom they came for advice on wills, suits against neighbors, and judgments. A man who did all that for you came to seem like family. And, like family, you could get right grieved with him. It is easier and far safer for a minister to keep apart from his parishoners, to refer them to others for help. It is easier, too, not to love them the way Bob did. The disappointments were often too keen. But then, perhaps the joys were that much greater.

Bob had few friends in Indian Valley so close to him as Blaine and Cora Quesenberry. They were like brother and sister to him. He would stop at their house to rest a few minutes between church services, or take dinner with them, or stop overnight. It was good to have friends like Cora and Blaine.

And then when their only child Muriel was twelve, she fell victim to an infection of the bloodstream, the same type that killed Calvin Coolidge's son. Bob went to the hospital whenever he could.

"Bob," the little girl would say, for she called him that, "did you bring me a pretty?" The preacher never forgot.

When she grew worse, he would stand with Blaine and Cora alongside her bed. "He knew just what to say," Blaine says. "And if he didn't know what to say, he was silent. He just stood there with us."

Muriel died, and there was no consoling her parents.

"Where was the Lord when our Muriel died?" asked Cora.

And Bob said, "Where was the Lord when his own Son was dying on the cross? Don't you think the Lord felt the same pain you feel?"

Blaine and Cora quit the church. On Sundays they would take out their car and drive mile after endless, aimless mile. Bob longed to console them.

For three years they avoided all churches. Then one summer day they drove past the Willis church and heard the congregation singing, and, above all others, Bob Childress's voice carrying like a trumpet.

They stopped. When Bob saw them at the door, the tears ran down his face, and he asked the congregation to sing "All Hail the Power of Jesus' Name."

Goats, Sawmills, and Roads

Not everybody was exactly eager to ride to town with Bob Childress, and it wasn't only the people who were fearful of cars. The preacher just wasn't particular enough about his passengers, some said. His family was the most critical. By 1934 the depression had settled over the mountains, and Bob had taken to bringing home all kinds of livestock to see how they'd fare. Trouble was, he'd get the idea while he was off below the mountains, buy the animal, and just shove it in the back seat, no matter how far he was from the Buffalo.

First there was the nanny goat and her kid. A minister friend had told him that goat's milk was good for the stomach. But Bob was more interested in the possibility that goats would be good for the mountains, being able to browse among the rocks and not minding irregular milking hours as cows did. The idea didn't work. No one followed his example. Instead of raising their own, mountaineers borrowed Bob's nanny whenever a mother was short of milk for her newborn. Folks say she must have fattened up a dozen babies.

Bob kept stocking the farm as the boys grew old enough to handle more chores. It never seemed to bother him that the livestock was hard on the car—and on his family. The night she arrived, that first nanny goat had chewed a hole right through the cloth top of the T-Model. Hattie told her father he'd need to build a pasture for the car, or the goat would eat it up. Nanny traveled in it so often, as she was lent out to serve as a mother for Buffalo babies, that she got real fond of it. She liked to jump onto the hood and stand there like it was her throne, scraping the paint down to bare metal.

Another goat and her kid came home all the way from South Carolina, where Bob had gone on a preaching trip. This time the car was a brand-new Ford that Conduff had helped buy.

That night, when Bob was resting from his trip, Conduff, preparing to take the car on a date, burst into the living room.

"Papa, I can't get that old goat smell to leave!"

His father looked up from his reading. "Whyn't you sprinkle on a little perfume?"

"Sprinkle!" he exclaimed. "I've near poured on a whole bottle, and it's strong as ever!"

Conduff told Hattie after he got home that the girl hadn't seemed to mind. It was Hattie her brothers confided in. And if they had plans or dreams or sometimes worries it was Hattie they went to.

The goats were only the start of the animal passengers. If it wasn't a dog, it was a yellow kitten for Hattie. Or if it wasn't a pig, it was a wide-eyed calf. Bob would come flying into the house from one meeting bound for the next, and on the way upstairs to wash and change clothes he'd call out, "Bryan, you wash the car for me, will you? And take that calf out first and find him a home." Washing the car was a task the boys despised, for once a calf or sheep or goat or pig had soiled it, the smell lingered. Conduff said that his car smelled of goat until the day it was sold.

One day the younger children were at school at recess time when they heard a car laboring up the hill and saw their fellow students pointing and laughing. There was their father in a brand-new Chevy with a Jersey cow and calf in the back seat, the cow's head sticking out the window.

"I felt like hiding, Papa, I was so embarrassed," said Marie.

"Why didn't you then, girl?"

"I was too interested. I just had to watch."

"Dad," said Bryan, "why don't you get us a truck?"

"Because preachers haul people mostly, and cows only in a pinch."

Then he added, "You know, Bryan, some people treat cars like they were holy or something. But around here they just get respect for getting us from one place to the next, and I keep 'em in shape for that."

But it wasn't long before he signed a note for Conduff to get a truck.

*Mountain winters were hard
on Bob's Brahma cattle.*

He introduced Brahma cattle to the Buffalo, too. (When he called Conduff to ask him to bring the truck down to South Carolina to pick up six head, Conduff asked why he didn't just put them in the back seat.) Big and rugged, Brahmas should stand the rigorous mountain climate, Bob thought. He was wrong. They shivered and froze and got sick.

Bringing in livestock wasn't the only way Bob was trying to bring new economic life to the mountain. He also thought about newer ways of farming, but the small patches of rocky fields didn't seem right for tractors and most other machinery. Besides, he had no capital. He had to wait for donations that came from people who had heard him speak.

Again and again he came back to the trees that covered the hills, and to the idea of a sawmill. Again he told presbytery that, if need be, he'd start his own, but they argued against it. A minister had no place in a business. And while he agreed in principle, he knew the urgent need of some kind of industry. The depression hadn't hit as hard in the mountains as in other places, but still the prices for hogs and eggs and anything that brought income were way down.

Folks normally optimistic were gloomy. One day Bob took dinner with the Quesenberrys at Indian Valley. "I declare, if things don't get better," said Cora, getting up from the table to bring in dessert, "I don't know how we'll carry on." When she returned from the kitchen Bob leaned back and hooted.

"Corey's got a cake she can hardly carry to the table, and she talks about hard times!"

But Bob knew his humor sounded hollow. Hogs were no longer worth walking down the mountain to market. Chestnuts had long since disappeared. Except for liquor there was almost nothing to sell.

Idleness had always been an evil giant in the mountains. Now there was even less to do. Folks walked the roads aimlessly or sunned themselves outside storehouses or sat on their doorsteps whittling. Or drank. Or fought.

Then out of nowhere there came a two hundred dollar check from someone who'd heard about Bob's work, with a note: "Use as you see fit."

Bob made up his mind quickly, putting doubts and caution aside. There was a secondhand sawmill at Mayberry that he could buy for very little, and at Meadows of Dan was a man he thought could run it. Both needed some fixing.

Bob had known Howard Webb since his summers as a student pastor. Tall and slender, with flashing eyes and black hair, he loved excitement and action. Folks said he was a liquor-head, although he never would let Bob see him drunk. He was hot-tempered, too, quick to fight and quick to forget it.

"Why, when we saw him a-comin'," one woman recalls, "we

girls would pull the shades and start in singin' so Daddy couldn't hear him go by a-whoopin' and a-cursin' and a-shootin'. We were that afeared our daddy would be provoked to a fight. If we were alone, we'd hide under the bed till he was past."

Howard had gone to services now and then. That's where the prettiest girls were, and the preacher told him that Sunday on the church grounds was a proper time and place to court. Bob liked the youth from the first, and when someone had said that Howard was a boy who needed soul-saving, Bob had replied: "What you talkin' 'bout? He just has lots of spirit. I wish I could fill the church with boys like him!"

Howard had married after that and had two daughters, but he continued to drink as bad as ever. It had been four years since he'd seen the preacher when Bob came over and made his proposal.

"Howard, I've a chance to buy a sawmill, but I'm not a-goin' to do it unless you promise to saw for me."

"Mist' Child'ss, what you fixin' to do? You know I've never sawed. Swung an ax considerable, but never sawed. I'll come work for you, but you got to get you a man who knows how to saw."

"Howard, you're the only man I'd have."

Finally he agreed and went to live in the little log cabin across the road from the manse, vacant since B. B. Franklin and his wife had died.

Setting up the mill went fast. The big gas engine was in surprisingly good shape, and parts missing or broken on the mill itself or the carriage, Bob could have made at the blacksmith shop at Willis. Sometimes he took off his coat and hammered out a few missing pieces himself. He located the mill on a slope half a mile east of the church. There was plenty of water and enough grade for the skidways where mountaineers could haul in their logs and stack them, awaiting a nudge from the canthook to start them rolling towards the carriage. Bob bought logs, for the most part, but also hired men to cut from his own woods and sometimes bought stumpage. Soon loads of oak and tulip poplar started coming in by oxteam, and the wail of the saw and the high whine of the planer started filling the cove. Getting the lumber out by truck to Galax, thirty-five miles away, was another matter. When the creeks were high or the roads too deep in mud or snow and ice, there was nothing to do but wait.

Bob's sawmill provided work during the depression. Conduff is at left.

Howard was quick to learn to saw and to manage the men. But he couldn't manage himself. For weeks he worked from dawn till dark in his tattered, pitch-blackened overalls. Then, generally when he knew the preacher wouldn't be stopping by the mill, he would be off on a long drunk. His wife would come over to the manse.

"We can keep on praying, Maggie," said Bob.

For long stretches, Howard seemed like a well man. He'd take his girls to Sunday school while Maggie watched from the kitchen window, so proud, she told Bob, she thought her heart would burst. Then some night Howard wouldn't return for supper. And so it went. Much as Bob warred against alcohol from the pulpit, he never mentioned it in the moments when the two men rested alone at the mill.

That winter Howard came down with rheumatic fever; the doctor said he couldn't work for a year. It was a brutal winter. Maggie dug overshoes out of a dump heap for the children and mended them with patches.

"Why you've got ornaments like a Christmas tree on your galoshes," Bob said. Next day he brought them new shoes. Hardly a day passed that he wasn't over joking with Howard and the young ones. And somehow he knew when there was nothing left in the cabin but a loaf of bread. He'd come in from the cold loaded with groceries, blowing on his hands as he pulled off his black bearskin gloves.

In the fall Howard was back at the mill. Once again the daylight hours were filled with the whine of the saw and the rumble of ox-drawn wagonloads of logs. Howard was happy. The mill satisfied his love of action. The sawyer's job takes a nimble brain. A man must make calculations in the flash of the carriage flying by.

A dozen men worked at the mill regularly now, with after-school help from the older Childress boys. Occasionally, too, there would be others: men that Bob brought out from court or jail. The first time he had a carful. Another time there were eight in a bus.

"Howard," he would say, "these boys have a little debt to work out for me." Sheepishly he would explain how he had paid their fines after having had them arrested for stopping church services with rocks or buckshot. They were more nuisance than help, yet when Saturday night came Bob thought he just couldn't send them home without a penny in their pockets. So he would start to give each of them a couple of dollars. That was enough for some fun, he thought. He reconsidered—no, that was just enough for a weeklong drunk! So he often piled his jailbird crew on top of a load of lumber and hauled them to Galax, where he treated them all to supper and a moving picture, unloaded the lumber, and took them back to the Buffalo.

Sawmilling was bound to make enemies. It nearly always did in a settled area with "techous" people, Bob knew. Roads got rutted from heavy wagons; gates were left open and cows left home; a cutover forest was a tangle of limbs and raw stumps. There was envy too: anyone who could hire as many as a dozen men must be up to his elbows in money. Bob tried to make sure the men were careful, and always went directly to anyone who was riled.

On a warm day in June, Bob arrived at the mill.

"How you today, Mist' Child'ss?" Howard called above the hum of the saw.

"Not so good, Howard, not so good. I haven't had a cross word th'owed at me in two weeks—"

He was interrupted by a man—sour as a hoptoad—who had been waiting in the shade of a lumber pile. A tree had dropped across his fence, and he was taking the matter to court. Howard nudged a log forward, drowning out the man's harangue with the scream of the saw. Bob soon calmed the man by offering to pay any damages or repair the fence.

Despite such troubles, the mill was doing what Bob hoped it might. Cash—the first in years—was trickling back to the Buffalo. The curse of idleness was beginning to lift just a little. "And best of all," Bob said to Lelia as he was packing for a speaking tour, "it seems as if Howard has become a well man."

That very weekend Howard went on a riotous drunk. His youngest brother Dinty, a hunchback, had just been jailed by Commodore Sutphin, a deputy sheriff, for cussing on the school grounds. Howard, furious, took down his shotgun and set out on foot to find Commodore. Maggie ran after him, screaming, then sank to her knees, helpless with fright.

Nobody, not even Howard, knows where he went. He never did find Commodore. Somewhere along the road, he rode in a neighbor's A-Model and shot holes through the top, one for each barrel, like two eyes staring up at the sky. Somehow he found his way home.

Bob was angry when he heard the whole tale. "Why am I wasting time on him?" he said to Lelia. He stormed across the road determined to turn Howard out, but when he saw him sick and helpless in bed his anger fled, and he walked back home.

"Lelia, let's go on into town to see Dinty," he said.

"What do you plan to do, fetch him on home?"

Bob felt his anger returning.

"I aim to lecture to him and leave him right there!" he said firmly.

Dinty was looking out through the bars as they drove up. Bob felt the need to swallow.

"Lelia, he does look mighty sad already, doesn't he?"

Then he called out, "Dinty, would you like to go home?"

Dinty's grin, says Lelia, like to pushed the bars apart.

Bob talked to the law, paid a fine, and drove him home.

Eventually Howard Webb gave up drinking, joined the church, and moved away to go sawmilling on his own. When the preacher visited Howard and Maggie in their home along a trout stream Maggie said, "It's not the finest in the neighborhood, but there can't be many any happier than ours. And you know, we owe it all to you!" She kissed him.

Bob couldn't answer. His eyes filled as he turned and left. Someday perhaps he could tell her how near he had been to failing them.

When Conduff was nineteen, Bob made the down payment on a hundred acres of timber on the slopes of Buffalo Mountain and made a deal with Conduff to take over. He signed a note so his son could buy a flatbed truck. Conduff hired a dozen men to peel tanbark while he skidded out logs with a team, using a stream as a sluiceway. Hattie liked to hear him tell about how if the water went to the horses' knees that was all right, for the logs floated easily behind. He used the stream for his truck road, too.

There were still no real roads on Buffalo Mountain, and the milling had made the need even more obvious. Bob had gone many times to highway officials at Roanoke. Often he would take along a carful of Buffalo men he had won over to his beliefs. He would point out that Buffalo people sometimes couldn't reach a doctor without hours and sometimes days of waiting.

"Roads are avenues of mercy," he said. Then he would ask one of the men to tell about fishing him and his car out of the stream, and of how not a week passed that he wasn't hauling someone to the hospital or the doctor.

Finally he decided he wouldn't wait for the highway department to act. He had heard that Washington had voted funds for roadbuilding, and he started schoolboys picking rocks out of fields and stockpiling them for embankments, giving their time after school and Saturdays. He borrowed Conduff's trucks, and Giles Harris donated gasoline. When WPA funds did come, to make them go farther Bob talked men into working one week for pay and the next for nothing. Soon the county set aside money for the bridge that would be needed at Little Flock.

"Never saw such a hand for getting men to work," says Mason Sumpter, the county engineer, who was there to help plan and supervise the building. Men came for the excitement as much as anything else. On a Monday morning a crowd would be waiting to begin, always more than there were jobs for, even at twenty cents an hour—or ten cents, under Bob's terms. The road from Buffalo Mountain started growing, beginning at the church and snaking down toward Willis.

There was still no bridge at Little Flock. There wouldn't be, as long as folks refused to sign easements—and they were suspicious of legal papers and "buzzardy lawyers." The road stretched uncertainly toward the stream.

Then one night Giles Harris knocked on the Childress door. He had just heard that the county money allocated for the bridge would go elsewhere unless easements were in by next morning at eight. Bob slipped on his clothes, and the two men set out in the dark. All night long they pounded on doors and talked, persuaded—some say threatened. The very presence of high-tempered Giles Harris was a threat. By daybreak they had the last signature and were on their way to town.

So in due time a steel bridge went in across the stream—the

first in the history of Buffalo Mountain. It was a proud day when folks started rumbling across in their wagons. Town was still a long, slow way off over rocks and up long hills, but the worst obstacle had been overcome.

As roads improved, Bob found he could serve more congregations. By 1938 he was going to eight churches, preaching and holding Sunday school at least once a week at each place. He wouldn't serve a church unless he had services that often. "He means business," said an official at presbytery. "None of that once-a-month stuff for him." Not that he was trying to set a record. The people were there, and would otherwise have gone without. There just weren't preachers to go around, and there was no money to pay if they could have been found. He held five or six services on Sunday and two or three on Wednesday— full-fledged church and Sunday school.

He was driving forty or fifty thousand miles a year, and though the roads were improving there were still rocks that tore at tires and gouged oil pans. It seemed to Bob as though the radiators were forever leaking. As he came steaming up the mountains, he almost always had to stop in the middle of every creek he came to, scooping up water in his straw hat. When it was cold he often picked icicles from the rocks to fill the radiator.

Bob Zehmer, the pastor from Roanoke, tells about the time he was driving with Bob in a Dodge sedan that seemed hot, even though the radiator was full. About five miles from home the car began to knock, and Bob stopped in the middle of a creek, took off his shoes and socks, rolled up his pant legs and went round to the hood.

"My soul and body, we're out of oil!" he said. The measuring stick was dry.

He took a half-gallon bucket out of the back, scooped it full of water, and started to pour it down the oil pipe.

"Preacher," yelled Zehmer, "have you gone plumb crazy?"

"Not that I know," he said calmly. "I've got to raise the oil to where the dips can reach it."

He poured the rest in, then took another reading. Still the oil was low. So he dipped up another half gallon of water and poured it in.

"A gallon of water and a pint of oil," he said. "That ought to see us home if we take it easy." And it did.

That night Bob said to Lelia, "I declare that car seems bound and determined to destroy itself."

Only the week before, when the boys had driven it down to the spring after water, it had backfired and started to burn. The boys were throwing sand on it as Bob ran downhill and scooped sand along with them. Still the fire blazed.

Suddenly Bob stopped. "Stand back, boys, it might explode!" he cried. "What difference does a car make when human lives are in danger?" He quickly brightened. "Besides, it's insured."

They stopped and watched, but only a few seconds.

"I let that insurance lapse! Start throwing sand!" They did, and put the fire out.

Winter was worst on the cars. Snow could turn to ice within hours. One car that Bob traded for he never did get home. It got stuck in the snow, and he banged it up so bad in getting it out that he took it back to town and traded it for still another.

The road from the Lee place up to the Buffalo seemed always to be slippery. Big Early Sutphin who lives nearby says, "Many a time Bob Childress hollered me out to help. The two of us were pretty stout, and together we could usually roll the car up the hill, but it was a long roll."

The road up the other side of the mountain was just as bad. The Alice Sutphin hill three miles from home was deep with snow when Bob got stuck just before eleven o'clock on a Sunday morning after driving all night from a speaking tour in Tennessee. He had with him a new coat given him for the trip. He felt worn out and irritable, for he'd been trying to be home in time to preach. He looked in vain for a fence rail to pry with, or brush to give traction to one wheel that kept spinning. In desperation he pulled off his coat and threw it under the wheel —which sliced it into two neat pieces. Well now, he thought, one for each side. He laid one piece ahead of each wheel, started up, and went on up the mountain, arriving just ten minutes late.

When Bob took a worn, mud-spattered car into Floyd to trade it in, the dealer, who was new to the mountains, greeted him. "Friend, they tell me around here a car that muddy is either a minister's or a bootlegger's. I don't know which you are, but if it was me, they'd say I was a bootlegger."

Coming back from Mount Airy he picked up a woman whose car had gone dead. It became clear that she was trying to discover whether or not he was a bootlegger. Finally, as they neared Hillsville, she asked him point-blank.

"What would you guess?" he asked, grinning wickedly.

"Well, it's clear you're not a preacher, so you must be a bootlegger."

Bob only laughed.

"I'll give you a right smart price for some whiskey," she said.

As Bob slowed down to let her out, he opened the glove compartment and showed her his Bible. She flustered, muttered a thank-you, and hurried off without a backward look.

Some say that cars were Bob's second pulpit, they were that important to his ministry. Just getting him from place to place was one thing. Every week he was preaching to a combined total of seven hundred people, according to the minutes of presbytery. But he and his boys were picking up many of those people and taking them home again, and doing the same with a thousand or so Sunday school children. It was hard to say what vehicles the Childresses might have at any one time, from pickups to trucks to carryalls. They saw use on weekdays for prayer services, funerals, and Bible camps. Most of all, they carried people to town and back in time of need or illness.

Bob's boys learned to drive as soon as their feet could touch the floorboards.

"You'd better know how," he said. "No telling when someone has to be carried to the hospital." They needed little coaxing for that, but sometimes they grew weary of forever picking up people for church or young people's meetings.

When they asked for a vehicle to see their girl friends they were seldom refused.

"Course you wouldn't mind taking the bus, would you, so's

you can pick up that Sunday school crowd," Bob would add. Or it might be churchgoers, Bible schoolgoers, or prayer-goers to be picked up and delivered home again.

Paul told his dad, "Every time I take that old pickup I've got the cab so full of old people that the girl I'm sweet on has to ride behind on the platform." Bob chuckled.

Conduff added, "Papa, you sure do get lots of mileage out of our courting."

There are those who say that Bob Childress did as much good with roads and bridges as with churches and sermons. There are others who say he did it with cars, hauling people in and out. There are still others who say that his sawmill did it. He helped other mills get started up, using engines from cars that he got at junkyards for power. Men of the Buffalo got jobs skidding, piling lumber, and running the planer. Loads of lumber started moving down the valley. The whole tempo of Buffalo Mountain speeded up. Horses began replacing oxen everywhere. They could make the trip to town faster. They were quicker, too, in skidding, and seemed to sense when to sidestep to keep from being crushed by a runaway log; some were even trained to skid a log to the crest of the bluff, step aside, and let the log unhook and crash down the mountain toward the mill. Lumbering added excitement to Buffalo Mountain, an excitement that Bob had longed for as something to replace fighting.

Logging trails started to zigzag over the Buffalo. Sawyers toppled the dead chestnut trees, gaunt gray skeletons to be sawed into lumber or to be ground for acid wood. Millions of feet of poplar and water oak went rumbling over the Little Flock bridge to market. The Buffalo was coming out of the depression better off than it had ever been before.

Idleness and isolation, those twin giants of the Blue Ridge, were giving ground fast.

The King of Slate Mountain

They called John Whorley the king of Slate Mountain at the time Bob first went there to preach in the school at Stamping Birches. Big John had been brought up in a cove nearby, had carried a gun from the time he was eight years old, had been a Marine sergeant in World War I, and had then been toughened by the jungle laws of lumber and coal mining camps in West Virginia. When he returned to the Blue Ridge with his brass knucks and knives and two police dogs, his reputation had already beat him home. He was six feet, two hundred pounds, and looked hard as a chestnut log. Folks looked at him with awe, and he liked being known as a man to be reckoned with. He drank a lot, but always seemed in control. Though nobody knew quite all he had done in West Virginia, few wanted to cross him. And anyway, he was now a deputy sheriff.

Slate Mountain is off to the east of the Buffalo about five miles, a softly rounded summit encircled by a brood of smaller hills. Today, the Blue Ridge Parkway cuts across it, but tourists seldom see the people or their homes, hidden by the dark of rhododendrons. A few rods back from the asphalt is the mountaineers' own road, two centuries old, crisscrossed by dusty trails where you feel the pulse and beat of Slate Mountain.

Bob Childress had wanted to carry his work to Slate Mountain ever since he had come to the Buffalo. Some of the men there who had heard about him asked if he could make it across now and then. Finally he said he'd preach every Sunday. And when he came, his effect on people was something John Whorley couldn't understand.

*John Whorley was feared in the lumber camps
for his guns, brass knuckles, dogs, and courage.*

Here was a man people listened to. They crowded around after services, unwilling to leave. He seemed as big and rough as any man John had run across, yet somehow different, unlike anyone he had met up with before. How could anyone who wasn't even carrying a gun command that respect?

John began making conversation with the preacher, man to man, after prayer meetings, and after a time the preacher asked him to go with him on home visits. So they made rounds together, and each time before they parted they would sit in the car while Bob prayed. John just listened.

"May we learn true fear of thee," Bob would ask. "May we

understand that just as asleep we are as helpless as a baby, so by day we are just as helpless without thy loving guidance."

Helpless? Fear? What kind of talk was that? John Whorley had never feared anybody or anything, and he'd never been helpless in his life. Even after a shrapnel burst in France had caught him in the arm, he'd been back in action a few days later.

When the time came that Slate Mountain people decided they wanted their own rock church like the one at Buffalo Mountain, Bob went to the big handsome blond man for advice, for John had good ideas and his opinion carried weight. John suggested that each man make a money pledge, then work it out at a dollar a day. The plan was accepted and the building began.

"It was hard work," John recalls, "for we met up with a knid of shale that had to be picked loose, piled into a barrow, and hauled off. Nearly all of us were farmers, so we'd work a week, then go home and catch up on farming for a week." They got gravel from Laurel Fork Creek, already washed clean by the stream, and it was good to have the gravel close, for the eighteen-inch walls took a lot of mortar. Conduff hauled rocks on his truck. Presbytery could give a thousand dollars, and that went for a furnace. Bob went to the bank at Willis and, as John says, "they just ran his face" for the two thousand dollars needed for cement and nails and other materials. He still owed five thousand dollars on the Buffalo church, and money was scarce just then.

It was an exciting summer. Most everybody worked on the church, and that used up time and energy. But one night John Whorley had been drinking and got into an argument with a stranger and was challenged to shoot it out. The two men exchanged fire for upwards of a mile until the other man backed off the mountain. (Today John can't remember who it was or what the argument was about.) Conduff heard the volleys, and later told his dad admiringly about how the big blond man fought it out.

Bob cringed inwardly. A drunken fighter was his son's hero. He thought of lecturing him on the spot, but reconsidered. He himself was torn by respect for Whorley's good qualities and anger at his tough and violent ways. Maybe Conduff saw the deeper virtues in the man, the honesty, decisiveness, and energy that had drawn Bob himself to him.

Bob decided on a direct approach. One afternoon he asked John to make profession and join the new church. John thought a moment and shook his head.

"A man doesn't meet up with God one day and then make promises that bind him the rest of his life," he said. To him joining meant not only quitting his profitable bootlegging but swearing off liquor, and that was something he feared he couldn't promise. He wasn't sure he wanted to stop, and he wasn't sure he could if he wanted to.

But he was curious about the preacher and the things he said. Each time, after a day of driving together, making visits and talking about Scripture, Bob would pause for a moment, bow his head, and give thanks for safe care and guidance. After the preacher had gone, John would go inside and pore over the Bible, marking the passages he wanted Bob's help with the next time they were together. Some the preacher himself didn't comprehend for sure.

"John," he would say, "when I come into water too deep for me to wade through, I simply back out. Someday maybe I'll be able to swim it."

One day, when the church was almost completed, John said simply, "I've decided to join."

The day when he professed was long remembered at Slate Mountain, for now the most feared man there had cast his lot with the church. Leaving for home that night Bob seemed to hear church bells chiming in the empty steeple.

John took any decision seriously, and now he threw himself into the work, the more so because quitting drink was even harder than he had imagined. "Preacher," he said, "I thank the Lord you've got plenty for me to do, for the more work I do the easier it gets."

The Slate Mountain congregation grew fast. Bob opened the church to all the denominations. A Hardshell began helping conduct services, then a Brethren and a Methodist. Folks were

Bob Childress on the steps of the church at Slate Mountain.

proud of their new church; it was the finest, they said, in all the Blue Ridge. From its roof you could see all the way to Buffalo Mountain. What's more, they discovered that the rain that fell on the east roof ran on down to Albemarle Sound and the Atlantic; on the west roof, to the Mississippi River and the Gulf of Mexico.

Bob loved the Slate Mountain people. They were happy, out-

going, quick to show affection. They loaded his car with string
beans and apples and cornmeal, ham-meat and ham-bacon. Slate
Mountain always lifted Bob's spirits and sent him home singing.

Getting there and back was still a trial, though, especially
when the water was high, because there was no bridge to the east
of the Buffalo. He had an A-Model now, and much as he had
loved his T-Model—his "mountain Cadillac"—the A-Model was
better at fording streams. The switch was waterproof, and the
distributor rode high; with an extension welded atop the oil
breather, he could roll through a torrent. Sometimes the water
was so deep that the car floated, and he had to be fished out
with a plowline lashed to the windshield post. The first time
that happened, he sat in the car, water to his waist, joking with
folks on the bank who were pulling him in.

"Bet you never hooked yourself a Presbyterian before!" he
called out.

If Bob was late for services, the congregation would start up
without him. During the winter he got stuck in a snowbank and
showed up, two hours late, riding a draft mule. The big mule's
tongue was hanging out so far folks say you could have tied a
knot in it, but the preacher was laughing as if he weren't tired.

"I've been hearing your singing for the last mile," he said,
"And if the wind was right, I'll bet even heaven could hear
you!"

Perhaps he was making too much progress too fast for the
Primitive Baptists. Or it might have been that bootleggers feared
the way he was moving the mountain towards temperance. Bob
never did know which. Anyway, he was coming home from
Slate Mountain near midnight one Sunday when he came upon
a bonfire in the narrow trail ahead of the car, with half a dozen
men sitting around it. His daughter Marie, twelve, and a girl
friend who lived at school were with him. Bob pulled to a stop.
The men around the fire were drunk and had guns, he could see,
and that didn't look good.

One of the men called out, "Come on out here, preacher.
We've got you this time."

The girls begged Bob to turn around and leave. Marie tried

to throw her arms around her father's neck to keep him in the car, but he opened the door and got out. As he walked boldly toward the fire, he called one man by name and asked him to scatter the fire so he could pass and get the children home. None of the men got to his feet. They seemed to shrink as Bob stood over them.

Then one of them cursed and said, "You're not a-goin' to hold any more night meetin's or Sunday schools. They're agin the will of God. Don't never come this way agin!"

And all Bob said was, "I'll be back again tonight."

In the firelight, her father's face looked to Marie like the angry Moses in her Bible history book. When he turned his back on them and started toward the car Marie was certain they would shoot. But not one made a move.

Bob started up the car and backed away, maneuvering around curves and up and down hills until he found a place to turn.

"Girls," he kept saying quietly, "don't be afraid."

They pleaded with him not to return.

"Papa," cried Marie, "you've always told us to reason or even to run rather than fight!"

"But girl, if we don't go back, they'll keep that road blocked," he said. "Just don't worry."

He drove to John Whorley's. John got up and dressed and started back with them over the same road. In the back seat the two girls shivered with fear. The men were still at the fire. John just walked up and arrested them. No one resisted.

At the trial Bob begged the judge to withhold sentence, saying that the men had been drinking and they had promised they wouldn't bother again. Why he should intercede for a guilty man Bob himself couldn't be sure. As a minister he knew he should show compassion, but as a man of the mountains he got sick in the pit of the stomach at the very thought of a man in jail. When Bob told his family that he had taken the men home from court in his car, the boys knew better than to laugh.

Then came the time when all of Slate Mountain turned against Bob Childress.

A band of fifty gypsies—the first that anyone in that part of the Blue Ridge had ever seen—had come to winter in the mountains. They came by covered wagons and pitched their dozen tents along a stream not far from the church. The women with their spangled earrings and bright clothes were the talk of Slate Mountain.

Bob stopped to visit with them one day, and they acted surprised and suspicious. But as he talked and joked they seemed to ease up. And before long they were talking about swapping and selling things. Almost before he knew it, he was bringing back a team of horses that looked as big and strong as elephants. But it turned out that one had distemper and the other couldn't find the water when the boys led him to it.

"Oh, he just doesn't know his new place," Bob said. But when he waved his hat in front of Old John, the boys snickered. The horse stood so still they said they could see the reflection of the hat in his eyes.

The gypsies told Bob the horse was only moon-eyed. "He can see when the moon news but not when it's full," they said.

"I can't understand," Bob said to the leader of the gypsies, "that such nice people as you would cheat a man."

"Oh, Mr. Chilla," he replied, "we don't cheat you. No sir! We cheats other people, but not you!"

He kept on swapping horses with them. He needed the horses for his logging and milling. Besides, he loved dickering. The gypsies fascinated him; he was sure that if he treated them fair and honest they'd eventually act the same way.

But that didn't happen. After an especially sour trade he talked to the oldest gypsy.

"It looks to me," he said, "as if you'd be better off to go out and get a job and work for your living."

The gypsy thought for a moment and answered. "I don't know, Mr. Chilla, I do pretty well. I start out in the spring, buy a horse for fifteen dollars, and by fall I have a thousand or two dollars. A person can't do much better than that." Bob had to smile as he shook his head.

The gypsies liked to have Bob around, it seemed, and if they bested him in a trade they would sometimes give him money in return, without even being asked. Several times they asked Bob and Lelia to dinner.

When they told how they toughened a baby by dipping it into the icy water of a winter stream, Lelia gasped, "I don't see how even a little pig could live through that." They only laughed. There was no talking them out of it.

It was late the following summer that the gypsies drew the wrath of all Slate Mountain. They had stopped at Old Boyd's cabin next to the millpond below the church. Boyd's wife had left him, but she came in every day to clean up and make his bed.

The gypsies asked if they could make dinner in his house, and if he had any grain to sell for their horses. He told them to get what they needed from a pile of corn upstairs. And then, when they were downstairs cooking, he remembered that his money—$155—was stuffed in a Prince Albert tobacco tin hidden in the pile of corn.

He went upstairs and looked. Not a trace of the money!

"Mr. Chilla," the gypsies told Bob, "when that old man came downstairs he had a pistol in his hand as long as your arm, and his eyes were sparking. He would have killed us. We told him we didn't take his money, we hadn't seen his money, but he wouldn't believe us." They left their horses and ran for their lives, plunging into the millpond, not realizing it was over their heads. "We were swimming and he was shooting. Mr. Chilla, that man tried to shoot us dead!"

That night a crowd of fifty armed men waited for the gypsies to return for their horses. When they didn't come, John Whorley, as deputy sheriff, took the posse to converge on their tents. John had his knife ready, he said, for he expected trouble. They found the gypsies in bed with their pants hanging up to dry. John took them to jail.

When Bob interceded for them, John Whorley felt betrayed, and so did most of Slate Mountain. John told the preacher he was upholding evil people. Slate folks would have killed the gypsies that night if they could have laid hands on them.

"But John, nobody knows for sure that they're guilty," said Bob. "They say they didn't do it."

John looked at him in amazement. What sort of man was this who didn't know right from wrong? He could hardly believe it was the same man who had been leading him through the Scriptures. All he could do was warn him.

"Just see that you stay away from jail," he said, "for folks are mighty mad."

But Bob kept visiting the gypsies. He went to the judge to try getting them released for insufficient evidence.

At Sunday services he faced a very quiet congregation. Some faces were hostile and hard. More of them evaded his look. The joy was gone from the singing, and when he shook hands with them at the door, they seemed anxious to get away. He had almost never felt so hurt.

"Perhaps I've been wrong," he thought to himself, "to interfere in what my people say is none of my business." No, he had to act on what he believed, no matter what they thought.

Two days before the trial John Whorley saw Old Boyd's wife in town and stopped her, intending to ask to buy her cow.

"I'd like to talk with you," he said.

She pulled away. "What do you want? I didn't steal that hundred and fifty-five dollars." John's thoughts raced. For the first time he considered the possibility that the gypsies might not be guilty.

He whispered to the woman, "We're right soon going to find out who did, for we're putting a pair of bloodhounds on the tracks."

The woman looked startled. "Reckon those bloodhounds would hurt a body?"

"Can't say for certain," he said.

The day before the gypsies' trial, John went to the Boyd cabin. As he talked with the old man he noticed a tobacco can above the kitchen window. When the old man went outside John checked it. Sure enough, the money was there. Old Boyd seemed really surprised. It had been empty last time he looked.

Bob tried to get the court to pay the gypsies for their time in jail, but they didn't wait for a settlement. They left that night and never returned to that part of the Blue Ridge.

John Whorley came later to apologize for having deserted the best friend he had ever known when nearly all of the mountain had turned against him.

John seemed abject, confused. Something had happened to the man, Bob could see, and when he questioned him, John confessed he had given up his job as deputy sheriff and had slipped back into drink.

"Brother John," said Bob, slipping an arm around his shoulder, "there's nothin' wrong with you that a little work won't cure. Come with me and help a few lame dogs over the stile."

He took John for a week of revival meetings at Mayberry. Like a man possessed, John beat the bushes for people to attend. He called on fifty-four mountain homes in a week. No perfunctory calls, either. At one place the man of the house slipped out the back door when John and a co-worker pulled up. John told the preacher about how he got away.

"Why not take out into the woods after him?" Bob said, then added slyly, "Of course, he's a mighty stout fellow."

John gave him a sidelong look. Next day, John went round behind the house while his co-worker knocked at the front door. John caught up with the man as he slipped out for the woods.

"I was a-goin' for a walk," the man said.

"I thought I'd take a walk, too," said John.

The man turned on him. "You've got my family. Ain't that enough?"

"It's yourself we want, brother." They sat on a log and talked. For the rest of the week the man came to revival, from fear either of the Lord or of John Whorley.

John went along with the preacher to a revival at Shooting Creek and again at Conner's Spur. They had become a team, both big and imposing men, and some who professed said it just looked like the best side to be on.

The revival did something to John Whorley, too. He finally felt that he had won out over drinking, and that the Lord had done it for him. Doing the Lord's work gave him a kind of excitement and peace at the same time.

Within a month, the king of Slate Mountain was ordained a Methodist minister. He went on holding meetings in Carroll, Floyd, Patrick, and Franklin counties. "Bob," he said at the end of the summer, "I reckon by now I've preached everywhere I ever bought liquor, made it, or bootlegged it."

Signs of New Life

Some days Bob Childress would think the clouds of fear and death were at last lifting from the Buffalo, but the next day would bring news of another tragedy. Coming home from an afternoon of calling on sick families, he stopped to visit Conduff at his logging operations. He found his son shaken and depressed. That day Conduff had been out looking for woodcutters. When he got no answer to his knock on the door of a farmhouse, he walked inside. There was the wife lying dead on the bed. Kneeling on the floor beside the bed was her husband, also dead, his pistol still in his hand.

Bob's youngest boy, thirteen, was helping with the chores, hauling the milk in an old car out to the road, where it would be picked up by truck. Robert paused to talk with Steve Kemp. Suddenly there was a shot, and the sound of a woman screaming, from a house a few hundred yards away. The two hurried to the house. They found the husband in the yard, his head blown off, and the chickens already picking at the brains. The man's wife stood on the porch, motionless.

"I got up to make breakfast," she said, "and he asked me to come lie down with him. I wouldn't. So he got up and dressed and went outside and took a shotgun to himself."

It was a gory sight for so young a boy. For days afterward Robert kept saying, "Mama, I wish I'd never seen it."

With all the violence at the Buffalo it was strange, visitors said, how little had been aimed at Bob Childress himself. There were others besides Hardshells and stillers who had reason to resent him. For he was continuing to upset every area of the lives of mountaineers, asking them to give up drink, to send their children to school where they learned to cast off mountain traditions and superstitions that were generations old. Besides that, there was hardly a family whose life he hadn't somehow personally touched, and he had crossed a good many people.

With all the people he had riled, wasn't he afraid, outsiders asked, that someday one of them would retaliate? It seemed inevitable. Bob only laughed. He'd go when his time came, and not before. No one could grow up in the mountains without that much of Hardshell belief. Besides, all the Blue Ridge knew he never carried a gun, and no one could plead self-defense in a fracas with him.

Changes were coming fast to Buffalo Mountain. Bob kept on pressuring the county to build more roads and all-season bridges. More and more cars were appearing.

Outside influences at last began moving up the roads and across the bridges. At Bob's invitation, a dozen Boy Scouts came for a visit. Buffalo boys were mystified by the uniforms. If they were soldiers or revenuers, where were the guns? Bob urged national headquarters of the Boy Scouts to consider building a summer camp on the Buffalo, but got no response.

A busload of young people from Bob Zehmer's church in Roanoke came to stage a melodrama at the Buffalo school. They were a little frightened on opening night when a tall boy walked barefoot down the center aisle and leaped onto the stage with them. But all he did was quietly lift an artificial rose from the table and walk out. The play drew bigger and bigger crowds as it moved from one community to the next—Slate Mountain, Indian Valley, Meadows of Dan. At its return to Buffalo Mountain, people started gathering in the afternoon—walking, riding horses, driving T-Models. By curtain time there were five hundred, half of them gathered outside around the windows.

The mail came through regularly now, not just on favored days as it had used to. It brought catalogs and magazines—strong inducement for older folks to learn to read. When Henry Mayberry had started hauling mail to the Buffalo only a few years earlier, older folks had asked him to read their letters and write replies for them. Now there were many who had made themselves semiliterate. One seventy-year-old, on receiving a typewritten letter, replied in indignation: "What made you write to me in reading? I read writing, too."

The new roads permitted Bob to make the rounds of his churches more easily. But still he couldn't serve his people as he should. He longed for the companionship of another pastor, and for the help he would give in ministering to mountaineers. The children of Ernest Boyd, the fisty little man who had been drunk long ago at Bob's first service at Mayberry, had sent word that their daddy wanted to see him. Bob was his brother and counselor and daddy all wrapped up in one. But his schedule was so full that he couldn't get there for days, and that was too late. Ernest had shot himself in the head.

Church headquarters was taking big chunks of Bob's time, too, asking him to tell the story of home missions, and especially of the mountains, at places all over the South and East. Usually the trips were brief and full. On the same morning he spoke at Washington and at Alexandria. Then he drove to Baltimore for an afternoon service and back to Washington for another that night, then started back. He reached home just as the sun beamed its first light through the trees toward the top of Buffalo Mountain. He felt he couldn't afford to be away long. With Conduff he once drove five hundred miles to Nashville, where he preached to a crowd of six hundred, then turned right around and drove home. From the time she was fifteen, Marie sometimes went along, and when he'd stop along the road to sleep he'd ask her to waken him after five minutes. A few times she let him sleep longer, but he didn't like it. She learned he meant only five.

It took Marie days to recover from some trips.

"Papa, how do you do it?" she asked.

Her dad laughed. "Someday you'll understand. You'll have so much to do you'll forget about tiring yourself."

The name Bob Childress drew big crowds. People found it hard to believe they could be laughing one minute and wiping away a tear the next.

He might tell the story of a young mountain couple who came to the manse with the boy's mother and asked to be married. They had no license. Before Bob drove them to town for it, he found the boy a suit of clothes in the store-house, then hauled them all into Floyd, where he bought him a pair of shoes. At the courthouse Bob waited and waited for the boy to get out of the car and buy the license. The boy only sat. Finally Bob asked what was wrong. The mother spoke up.

"Mr. Childress," she said, "I reckon he just hates to ask you for the money."

Bob told the crowd: "All that boy had was the urge!"

From humor, Bob switched abruptly to reveal his love and respect for the mountains and their people, and to give his hearers something of the same regard.

"I often think the mountains are a hatchery for the cities," he said. "We rear our young ones the best we know, teach them to love God, and send some of them to town to sweeten the churches there and bring the freshness and freedom of the mountains with them, without which city churches grow cold. Several mountain boys, from our poorest mountain homes, are leaders in city churches.

"We go to the mountains for their sake, but for our own sake, too. If the world had nothing to do, would we have a happy world? If a church had nothing to do, would we have a happy church? The church must go with the gospel for its own happiness. For the greatest joy we have is the joy of helping somebody.

"Yes, we go to the mountains for their sake and for our sake. And we go for Christ's sake. He loved them all, whether in the hills or the lowlands, whether white or black, simpleton or scholar, rich or poor. And in the last day our greatest joy will be to hear him say, 'Inasmuch as you have been faithful unto one of the least of these, you have been faithful unto me.'"

When Bob finished talking the crowds would press around him to soak up his warmth and magnetism. They pressed money on him, to be able to feel themselves part of the powerful force that was shaking the mountains.

"If a man like Bob Childress gives his whole life to a cause," one man got up and said, "the least we ought to part with is a ten dollar bill." The money poured in.

"A strange feeling comes over you when you hear Bob Childress," a man wrote presbytery, "and it stays with you all your life, so that whenever you think of him up there on the mountain you want to send him a remembrance."

Businessmen's groups across the South begged him to speak. Most of these he had to turn down because his job, he said, was the mountains. But when he spoke in big factories it was strange, people said, how he could talk to manufacturers, union leaders, and workers all at the same time.

With all he was doing, there was bound to be envy and criticism of Bob Childress. Some said he was bribing his people into membership. At Christmas he'd give presents to everyone in his churches—a bag of candy and nuts, with perhaps pickle dishes for the women and whittling knives for the men, and small toys for the children—not every year, but when he saw something he thought his folks would like. Some years there might be a thousand presents. And when a minister criticized him for it, all he said was, "It never occurred to me it was ever wrong to show your love for anybody."

Envy caused one lay preacher to tell folks that Bob Childress was sweet on girls. Everywhere Bob went he seemed to have someone with him, most often one of the women who needed a lift to town or to kinfolks across the valley. Usually it was a different one each time. An ordained minister near Indian Valley went so far as to have Bob shadowed for a whole week. When Blaine Quesenberry heard, he sought out the man immediately.

"Well, what did you find out?" Blaine asked.

"That's just the trouble," the preacher said, perturbed. "Nothing at all!" Then he added, "But I know he's a woman-lover."

And big, hearty Blaine said, "Yes, I know he is. And he's a man-lover, too, and a children-lover. He loves everybody. I've heared him say, 'There's hardly a soul I don't love, no matter what they say about me.' " Then he took the man by the lapels and spoke into his face. "You and I say that and hit wouldn't mean much, but when Brother Childress says it, hit's true!"

There was one woman especially who kept the gossip alive. She was powerful in the Blue Ridge, for she had a strong voice at the courthouse and she advised officials on exactly who deserved relief groceries. Either post was important; together they gave her real power. She saw her influence decline after Bob Childress was made adviser to welfare officials in both Floyd and Carroll counties.

She told a young woman at the store in Floyd, "Why, I've heard tell he put his arm around the girls right out on the steps after services!"

"That's true," the young woman replied softly. "Why, I wouldn't feel as if I'd been to church if Mr. Childress didn't give me a little hug on the way out. He's done it since I was a baby. He's really the only daddy we ever knew." The young woman paused, then added. "As I see it, the harder a man works for the Lord, the harder the devil works against him. He doesn't bother much with a man who's sitting still."

Others who tried to keep the gossip alive were the men who persisted at trading in liquor. When one of them saw Giles Harris's wife driving with the preacher, he went to Giles and hinted it seemed mighty queer. He counted on Giles' temper, swift and strong.

But Bob got word that Giles had been told something damaging, and he drove over to Giles's place and got out of the car. He was met on the porch.

"Giles," he said, "you're mad, and I don't blame you."

Bob thrust out his hand and the two shook.

"Bob, I don't believe a word of it," Giles said. But he looked dark.

"Brother Giles, I wanted to make sure you knew that the only time Nancy rode with me is when I drove her over to the mill."

"I know, Bob, I know, and there's only one thing for me to do. I've got to go get the man who started the story!"

The preacher studied. "Giles, what good could come of that? And what would the Lord think of it?"

"Bob, I've got to do it."

"And I've got to stop you. Sit down here with me." Bob knew how a man's anger can weaken when he is comfortable. He went across the porch and draped his big body down the steps. Giles sat down beside him.

"Brother, you and I are men with high tempers, and everybody knows it," Bob began. "But temper isn't all bad. A good ax has to have it. But, mind you, it's a better ax if you don't hit it against a stone and dull it. Keep it sharp, but don't let it go, I keep telling myself."

He turned to Giles. "The manliest thing to do when folks taunt you is to laugh. Now isn't that true, Giles?"

"Could be, I s'pose."

"And it's the Christian thing too, Brother Giles, it's the Christian thing."

"You're right, Bob, I guess. But I just hope I don't run across that fella too soon, for the sake of my Christian temper."

The gossip didn't disturb Bob Childress or even Lelia, but it preyed on his children.

"Why don't you defend yourself?" they asked.

"Law, children, if I tried to straighten out the tales they tell about me, I'd never get anything done for the Lord. If what they say is true, eventually it will be found out. And if it's not, the rumors will die."

Another man might have stopped driving folks to the doctor and the hospital and might have gone from one service to the next without a girl to play the piano and teach Sunday school. But Bob just kept up his ferrying service.

Liquor dealers from Roanoke and elsewhere who made their way to the Buffalo for supplies felt pretty sure by now that Bob was no spy. He was something harder to deal with—a turncoat mountaineer who seemed to be sweeping the whole mountain into temperance. They didn't like him or his sermons, but most of them didn't go out of the way to get him. Bob avoided open conflict with them, since he didn't believe it would do any lasting good. A visiting Roanoke minister who had happened upon a still while hunting quail had shot the kettles full of holes and smashed the coils, and that night at supper proudly told the Childresses about it. There was silence. Bob tried to keep his voice from betraying a sudden surge of anger.

"Friend," said Bob, "I'm against the stilling up here more than you are. But you've got to know how these folks have lived for years and years, and how they feel about their business. What right did you have to destroy another man's property? Or to take the law into your own hands? You can thank God you weren't shot. And, much as we love you, it's better that you don't return to hunt, for mountain folks will never forget you."

One night in the late summer of 1939, Bob was driving home from a night meeting and had shifted into low gear for the long climb up the hill from the Lee place when half a dozen men jumped out of the woods ahead. They had guns and were clearly drunk.

The leader shouted, "All right, preacher, get down out of there. We're a-goin' to settle up with you!"

Bob stopped his car beside them and jumped out. He could feel the anger pulsing in his neck. He grabbed the ringleader by the collar and boosted him into the car. The others stood silent as Bob started up and drove off. How strange, he thought, that I should feel no anger now. Is it action that quiets me? All he could feel was a protectiveness toward the man who sat, frightened into silence, beside him as he drove.

Bob didn't ask the man about the grievance he and his friends felt. He guessed that the man was a stiller who resented the loss of local trade. Bob just asked where he lived and drove him home.

Alone again in the car he suddenly remembered he hadn't thanked God for his safety. The truth was, he thought, it had never occurred to him to be scared.

Bob could never quite figure what men planned to do when they barred the road and made him get out. Did they think they could provoke him to fight or draw a knife or gun? Surely, all the mountain knew he was unarmed. That might be why they generally backed down, knowing that in court they could never plead self-defense. More likely, it was that Bob didn't give them a chance to act. He had long ago learned that a man with a purpose—one who shows no hesitation—wins many a battle without a blow. At least that's the way it seemed to work out most of the times he was stopped. But there were other times when he could only feel it was pure grace that brought him through.

That same fall, as Bob was driving home from Indian Valley four men flagged him as if they wanted a ride. The moment he stopped, they pulled him out of the car. He hadn't seen them before and couldn't call them by name as he sometimes did to calm those who threatened him.

"What is it you want of me?" he asked.

"We're just a-goin' to kill you, is all," said one.

Bob couldn't tell if they had been drinking. Certainly they weren't drunk. When he saw they were each armed with a long knife, his heart started thumping. And the sudden thought came: Is this what is meant by fear? Am I really afraid to die? He had sometimes wondered what it would be like, but he had never thought he'd be afraid when the time came.

The men didn't move. They stood all around him, just out of reach, as if waiting for a signal.

"Just what is your grievance with me?" he heard himself saying.

There was no answer, but Bob thought he could see a weakening of their resolve.

"Tell me what I have done or what I can do to make amends."

One of them spoke fiercely and advanced a step. "You don't need to do nothin'. We're doin'!"

Bob found his voice again, and it was so calm it surprised him.

"If you're going to kill me, that ought to be easy, for there are four of you," he said. "But let me have a prayer before I die."

He went to his knees, and when he prayed, he prayed out loud for the men and their eternal souls and for their families and for all the people of the mountains who had never learned to love. So earnestly did he feel what he was saying that he almost forgot about the men. When he glanced up he saw them standing by the car listening intently. He concluded with the Lord's Prayer, asking them to join in. There was no sound from their direction until he finished, when he heard a single "Amen."

He got to his feet. No one moved. The men had sheathed their knives. He asked if they wanted a ride. They all climbed in. On the way, someone told him they heard he had steered the revenuers to their still.

In November of that same year a snowstorm swept the Blue Ridge. Bob found himself stuck in a drift on a hill in the early moonlit hours of morning. He kept backing down the hill, then racing forward, plunging into the drift. But each time the car slid a little closer to the road's edge. He knew where the nearest house was. It belonged to a man he had once caused to be jailed and fined for having been drunk and barring the road. He hesitated a moment outside the car, then started off toward the house through drifts that sparkled in the moonlight. He knocked at the door.

"This is Bob Childress!" he shouted. "I'm stuck on your hill!"

There wasn't a sound inside.

"You've got every right not to help me," Bob went on, "and if you don't, I'll understand."

There was the sound of footsteps as a lamp was lit, and the man came to the door in his nightshirt. He asked Bob in and told him to sit while he pulled on his breeches. Then he went out and yoked up his oxen and hooked them onto the car. As the team strained through the snow, their breath plumed above their backs. When they reached the top of the hill and Bob got out to thank the man, he found he could hardly speak.

"For what you have done," he said haltingly, "but for your Christian forgiveness far more—I'll never forget this night." The oxen bawled, impatient to return to their warm barn.

When Bob returned home, he talked long with Lelia. Something was changing at Buffalo Mountain. It was no longer so filled with hate and vengeance. He felt it in his bones.

"There's a better day ahead," he said as he dropped off to sleep.

Once again, Christmas was peaceful. As the family gathered around the tree, Lelia was the first to open her present. The children could see it wasn't the set of frying pans their practical mother had wanted—but a necklace that flashed like sunlight on morning dew. Then it was time for the children to open presents, and while they were lost in the excitement there was a clatter in the kitchen. When they rushed to look they found their dad and little Hattie in aprons, pretending to cook, mischievous grins on their faces. All around on the big black range were shiny new frying pans.

A little later Hattie was nowhere to be seen. Bob started upstairs after her.

"Hattie and I have a special surprise for you," he said. But she was already coming downstairs on her unsteady little legs. Partway down, she stopped. She had written a poem of thanks to her family for all the gifts, and as she stood, painfully frail, she read it in a clear strong voice. The others clapped.

Her face was aglow when Bob lifted her to the floor.

"And now for our big surprise," he said. He turned and faced her, bowed deeply and took her arms. Slowly and haltingly, they waltzed around the room. Their secret had been a poorly kept one. Hardly a day passed since she had first stood alone that he hadn't helped her with walking and balance, and since Thanksgiving there had been strange thumping sounds from a room upstairs.

As they danced, Bob hoped he wasn't tiring her. Each time they had practiced she had seemed a little weaker, and now she was leaning most of her weight on his arms.

Changes on Buffalo Mountain sometimes came too fast for people to adjust. A gravel-crushing plant moved in to speed up roadbuilding. When its operator, an outsider, found no workers one morning because of a burying, he stormed out to the cemetery and tried to get his men to come back to work.

"Look here," said Claude Harris slowly. "Up in the mountains we have respect for the dead, but not necessarily for the living." And the way he said it, and the way he looked, the stranger just up and left the cemetery without another word.

Bob got a Delco electric light system installed in the church, and a set of chimes. The first time the chimes were played, the Spence children who lived down the hill darted wild-eyed past their mother in the doorway and hid under the bed.

"It's the end of the world, Mammy!" they cried. "Music, music, a-comin' right from the clouds!"

When the first airplane roared up over Squirrel Spur, folks say that chickens flew to roost and children ran and hid and whispered to one another, "It's a saw-mill a-busted loose and flyin'!"

The Spangler girls thought it was a buzzard, for it looked about that size.

Old Abe Webb had been coming back from Mount Airy, and folks asked if he'd seen it.

"Seen it?" he snorted. "Why, the blame thing stopped and asked me the way to Jar Gap!"

There were changes all across the mountains. Young folks still climbed the Buffalo in spring, but they were happiest when Bob Childress was with them. Sometimes they took supper. Now and again they went before dawn and cooked breakfast as the sun rose. There were sociables in the church basement, too, and lively ones. The older folks couldn't help but talk about how times had changed.

Bob Childress felt it, too, with every fiber in his body one day in spring when he was out cutting firewood. He came across whole rings of chestnut sprouts coming up around the trunks of dead giants.

"Look here," he shouted to his companions. "Those chestnuts aren't dead at all! There's a whole circle of young'uns. Some day your young'uns will be picking those old chestnuts again. Just you see!"

Out from the Buffalo

It was the young folks, Bob Childress had always known, who held the future of the mountains in their hands and hearts. Their quick and warm response to him along the roads, in the cabins, in the school and Sunday schools, had lifted his spirits in the darkest days. Even as he struggled to stem the drinking and killing, to heal old hatreds and bring in love and work and self-respect to their parents and grandparents, he wished he could spend more time with the young. What he did try to do was give each of them a feeling of being somebody who mattered, who was loved, whose life could amount to something.

Hazel Bowman was a slender, pretty girl whom Bob first saw after her father had gone berserk and nearly killed her sister with an ax. She says, "It seemed like Mr. Childress was the first person who ever noticed me, for I was the youngest of seven. It made me so happy that he remembered my name and teased me. When my daddy died he said he'd like to be my father—and that's what he really was." Hazel's words are echoed by hundreds whose names he never failed to remember and whose lives he changed. Most of the changes came from what Bob believed in almost as strongly as he believed in God—education.

"It was like he thought the worst sin a young'un could do was not get schoolin'," one man recalls. "I remember as a shaver how he just about hauled my big brother, kickin' and hollerin', off to Buffalo school when my folks gave in and said he could go. The preacher made books seem like big boxes full of candy just waitin' to be tasted. I never was much of a learner, but I still read some most every day even yet, and it was the preacher that got me goin'."

Bob kept a close eye on the Buffalo school over the years and boosted others wherever he ministered.

In the late thirties, scores of children he had started off were ready to graduate from high school. Bob had talked for years to some of them about college. His own son Conduff went off to Maxton Presbyterian College in North Carolina, and his girl Evelyn to teacher's college at Montreat, North Carolina. But it was the rare mountaineer who could see any reason why a boy should leave home for more schooling. Maybe a preacher, at least a Presbyterian preacher, should have it, but who else needed it on the Buffalo? Bob would only say that God meant for those with brains to fill them and work them. But the old suspicions died hard. When Steve Kemp, the first to be convinced, said he'd let his son Frank go, he still had doubts.

"Mind you, I want him to grow. I don't want him to swell."

At Meadows of Dan was a quiet, studious mountain boy named Dorn Spangler who had told Bob he had a leaning towards the ministry. Nothing could have pleased Bob more except his own sons wanting to preach, and none of them had showed any such desire. But Dorn had no money, for one thing, and the thought of living in a town the size of Stuart, with a population of six hundred, while he finished high school was frightening. Bob took the boy to town and arranged to take care of his board and room. Hardly a week passed that he didn't stop in and bolster Dorn's confidence. The boy was smart and did well. All the while, Bob talked up college to him even though in the history of Meadows of Dan only one person had ever gone. When the time came, Bob helped him get admitted to the college Conduff was attending.

At Indian Valley the high school closed for lack of money just two months before the school year was to end. Darius Flinchum, the oldest of eleven children from a poor mountain farm, and a brilliant student, was crushed. After speaking to the other students and him after church one Sunday, Bob made up his mind. On the next weekend he drove over to talk with all their parents, then took the six students into his own home so they could attend the Buffalo school the rest of the year. When classes started again in the fall, he arranged for the high school in Willis to take the children. But only Darius went. Later, Bob helped get him into Presbyterian Junior College in Laurinburg, South Carolina, where among three hundred boys he became president of the student body and valedictorian.

Lois Kemp, Jeanette Spangler, Marvin Sutphin, and two of Tom Boyd's daughters went to college. Bob's own quiet little Evelyn finished teacher's college. Late at night at his desk in the living room he wrote letters of encouragement to the students, all of them lonely for the mountains. To his own impetuous Marie, who threatened to return home from Radford, he sent encouragement. "If you don't eat, you're bound to be unhappy. Just fill your body and your brain. We're all thinking of you.

"Hattie stays busy walking to and from school. The teachers tell me she's the smartest one there. How I wish you could see her standing in a pew leading all the singing at Sunday school!"

Then, as Bryan and Paul were getting ready for college, the lightning flashes of Pearl Harbor thundered along the Blue Ridge and rumbled far back into the coves, farther than any news from the outside ever had.

The call came for trees. Shipyards at Newport News and Baltimore were eager for the white oak and chestnut oak of Buffalo Mountain and for the yellow poplar, sound and true, smooth of trunk and straight as a rifle barrel for sixty feet up to the first limb.

The next call came for quartz. Men spoke to the pupils at the Buffalo school, asking them to look for glass rocks to be used in making radio crystals. When they returned and rewarded the youngsters with candy, word raced round that the men were spies and the candy was poison. Agitated mountaineers knocked at the Childress door. All Lelia could say was, "If it's poison, it tastes mighty good. I declare we've eaten ours all up!"

Finally the call came for men, the stalwart young men of Buffalo Mountain, so sound of limb and keen of eye. The war was hungry for them. Slim little Vernon Sutphin, such a hand at shooting squirrels, went to the Pacific, and word came back later that he won the Bronze Star for cleaning out a nest of snipers. Marvin Sutphin joined up early and became a major in the Philippines.

Then it was Bill Joe's turn to go. On the day of his departure the five Childress boys gathered down the hill by the spring and stood there a long while, talking. Bob watched them from the window, uneasy, until they started up the hill. They filed through the front door and stood, a little embarrassed it seemed, in front of him.

"Dad," Paul began, "Bill Joe's going now, but soon we're all going to be away, maybe a long time, and while we're still all together there are some things we'd like to say."

Bob looked from one face to the next.

"We want you to know, Dad," said Paul, "first, that no boys could ever have had as fine a father as you."

Bob tried to swallow but couldn't, could only manage a crooked smile. Then Bryan spoke.

"And Papa, we want you to know that you don't need to worry about us in the service. For one thing, there's not a one of us who ever tasted liquor in our lives, and we aren't about to start. Don't know if you've ever worried about it, but we wanted you to know."

Bob felt faint for an instant, and reached for a chair. He thought he could hear the doxology ringing in his ears: "Praise God from whom all blessings flow"—interrupted by a sense of guilt that he had ever doubted them.

Just then Lelia called them all to eat, and oh, how they made away with her fried chicken and corn bread and apples fried in butter with a touch of sugar, and applesauce cake, and all. Lelia's cooking had a way of easing pain.

One by one the Childress boys went to war: Bill Joe, Paul, Bryan, and even Robert, the baby, when he was seventeen. Only Conduff, who had a family, was spared.

Buffalo Mountain was a lonely place for Bob Childress without its young people. Almost all the boys seemed to be in uniform, and the girls had mostly gone off to work in defense plants in the valley towns. A few were still away in school. Dorn Spangler had gone to Westminster College at Fulton, Missouri, and then to Louisville Seminary, and Bob had high but secret hopes he would come back to serve in the mountains. It was hard, then, to read the letter that came from Dorn one fall morning. "I just don't feel the call to preach," he said. "But Mr. Childress, as a teacher I can serve the mountains, too. So I'm changing schools." Bob covered his disappointment and replied at once: "Dorn, you have already blazed a trail for others from Meadows of Dan to follow."

It seemed to Lelia during the war years, Bob never rested. He felt he couldn't stop, with all the work there was to do. Sometimes he'd preach in fourteen churches a week. He couldn't rest knowing that there were people who didn't have services near their homes.

The Childress men during the war years. Left to right:
Robert, Jr.; Bill Joe; Paul; Bryan; Conduff; Robert, Sr.

More than that, he kept right on building new churches. Mayberry wanted its frame church to be transformed into a rock one like the others. So with Bob's help they encased it in the same tawny rocks as the rest.

He encased another church at Bluemont, which looks down the mountain to the blue of The Hollow where he grew up. Nearby were Granny Puckett's cabin, and Hard Smith Mountain —places dear to his heart. Perhaps that is why he loved his Bluemont church so much.

Bob Childress got to building so many rock churches in so many places that it was a source of joking. Dump Yeats's son, Hassell, said to his daddy when they came to a wooden church, "Mr. Childress never saw this church."

"How's that?" Dump asked.

"He'd have rock-sided it afore now!"

One day Henry Mayberry, the mail carrier, asked Bob to come into Willis and start a church. Bob laughed.

"You've got churches already—enough for the town," Bob said.

"But we don't have you," said Henry. He kept after Bob, pointing out that, despite the three churches there, the town had services only once a month.

So Bob raised money to buy the bank building, knocked out the safe, brought in chairs and pulpit, and started weekly services. Nineteen people joined the first month.

Every three months one of Bob's churches played host to all the others at a midweek night service where they discussed problems, compared notes, and closed with all joining hands and singing "God Be with You till We Meet Again." Folks said it gave them a good feeling to know they were part of something bigger than their own church.

One day Bob was invited to preach for a week at a crossroads community called Dinwiddie. He found it a strange sort of place. He could see that folks were better off there than in the hills. They worked on the Betty Baker railroad or in a nearby zinc mine. Most of them had seen the outside world. Few depended on farming. And yet the church building he was speaking in was a ruin. And he heard so much gossip and backbiting, especially about religion, that he remarked on it to one of the men.

"I don't know why it is," the man replied, "but we can't seem to forget that we're Methodists, Democrats, Presbyterians, Republicans, and Baptists."

On the last night of the week of services someone passed the hat and offered Bob the cash.

"What's that for?" he asked.

"To pay for your services."

Bob turned red. "Well, I don't want it. I want you to get more of it together and use it to turn this pigpen into a church. Save it and build something fit to hear the word of God in!"

People were angry. One man came up fuming.

"If there were a new church," he said, "and I'm going to fight it tooth and nail—and if you were to be our preacher, I'd never come!"

But a week later, Bob got a letter from the same man, asking him to come over for dinner. A day later there was another letter, this time from an elder, Arthur Mitchell, saying simply, "Please, Mr. Childress, come back and help us build a church."

Bob went back the following week, and for the next three years he never missed a service. Dinwiddie people weren't accustomed to such a minister. In the past there had been Sunday school only during summer and preaching if the weather was good. This man came through mud or snow, and the worse the roads, the happier he seemed. People who'd never been before started coming to church, and many, including even Hardshells, were baptized. Young folks seemed to think that no one but Bob Childress could marry them. He tore down the walls of jealousy and spite without their knowing it, got a Primitive Baptist in one job, a Methodist in another, and a Brethren doing something else.

When it came time to build the church, money poured in from the people of Dinwiddie and from others outside, but the biggest contributor was Bob Childress.

"I've seen him put a hundred dollars in the collection plate, a gift from someone that was really meant for him personally," says Arthur Mitchell. "And when we tried to give it back he said, 'Arthur, if I die with more than two hundred dollars I'll feel I've robbed God. I've got insurance for my wife and Hattie.' "

The building turned out to be a beautiful one—another rock church, but perhaps even handsomer than the others he had built. It rested on a hilltop with the same solidity and grace as the ageless churches of Europe. The stage and altar were of the same yellow and white stones as the exterior. A loudspeaker on the roof sent out chimes and songs that could be heard for a mile.

Then, one Sunday, another preacher stood in the pulpit. There hadn't been any warning, but now the new man announced that Mr. Childress wouldn't be able to come back. People wept during the service. Perhaps he hadn't wanted to say good-bye. Or did he know that the congregation would never have let him go? His work was done, though, they admitted. The community had been welded into one. No one knew quite what he had said or done. It was hard to remember that they had ever been divided. All they knew was that they were a grateful people, but lonesome without the man who had changed their lives.

Hardly a day went by that the mail didn't bring a request—or more often a plea—for Bob Childress to preach or speak or hold a revival series somewhere. Other sorts of invitations arrived too— calls to serve churches in tiny hamlets and in large cities. Only one ever really tempted Bob.

The forceful secretary of the Synod of Tennessee, Dr. Goodridge Wilson, knew from the start that Bob Childress was the man he had to have to head up mission work along a strip of the Cumberland Mountains from Kentucky all the way to Georgia. He induced Bob to spend one weekend a month in the Cumberlands, then urged him to come full time. Bob saw the need. The area was a vast, forgotten region where poverty and ignorance and isolation ruled. Religion was as backward as the economy. At mysterious tent meetings, hundreds of mountaineers might be "struck with the jerks" and fall down stiff. Others gathered to worship rattlesnakes. There was violence here, too, as there had been at the Buffalo. On the second Sunday he was there, as he was eating a picnic dinner under the trees before a service, someone came running up to announce that a man had been killed just a few hundred yards away.

The prospects of a new field were exciting. It also seemed possible that now the work in the Buffalo area could go on without him. For years seminary students as well as ministers seeking new parishes had visited and worked with him, mostly in the summers. Some had come out of curiosity, some because the seminary or the mission board had nowhere else to send them. Only a few had shown the toughness of spirit that a mountain ministry demanded, and fewer still had felt a commitment that would bring them back. But now Bob knew just the two young men he would like to have take his place. One was a brilliant student, James Booth, who had just begun lay work there, the other an equally outstanding young minister, Ralph Arbaugh, who was married to Johnny Sutphin's daughter. It would be good for the Buffalo to have new blood. He came home ready to accept the Cumberland offer.

"Leave Buffalo Mountain?" said Lelia. "It's going to be hard on Hattie."

It was true that Hattie, now eighteen, loved the mountain the way few of the others had. It was also true that she was failing, having more fainting spells and losing weight.

Hattie said, "Papa, if we can take the whole family along, it won't be so bad."

And Bob said, "Yes, Hattie, if it was like when we came here we could, but the children are grown now, and some even have families."

Bob gave up the idea, because Hattie was all but sacred to him. It was the nearest he ever came to leaving Buffalo Mountain.

Instead, Bob Childress drove over to the Cumberlands with the same two young men he had been counting on to replace him at the Buffalo. After working a few weeks they agreed to accept the offer to serve there. Many at headquarters protested about sending such brilliant young leaders to the area, but the president of King College at Bristol, Tennessee, disagreed: "We must send our best. They need all the brains in the world to go into a murderous wilderness and come out alive. I believe that as strongly as Bob Childress does."

After years of worry and waiting, the war was finally over. Most of the Childress boys came home about the same time. Bryan, who by now looked enough like his father to be a twin, took up sawmilling like Conduff and did well. He married Doc Vaughn's granddaughter and built a fine house just across the road from the Buffalo church. Paul, the quick-moving, humorous one, took up garage work in Hillsville.

Bill Joe, home on furlough, seemed to have a special curiosity about his Dad. He plagued him with questions. "Why in the world do you keep bringing groceries to the Lorimers and carrying them to the hospital? They'll never do anything for the church!"

Bob looked up from his paper absently. "Why, Bill Joe, it's not what they can do for the church, but what the church can do for them."

Next day when Bob returned from driving a woman two hundred miles to Charlottesville to the hospital, Bill Joe asked, "What did they pay you for it?"

"Why, nothing, Bill."

"Nothing at all?"

"No, Bill. The Lord does that, in other ways. Just the other day I got a hundred dollars from a man in Washington."

After Bill Joe was discharged from the army, he went back to finish high school and then on to King College at Bristol. On a summer Sunday after Bill Joe's first year there, Bob rose to his feet after a service at Buffalo Mountain.

He was visibly shaken, even pale. Folks saw that he trembled.

"This is an announcement I never dreamed I could ever make—" he began, and faltered.

All eyes went to the Childress family in the pew, but most of them too were goggle-eyed. Was he going to accept a call somewhere else?

Their father finally went on. "Next Sunday my son Bill Joe is going to preach his first sermon." Then his voice broke, but he managed to say, "Bill Joe is going to be a minister."

The next Sunday the old Buffalo church was filled to over-flowing. Folks stood outside the open windows and listened as Bill Joe preached. Not quite like his Pa, some said, but fine for a start.

It was the year after, when Hattie lay sick, that Robert, the youngest boy, wrote from school that he had decided to go into the ministry.

"Oh, I just knew he would," said Hattie from her bed. "It's another of my prayers answered."

At Christmas in 1949, Hattie wrote several little poems—sad ones they were, one of them a message of good-bye. Then, after Christmas, she was gone, and it seemed that the fires had turned to ashes in the big house. For just as everyone used to cluster around the fireplace to keep warm, so they had gone to Hattie first to tell about their adventures, their dates, to hear the warm tinkle of her laugh, to tell about their successes and their dreams for the future. The child who was not supposed to have lived at all had made their lives rich.

Bob walked in the woods one afternoon after the next, for he couldn't stand the cold, silent house. Lelia was stricken. The quiet resolve, the courage that had been a foundation for the family through every other crisis, was shaken. There was no getting her out of the house. It was months before she was herself again.

But big, quiet Bryan surprised everyone most. The day Hattie died he paid off his crew of woodcutters and never again went back to the woods. He knew he must become a minister—Hattie's spirit and faith and courage had something to do with it, though he couldn't explain just what. He and his plucky wife Polly left their new home across from the Buffalo church and set out for college.

There would be three Childress sons in the ministry.

Only now did Bob admit to himself how much he had secretly hoped for it. It was a pleasure beyond expressing to know they had affirmed his own lifework by choosing it themselves. He watched their work intently, chuckled as they sweat over theology, listened to their sermons, and hoped that seminary wouldn't wring out their spontaneity.

Even as they began their seminary work, he got to thinking how the needs in the mountains were changing. People who had lived and worked and gone to school outside the Blue Ridge during the war years returned with a different view of life. There was something better than drinking and fighting. They had children to educate, homes to build.

There were still a few old hostilities, and as long as they remained Bob couldn't rest.

Grandpa Sepie Scott and Grandpa Elim Reynolds had been the best of friends. They'd been raised up together, and their grandchildren had even married back and forth. Grandpa Sepie was postmaster and storekeeper at Laurel Fork, and the best part of Grandpa Elim's day was at the store playing checkers with Grandpa Sepie—until one day they fell out over a game. They stopped speaking to each other.

Bob went from one to the other.

"It's late, Grandpa Sepie," he'd say. "Don't let the night fall on a quarrel."

He'd tell Grandpa Elim, "Our time's too short for anger. It may be the last time in your life you'll ever see Sepie. Go tell him you love him."

He finally got them both to church, and the sermon he preached folks still remember word for word.

"Only death is certain, and before death comes, let's settle all our accounts. If you've done your brother wrong, shake his hand. If he's done you wrong, forgive him. For it's vain and foolish not to forgive."

The congregation watched expectantly. "If you've someone to forgive, go to him now!"

Grandpa Sepie got to his feet at the rear of the congregation and walked slowly to the front. Grandpa Elim didn't budge a muscle, but he must have heard the footsteps, for the moment

Sepie turned to him in the pew, he pulled himself to his feet and thrust out his hand. Before anyone knew it, Bob Childress was there, putting his arms around them both.

There were checker games again in the store, such happy ones that folks didn't mind waiting a while for their stamps and money orders.

Bob got two men to join the church who hadn't spoken in forty years. When he asked one why such close friends had fallen out, the man looked embarrassed. "I just don't recollect," he said. Bob persuaded them to shake hands and forget the past before the entire congregation, since they were outstanding men and all the mountain knew of their enmity. And just what does a man say to his best friend after forty years of silence? He says as the other takes his hand, "Be a mite keerful. I've got a sore hand. Don't mash it."

Bob told his congregations, "Forgiveness is its own reward. Just try it on the person you like least in all the world, and see how good it makes you feel."

One old man made a real effort. He rose in a prayer meeting and prayed with fervor. He told of his years in the legislature, of his carpentry, of how he had always tried to help the poor, and then went on: "I fully forgive Brother Lorimer, and I pray the Lord will clear his mind of that get-rich-quick scheme!"

When he paused for a breath, Bob said quickly, "Amen. Let's close with a hymn."

For the most part, though, the old rancors were disappearing. When Bailey Goad went along with Bob for a service at Indian Valley, Blaine Quesenberry was amazed at seeing the man in church. Ever since he was a child Blaine had heard about the time Bailey had shot Jim Dickerson and how he was the meanest man on the Buffalo. Blaine whispered to Bob, "Is that really Bailey Goad?"

"Yes 'tis," said the preacher. "It really is."

Blaine said, "He's the fellow that shot my cousin once."

"Dickerson was your cousin?"

"Yes, he was."

Then Bob laughed so loud folks say you could hear him all

over the crowd, and hollered, "Bailey, Bailey, come on over here!"

Blaine tried to stop him, kept saying, "He won't want to see me."

But Bob just hollered again, "Bailey, come here and meet your kinfolk!"

Blaine says, "That's how Bob treated us. He made jokes about our fights. He just wouldn't let us keep on hating."

Things were getting so quiet at the Buffalo that it was something of a surprise when Will Goins had another mean spell and set out after his wife with a shotgun. There was something more than quick temper wrong with that man, Bob thought. Bob talked to him after he had cooled down some, and asked if he didn't want to go to the hospital. Bob and Will's brother (whose finger Will had once almost bitten off) had made a decision. Will, big and husky though he was, had always believed he was a sick man and longed for a doctor's attention. It took no coaxing to get him to go to a hospital, and, not being able to read, he wasn't aware when he passed through a gate that he was entering a mental institution.

But by the time Bob and Lelia returned to visit him he knew it, and he was frantic.

"You know what this is? It's a nuthouse! A regular nuthouse! See that man thar? He's looney! Looney as a barred owl! You've got to get me out of here!"

Bob tried to tell him that the doctors believed he was sick, and they could best decide when he might leave. Will pleaded. There was no more fight in his system.

He looked furtively around him. "Just sneak me past the guards and carry me home with you."

The doctors said Will's meanness and unpredictability were pathological, and they could do little more for him. It might have been then that Bob devised a scheme with them, or it might have been when Will had first been admitted. Anyway, two months after Bob and Lelia's visit, a man from Buffalo Mountain hid in the shrubbery at the edge of the grounds.

Will, who was outside gardening, heard a voice call to him

softly: "Will Goins, drop your hoe and take out after me. I'll carry you back to the Buffalo."

Will made his escape. When he appeared at the manse his eyes glowed.

"Will," Bob told him, "unless you live like a saint and never again have a mean drunk, those hospital jailers will find you out and have you back behind those walls quicker than a fox."

From then on, Will Goins lived a quiet, almost respectable life.

Will's wild spell was about the last gasp of violence at Buffalo Mountain. It was coming to be known as a staid, almost conservative area. There hadn't been a killing for years. Elsewhere in Carroll and Floyd counties there was still a killing now and then, and some malicious wounding, but not at the Buffalo. The people were different there. The past had passed into legend—unreal, hard to believe.

It was true of stilling, too. After the war it had begun to boom in the southern highlands. Once, when a Navy plane crashed and searchers scanned the horizon for signal flares, every column of smoke they investigated came from a thriving mountain still. Bob knew that his parishioners too must be sorely tempted to resume their trade. A pint of old popskull sold for a dollar—less than the tax on legal whiskey—and millions of southerners preferred its raw, fiery taste to store liquor, which they said barely tickled the tonsils. A magazine article singled out Franklin and Patrick counties, Virginia, where the entire economy depended on moonshining. A still that cost as little as one hundred dollars might bring in that much every week. A big still might bring in one thousand dollars, and the transporter who bought it, diluted it, and sped it to market might make considerably more, if he worked every night.

But, much as the liquor traffic surged below the mountains and in the valleys to the west, Buffalo Mountain and Mayberry and Meadows of Dan and Indian Valley and Bluemont and Dinwiddie remained quiet and respectable. A different yeast was working there.

It wasn't just the mountain that was changing, either. Now and then Bob would get word from scores of young folks he had helped on to college. Darius Flinchum, the boy from Indian Valley who had lived at the manse, had written Bob long ago for advice. He had been appointed to West Point, and didn't see how he could turn it down.

"Mr. Childress," he wrote, "what I really want is to be a doctor."

His answer came immediately. "Have faith, Darius, and you'll find a way."

It worked out that way, too. He turned down the appointment, and when his money ran out at the University of Virginia medical school, the dean helped him get a Du Pont scholarship and, later, other scholarships that saw him through. He finished among the top ten, and returned to general practice in the coal fields near home. Working with the victims of mine accidents, he grew interested in reconstructive surgery and went on to specialize. His surgery worked wonders on wounded GIs in Korea and again at the Warm Springs Foundation in Georgia.

All his life Bob had thought of his work as a ministry to the mountains. Now he saw that the mountains could go out and do something in other places. Just imagine, he thought to himself, old Buffalo Mountain a seedbed for missionaries!

He couldn't help but think of it again when old Bailey Goad testified at a revival he went to with Bob in an area to the west that was still torn by fighting.

"Truth don't need no dressin' up the way a lie does. It's pretty all by itself." Then Bailey went on. "If my boy did wrong, I'd a whole lot rather he got caught at it the first time. I'd rather get him out of jail than out of a funeral home."

Here was a missionary from Buffalo Mountain—and every ear was tuned in, because even in the valley the name of Bailey Goad brought memories.

"When I die," he went on, "I don't care what they say at the service. The way I look at it, I preach my own funeral every day. A man's life ought to be his funeral. Oncet you're gone, nothing that's said can do a bit of good. You're in the hands of the Lord."

One day in early June when the flame azaleas were blooming

and the sun started the witch-water to rising from the road, Bailey walked up to Bob's house.

"Are you busy?" he asked.

"Never too busy to talk to a friend."

"Well sir, can we just walk around the place some?"

They did, and as they walked in the bright summer sun, Bailey took to musing.

"I've always been in debt," he said. "But now I'm out. I don't owe nobody. Except you. I owe you. We all owe you. It's something I need to tell you, and it better be now." He hesitated, searching for words. "It's that you've tamed this here old Buffalo. You've given us all our upright. You've made us see what fools we were with our drinking and fighting. And we never gave you anything back but—"

Bob stopped him. "Yes, you did, more than you guess."

Bailey must have known that his time for paying debts was running short. For it wasn't but a week later that the doctor was called, and they laid him away. He was the first person to be buried in a new cemetery across from the Buffalo church.

Whenever Bob's sons would return from seminary he'd have them preach in one or more of his churches. And all of a sudden, it seemed to Bob, there were many others at Buffalo Mountain who were becoming ministers of one kind or another. Owen Starr, a gentle, soft-spoken farmer who had long taught Sunday school, was ordained in the Missionary Baptist church, and preached whenever Bob was away. Then there was Doc Jennings, a dentist at Willis, who served the church there in Bob's absence. And big, hearty Ed Gardner, a game warden, did the same thing at Bluemont.

And there was John Whorley of Slate Mountain. The same energy that had once impelled him to chase every competitor off the mountain found a new outlet once he was ordained. Right away, he had converted a gunman who had six notches on his pistol. He substituted in the pulpit when Bob was off on tour. And when the government founded a work camp in the mountains, he was put in charge, and, first thing, he started a Sunday school. When he was stationed at Fort Bragg during the war, he organized Sunday schools in several sections of the post and was assistant pastor at nine nearby mountain churches.

*John Whorley used his great energy to preach
and teach wherever he went.*

He wrote Bob, "I'm just following the course you laid out for me."

Wherever John went, he taught. At Walter Reed Hospital, where he went to have shrapnel removed from his arm, he preached and visited other patients between treatments. After the war, he accepted a call to a church in Dublin, Virginia.

Bob was sorry to have folks leaving the mountains. But he cheered at the thought of what the mountains were taking to the land outside.

All the Upright We Ever Had

Doc Burnett had tried for years to get Bob Childress to slow down, but had finally given up. So had Miss Willie Mitchell, a salty little nurse in Dinwiddie who had often helped take care of Hattie and the other children when they took sick.

"There was no stopping the preacher from bounding around these hills," Miss Willie says, "any weather, any time of day or night, driving people here or there, hauling rocks for one church or the other, doing Lord knows what all. Sometimes I'd know he hadn't had a bite all day, and his furnace needed a lot of stoking, so he'd end up putting a hog's-bait of food away at one sitting. It wore you out just to watch that man move."

Bob was sixty when the Korean war broke out. He was still leading services in fourteen churches each week and, if anything, putting more miles on his car than ever. Church publications began commenting on his ministry.

"Mr. Childress has driven an average of 40,000 miles a year since he went to the Buffalo," said one. "His salary from the field wouldn't have paid car expenses, much less provided a living. He brings great sums of money in to Home Mission work. He holds great audiences in his hands, bringing them from laughter one moment to tears the next as he tells the story of his mountain people. Often he borrows thousands of dollars to pay for his building operations. His sons' lumber trucks haul many people."

Presbytery decided that "Mr. Childress covers more territory and has more travel than any other man, over roads that in most cases are poor and often well nigh impassable. Something must be done to relieve him of burdens incident to wear and tear

240

upon his car. We are taking a step in this direction for next year."

They added $150 to his yearly budget.

The Synod of Virginia published this testimonial: "Only eternity will tell the tremendous good accomplished in this unusual diocese."

On a desperately hot day in August of 1950 Bob was loading rocks on a truck for an addition to the Slate Mountain church and had to stop. He felt overheated. A few days later, as he was driving with Mr. and Mrs. Arthur Mitchell and their daughter to pick up church pews, he suddenly clutched the steering wheel and slumped. The car swerved, but Bob got his foot on the brake in just enough time to stop on the shoulder. Mitchell rushed him to the hospital at Christiansburg.

The stroke partly paralyzed Bob's right arm and leg, but his speech and spirit were unimpaired. Word traveled fast, and mountain folks began flocking to the hospital. They couldn't understand why they weren't allowed in—and neither could Bob, when he heard them at his door.

"Just li'l ol' Lige won't hurt me, or Jamie either," he would plead. He knew that some must have walked and hitchhiked the thirty miles.

He would tell his nurse, "Well I declare, that sounds like my brother." And when the visitor peered in around the door, he'd sing out, "Yessir, Brother Amos!" Next it would be Brother Posey or Sister Sally or Brother Hassell or a dozen others.

"Look here," said his nurse finally. "How many brothers and sisters do you have?"

"Sister," he said chuckling, "you'd be surprised. Fact is, I can't think of anyone just now who isn't!"

Another patient, hearing his hearty laughter, said, "Why, that man's not sick!" The nurse only smiled and said, "There's nothing wrong with his laugh, that's sure."

Margie Spangler, Babe's little girl who was just beginning to work, left a twenty dollar bill in his room as she slipped out, and the next time Bob said, "You think you're smart, Margie. But I'll pay you back. Just see if I don't!"

It seemed that all of Buffalo Mountain came to visit, as well as Slate Mountain and Bluemont and Dinwiddie and Willis and Mayberry-Meadows of Dan. And knowing how Bob would suffer from having them turned away, the doctor gave them each a brief visit. On a single day there might be fifty people waiting their turn in a line that stretched from his door all the way down the hall. If friendship could have cured him, Bob would have been healthy in a week.

But he got no better, and the doctor realized the visitors and his worry about the churches were tiring him. So in late fall he was ordered to Florida to rest in a hospital far from disturbances. Just before Christmas his money ran out, and he wrote his sons to sell his car. Someone must have guessed why. The week before Christmas he got dollar bills and five dollar bills tucked into cards, adding up to nearly two thousand dollars.

After he was well enough to rest on the beach, he met a Missionary Baptist minister there and took an instant liking to him. The man was fascinated with Bob's talk of the mountains. One day Bob offered to buy the man's car, on one condition.

"What's that?"

"That you drive it up to the Blue Ridge for me, and while you're there look over a field that needs you."

So the preacher drove the car up, loaded with oranges that Bob sent along for his mountain parishes. That's how N. A. Thompson became the pastor of Mount Hebron Baptist Church and the church at the nearby village of Floyd.

Six months later, just before Bob left Florida, his doctor there warned him he must not preach more than once a Sunday.

"Now look," Bob said, then lapsed into mountain talk. "You talkin' 'bout these ol' city preachahs. If they can preach oncet a Sunday, I can hold three services." And then, lest he sound boastful, he added, "You see, I don't preach long."

Back home, his doctor told him he must give up preaching altogether. "Take up fishing," the doctor suggested. So Bob did, but he didn't really cut down on other things. Once back, he couldn't give up. He continued to serve eight churches the same as ever. Otherwise he obeyed his doctor's injunctions to the letter, never once sprinkling a grain of salt on his food, and downing slab after slab of the white meat of chicken to stoke the furnace of his energy. His illness seemed like little more than an ax blow to an oak, which, though it feels the impact, carries itself as proud as ever. Besides, Bob Childress had something special he was set on doing, and it would take some effort. He told only Lelia about it.

*Lelia Childress still lives near the church
on Buffalo Mountain.*

"Bringing people together is the one thing I've tried to do, but we haven't done enough yet. And now's the time."

So one Sunday he drove down to Squirrel Creek to preach in the Negroes' chapel, noticing on the way how much the road, always so slow and dangerous, had been improved. A truck could make the trip now. After the sermon he asked the choir to sing for him.

"Now that sounds so much like the very heartbeat of heaven," he said, "that all Christians ought to hear it." Then he invited them up to sing at his Bluemont church, just a few miles above on the ridge, though almost no one from Squirrel Creek had been there. His friends turned silent and serious. One shook his head slowly. So Bob talked on about how much the other churches needed their singing. Finally he said he'd carry them up himself in the truck. But it wasn't till one old man said, "Well, I reckon we can try it, if you say so" that they agreed.

Bob didn't even tell the Bluemont congregation. He just marched the Squirrel Creek folks into the church and right up front and had them start off with singing. It was the best hymn-singing they'd ever heard, Bluemont folks said later, and they wanted to know how soon the visitors could come back.

A few weeks later Bob got them to a service at Willis, and brought the whole group home for dinner. While they were waiting to eat they played the guitar and violin and piano, singing spirituals and folk songs till the manse fairly shook.

"I never saw anyone so happy in my life as Mr. Childress that day," says Louise Hatcher, the Squirrel Creek choir leader. "He kept going around with platters of fried chicken and boat-loads of gravy, turnip greens, hot rolls, and mashed potatoes, then cake and peaches."

Soon other churches asked to have the Negro choir come to their services. Before long they were singing at six churches on a Sunday, and it would be two in the morning, Louise Hatcher told the preacher, before she got to milk her cows.

Bob was joyful those Sundays. Nobody showed even a trace of resentment. Whenever there was room in the truck, he piled in other members of the Squirrel Creek congregation, even if they weren't going to sing. Louise's mother at first was fearful of going inside a white church, but the preacher told her, "Now, Sister Nora, my skin is light and yours is dark, but there's no difference in heaven. It's the color of the soul that counts."

The crowds grew larger.

"Whenever we sang," said Louise, "Mr. Childress would have me introduce everyone. He asked Heywood MacArthur, 'Any kin to General MacArthur?' And we all laughed. After that,

Mr. Childress always called him Douglas. In all the time we worshiped together, not a thing unpleasant happened. We stopped for a picnic in the old Lee yard near the fishpond, and the only thing the owner said was he'd appreciate it if we sang before we left. Another time we stopped at a restaurant at Fancy Gap. Most of us had never before been inside a restaurant. The owner said all he hoped we'd do was sing for our supper. It was just like we were one people. You can't know what that's like, not to feel unwanted. You'll never know."

"Folks loved to hear us sing," says Louise, "especially those at Slate Mountain. Last time we were there, a host of us went. We sang, 'Git on Boa'd' and 'Stan' by Me' and 'Ol'-Time Religion,' and afterwards Mr. Childress took up what he called a 'love offering' for us for our church."

Bob started taking some of his congregation down the mountain with him to worship in the Negro church. Soon he brought a whole busload.

And so for more than a year Bob's churches were holding integrated services, and everybody—white and black—was enjoying it. Bob said very little about it to his friends at presbytery. He wanted something more than simple fraternizing, he told Lelia. He wanted the brotherhood of black and white to be a deeper, working thing. And the church he chose to try taking another step in was his beloved, lively Slate Mountain.

Sometimes it seemed that Slate Mountain must be his favorite congregation. He would come home from a "poundin'" there with the car springs sagging with the weight of food: cornmeal, sugar, flour, dressed chickens, butter pressed into molds of sculptured beauty, syrup, honey, jelly preserves, and home-cured hams. Slate Mountain people were outgoing and alive, and they loved Bob Childress.

He had tried other experiments there before, like making deacons out of four boys only sixteen to eighteen years old. "Our churches must stay young," he said, "and I've known these boys and their daddies all their lives." The idea worked even better than he'd hoped. The boys continued as deacons right into adulthood. Once a month young folks took entire charge of the services. When Bob told the congregation that Slate needed a new pastor, a young man who could give strong, young leadership, they thought he was joking, even when he told them he was giving up Willis and Indian Valley, too, to round out a field for a new man as soon as one could be found.

Suddenly, when presbytery notified him of a replacement for those churches, Bob knew that he had one last chance at his idea. The last time Bob would be at Slate was to be Communion Sunday. He had planned to tell them about his departure, but he couldn't. Saying good-bye always tore him apart. Instead, after services, he broached his idea.

"You know, I've invited the folks from Squirrel Spur to sing for us again next Sunday," he said, "and that's the day we take communion. Now, I think it would be nice if we asked them to take communion with us."

There was silence.

"Sam Underwood, what do you say?"

"It's all right with me," Sam said.

"It's all right with me," Ted Sutphin said.

The preacher sensed a reluctance. He called on one of the women.

"Well, Mr. Childress," she replied, "I for one would love to have them take communion with us, but I don't feel like using the same glasses."

Bob paused. "I'm glad you told me just how you feel. Now if you'd rather not have them partake, you say so."

More silence. Then someone suggested feebly, "Couldn't the colored folks use the glass cups second, after refilling?"

Suddenly Luther Woods popped to his feet to say that Communion Sunday was not one week but two weeks away. They could decide later.

After services the next Sunday, when the Squirrel Spur folks were leaving, Bob told the congregation that another preacher was going to take his place. It was something he had requested a long while ago.

The congregation stared. It couldn't be. They had known no other pastor. He wasn't a minister, but father and brother. He couldn't do it. The women started crying. Bob hurried out the door, and some say he was crying too.

Carfuls of people drove over to the manse at the Buffalo. Had presbytery at Roanoke taken him away? It couldn't have been his own decision. He couldn't desert the church that he had fought over and labored over and suffered a stroke over, too.

Was it because of the colored folks and the people who complained that they didn't want to use the same glasses? Why, we'll drink and eat with them or after them, before we'll let Mr. Childress go!

Bob tried to make them understand that it was for the good of the congregation that they have a new minister.

Some drove to Roanoke to presbytery headquarters, belligerent. "We won't have Mr. Childress turned out!" they said. Presbytery began to wonder if Bob had changed his mind and wanted to get back. They grew irritated. There was no quieting the Slate Mountain people, for they loved him with a fierce, unreasoning devotion.

But eventually they realized that Bob's leaving was just a part of his effort to slow down. The doctors had kept on warning him to slack off, and he had tried his best. He took a few moments each day just to lie down, and took up fishing more regularly. Most of the time he let someone else do his driving for him, usually Hazel Bowman, a girl he had befriended and later helped through high school and college.

But in spite of all his intentions and efforts, Bob Childress couldn't stay still so long as there was a need. He couldn't stand the thought of one of his churches standing empty of a Sunday, so he continued to preach in at least four or five places. When a call came from a friend, a family, or a hospital, he was up and out no matter what the time or weather. The Buffalo folks could no more imagine him not moving, laughing, living among them, than he could himself.

Then suddenly he was gone, and it seemed nobody was ready for it or really believed it. The heart attack came just before Christmas, and three weeks later, on January 16, 1956, he died peacefully at Roanoke Memorial Hospital.

On the way to the funeral service, Blaine and Cora Quesenberry picked up a man from West Virginia who was at Willis
and who didn't know the way to the church. "I never seed Mr.
Childress, but I heared what he did for my daddy. Picked him
up and drove him twenty-five miles in the mud in low gear to
get him to the doctor. Burned up his new car and had to trade.
He saved my daddy's life, and that's why I come here."

Hundreds came, or tried to, that day. A blizzard had left the
roads covered in many places, and they were all but impassable.
There were cars in the ditch most of the way up the mountain.
Some who couldn't get there by way of Willis went around to
the Hillsville side and tried again. Still, enough made it so the
Buffalo church was filled up, with many standing outside or staying in their cars to keep out of the cold.

Several ministers spoke. "When the Master has a big work to
do," one said, "he raises up a big man to do it."

Said another: "He could, if he wanted to, have gone into any
big city church and been outstanding. But that isn't what he
chose to do. And that's made all the difference to these mountains."

One quoted from a speech by Woodrow Wilson: "I tell you
this, the only thing that saves the world is the little handful of
disinterested men in it. I have found a few. I wish I had found
more. I can name two or three men whom I have never found
thinking about themselves or their own interests, and I tie to
those men as you would to an anchor. Men who have no ax to
grind. Men willing to die in obscurity, if only they might serve.
The princes among us are those who forget themselves and serve
mankind."

The *Roanoke Times* wrote:

> In spite of snow and threatening weather, hundreds of people rode
> on those roads to pay tribute to one who loved his fellow man
> and never spared himself in the service of God. They crowded a
> large stone church and overflowed into the church yard for the
> funeral of the Sky Pilot of the Buffalo Mountain country, and a
> Good Samaritan to many a man, woman and boy and girl to
> whom, for more than a quarter of a century, he ministered.

A remarkable man, a remarkable career and a wonderfully fruitful ministry was Bob Childress. His personal friendship and his ministerial influence extended beyond the area dominated scenically by the lofty peak where he made his home, to include much of Virginia and portions of other states.

The *Carroll County News* carried a page of pictures of Bob's six rock churches and a story paying tribute. There was only one other item on the whole page, no more than an inch long. It read:

Carroll County Sheriff's Deputies destroyed two mash barrels and a copper still worm in the Little Vine section of Pine Creek. Other parts of the still had been moved. No arrests were made.

Bob would have been the first to laugh at seeing that news item alongside the account of his life, and the first to admit that a man's work is never done.

It seemed that the people would never leave the churchyard after the funeral service.

"If I'm worth anything, it's because of Mr. Childress," said Hazel Bowman. "He changed my life."

"It's going to be lonesome around here," said Hasten. "I used to look forward to his coming like a child to Christmas."

Miss Blanche Green, the schoolteacher, said, "I used to sit and look at him and think, if you only knew how many lives you've transformed!"

And old Doc Burnett said: "He was the savior of the Buffalo. And a sort of Robin Hood, too, getting donations from his rich friends and passing them along to the poor ones."

Little old Josephine Mayberry, who had propped for him at that critical funeral years before, said: "I'm tryin' to live so I can see him agin someday." She mused. "He promised to preach my funeral, and here he's gone first. He went into too big a strut workin' for the Lord."

Said another: "He done all the marryin' and buryin' and baptizin' for a quarter-century. No other man livin' could have done the work he done."

"He gave most of us all the upright we ever knew," Steve Kemp said. "He moved this ol' Buffalo."

After the coffin was lowered, two grizzled mountaineers lingered in the cemetery, reluctant to leave. It was hard to tell whether the one was addressing himself or his companion.

"Now Bob Childress is gone," he said. "You won't have another Bob Childress. There just won't be another."

His friend said, "There won't never need to be."

Epilogue

If you've never seen the Blue Ridge Mountains, plan to go there someday. Go in April if you can. That's when spring is born on Buffalo Mountain, and apple trees bloom beside the split-rail fences. Honeysuckles come later, like a pulse beat, then dogwood, then laurel, then flame azalea, then rhododendron, until the heartbeats of spring subside into deep, serene summer.

But it is at apple blossom time that the Buffalo is most beautiful. On years when Easter falls late and every hillside and hollow is decked in white, it seems as if the world is dressed for resurrection. It is then that older folks of the Buffalo shudder, remembering how it used to be.

Many are gone now: Steve Kemp, the Harrises, Mack Moles, Elder Marshall, Anderson and Lucy Carter. Doc Burnett is gone, and it's a pity. After fifty years of mountain practice he could have told you how to extract bullets from just about anywhere in the body, and how to tell the difference between fleabites and a blast of bird shot.

The Primitive Baptists are no longer a force in the mountains. Their little churches are torn apart over whether or not there is a hell, whether resurrection will be spiritual or physical, and whether or not to pay ministers. At last count by the *Christian Herald* there were nationally only sixty thousand members. But in August sons and daughters from Maine to Florida return for the festivities—fried chicken and apple pie and jollity and stories of old-timey days. Cars and trucks clog the highways, but no one seems to care, not even the highway police. It sometimes takes two hours to get past Big Bridge Church east of Hillsville.

Why not join the celebration? Go inside, hang your hat on one of the hooks that circle the room, and sit among the worshipers. You will sing "Shall We Gather at the River," while outside the creek is running, swift and glistening, with swallows skimming over it, and it seems as if the little stream must surely be flowing to the throne of God.

Afterward, when the hordes of people drive away and the churchyard lies empty and evening-gloam slips across the coves and hollows, the only sound will be that of the whippoorwills. You'll know then how lonely it is after the young folks have left the mountains.

"We thought they'd come back," says one old-timer, "that they'd get homesick for the hills. But they didn't. They just come to visit in their big shiny cars that scrape bottom on the rocks. It's public works that's the trouble, public works that ruint the country," he says, meaning any kind of work away from the farm for wages, like mining or road-building or factory labor.

Some will tell you that strange things still happen at the Buffalo. The woman who lives on the Lee place saw a blinding light, just at midnight, that lit up the whole cove bright as day. Nothing man-made about it, she says, it was straight from the Lord. More than one will tell you of seeing a great blacksnake, thick as a telephone pole, that lives on the Buffalo—maybe in the tunnel that runs clear under the mountain.

There are marks of Bob Childress in many places. Miles of graded road now wind through the hills, like the new one down the hanging walls of Squirrel Creek, once so cut off from the outside world. People are sending their children to college. Andy Howlett's daughter even went off to Exeter in England to study literature.

"The Buffalo used to be as wild as when Pocahontas was here," says ninety-year-old Ma Sue Hall of Floyd, with a twinkle and just a touch of regret, "and now Ph.D.s are getting as common as bootleggers."

They're still arresting old white mules and evil-doing horses and cars along the Blue Ridge, but very few around the Buffalo.

And in twenty years there haven't been but two murder cases.

"Now, we just don't think about whether or not we dare go to a gathering," says Mrs. Elijah Vaughn, who knew the Buffalo at its worst. "Never even stop to wonder if it's safe. Just the same, to this day, when I hear a shot the chill goes through me."

All of Bob's rock churches are active. Two of them you can see from the Blue Ridge Parkway, and the one on Slate Mountain is barely out of sight. Almost anywhere you stop you're likely to meet someone Bob Childress helped to stop drinking, to get through school, to bear a sickness, or simply to learn to love. You'll be welcome at the Buffalo church, where Mack Moles's son is an elder and Bailey Goad's grandson is the superintendent of Sunday school.

At the last service I attended at Mayberry, mountain people who scratch the soil for a living pledged hundreds of dollars to start new churches in distant suburbs. "That's the legacy of Bob Childress," said the minister there. "He rewrote the first commandment of the mountains. It's no longer 'My family is my care and keep.' Now it's 'Whoever's in need is my care and keep.' "

On a hot summer's day just a week before he died, Hasten Childress sat in the rocker on his porch and talked at length about his brother as the crickets were singing and the witch-water rising from the road beside his house. "Bob used to say that each of us is tending the little patch of ground God lends to us. 'Whatever comes to me in the pod,' he'd say, 'I want to pass on in full flower, and what comes to me in the flower, I'd like to pass on in full fruit.' Well, the plants he tended are still bearing."

Each year the sprouts around the chestnut stumps on the hillsides seem to grow a trifle taller before they wither. "Someday," Bob used to say, "the Lord's going to give us back our chestnuts. Just you see!" There are many folks who are beginning to think that's going to come true.